ONE HELL OF A RIDE

John Lawrence Reynolds

ONE HELL

> HOW **CRAIG DOBBIN** BUILT THE WORLD'S
> LARGEST HELICOPTER COMPANY

OF A RIDE

DOUGLAS & McINTYRE

D&M PUBLISHERS INC.

Vancouver/Toronto/Berkeley

Douglas & McIntyre
A division of D&M Publishers Inc.
2323 Quebec Street, Suite 201
Vancouver BC Canada V5T 4S7
www.douglas-mcintyre.com

National Library of Canada Cataloguing in Publication Data
Reynolds, John Lawrence
One hell of a ride : how Craig Dobbin built the world's largest
helicopter company / John Lawrence Reynolds.

ISBN 978-1-55365-363-9 (cloth) · ISBN 978-1-55365-491-9 (paper)

1. Dobbin, Craig, 1935–2006. 2. CHC Helicopter Corporation—Biography.
3. Helicopter transportation—Canada—History. 4. Businessmen—
Newfoundland and Labrador—Biography. 5. Businessmen—Canada—
Biography. 6. Industrialists—Canada—Biography. I. Title.
HC112.5.D62R49 2008   338.092   C2008-904109-7

Editing by Barbara Pulling
Cover design by Peter Cocking and Naomi MacDougall
Text design by Naomi MacDougall
Jacket photograph courtesy of Elaine Dobbin
Photographs courtesy of Elaine Dobbin and CHC Helicopter Corporation
Printed and bound in Canada by Friesens
Printed on acid-free paper that is forest-friendly
(100% post-consumer recycled paper) and has been processed chlorine free
Distributed in the U.S. by Publishers Group West

We gratefully acknowledge the financial support of the Canada
Council for the Arts, the British Columbia Arts Council, the Province of
British Columbia through the Book Publishing Tax Credit and the
Government of Canada through the Book Publishing Industry Development
Program (BPIDP) for our publishing activities.

FOR ELAINE

And to the memory of Captian Matthew William Davis
and the sixteen other victims who perished on
Cougar Helicopters Flight 491 on March 12, 2009

There shall be no wasting of victuals
nor time spent in idleness
but all industrious uses practiced
to set forward the enterprise.

JOHN GUY, first governor of Newfoundland, 1610–15

If Craig wasn't in a corner fighting for his life,
he'd find a corner to get into.

JEAN-YVES GELINAS, early business partner of Craig L. Dobbin

Introduction

For more than five hundred years ships from around the world have passed through the Narrows to the harbour at St. John's, where they flushed their bilges, dumped their waste and, on many occasions, sank to the bottom.

In the spring of 1960, while slush along the gutters of Duckworth Street melted in the sun, Craig Laurence Dobbin fumbled his way through the cesspool waters of the harbour enclosed in a rubber suit and brass diving helmet. A belt of lead weights held him on the bottom as he moved through the wreckage of a ship sunk during the Second World War. The vessel's steel hull had disintegrated into rust, but Dobbin was interested in the parts that had resisted the corrosive salt water—the ship's bronze and brass fittings, driveshafts and propellers. Removing them with wrench, saw or torch and hauling them to the boat floating thirty feet above his head would bring a reasonable payday to Dobbin and his two partners, brother Dennis and friend Bob Lochart, in their company Aquasalvage Ltd.

The work was risky, but Dobbin discounted the danger. At least he was doing it for his own company, not for one of the foreign-owned corporations along Water Street where executives barked orders in clipped British accents or the flat nasal tones of Ontario-born stuffed shirts. Craig Dobbin would work for nobody but himself. Not for his father, and certainly not for some Brit or mainlander who considered Newfoundland an edge-of-the-world outpost.

On this day, however, the risk became reality. Two lines stretching down from the boat above his head got ensnarled in the wreck. The one that divers call their umbilical line fed his diving helmet with air. The other, a length of nylon rope, represented his means of communication with the boat. Pinched between metal sections of the hull, both lines were now unserviceable.

Dobbin began wrenching at the lines, blindly trying to free them in the dark water. They held fast, and the more he exerted himself, the less oxygen remained in his helmet. He could swim the distance up to the boat if he could remove the diving helmet and the weighted belt. But the helmet was tightly bolted to his suit, and the belt securely fastened. He would lose consciousness, he knew, long before he could free himself from the equipment.

Later, Dobbin would claim that he prepared himself to say goodbye. "I was ready for it," he remembered. He could simply relax, drift first into unconsciousness and then death. By the time the men above him realized he was in trouble, he would be beyond rescue.

But the idea of dying in those filthy waters and, worse, never achieving the success as a businessman he had planned for himself was not acceptable. He would not wait passively for death. If he were to fade from life, he would fade while fighting for another breath. He resumed swinging the lines back and forth, applying his considerable strength in an attempt to free himself.

It worked. The lines released. Air began flowing into the helmet again. He breathed deeply and willed himself to grow calm. Then he tugged on the rope, signalling to be pulled out of the near-freezing water. The work day was over.

The three men piloted the boat to shore, walked to a nearby bar and consumed several pints of beer before heading for home. The following day Craig Dobbin pulled the diving suit on again and returned to the water in search of salvageable brass and bronze. For now, that was his work. But he was already searching for another career, and eventually he found it.

Like a dragonfly that spends its immature years in water, then emerges to soar though the air, Craig Dobbin rose from the harbour water to create the world's largest helicopter company, a multibillion-dollar corporation performing complex operations for governments and petroleum industry giants. Stubbornly insisting on remaining in St. John's, he came to count presidents, prime ministers and royalty among his friends, and his antics and generosity became legendary far beyond Newfoundland.

Almost a half-century after his near-fatal dive, Craig Dobbin's life ended with some irony, cut short partly by a disease that robbed him of air. His achievements—including an estate valued at half a billion dollars—left many who knew him shaking their heads at his triumphs and his audacity.

"No one could ever tell Craig Dobbin he would fail, or that he *could* fail," a Dobbin business associate recalled. "His life is a lesson to everybody who chooses to go into business for themselves. The trouble is, to succeed at Craig Dobbin's level you have to *be* Craig Dobbin. And we'll never, in our lifetime, see anyone like him again."

When Craig started as a developer, and later when he launched
the helicopter business, none of the banks would touch him.
He was a wild man, sure to go broke, they said. And near the
end, they were all lining up to kiss his arse.
PATRICK O'CALLAGHAN, president and CEO, East Coast Catering Ltd.

THE IRISH CITY OF Waterford is famous as the source of exqui-
site and expensive lead crystal vases, goblets and sculptures purchased more for their heirloom value than for any practical
purpose. Founded by ninth-century Vikings, Waterford grew second only to Dublin in size and importance through its first thousand years of existence, and its mediaeval city walls remain the
oldest in Ireland. Much of Waterford's growth was based on trade;
located in the southeast corner of Ireland, it is the country's nearest
port to Europe.

Sometime in the late twelfth century, a Norman knight named
Reginald d'Aubin settled in Waterford, launching the line of Dob-
bin/Dobbyn. The knight, whose ancestors had intermarried with
descendants of William the Conqueror, may have bequeathed admirable personal qualities along with his name. A number of Dobbin/
Dobbyn citizens (the variation of the name's spelling appears to have
little connection with religion or social standing) served in political
office and local militia duties in the Waterford area.

The surname appears in other locales, most notably among
the Irish Republican Brotherhood, one of the most active secret

organizations advocating Irish independence. Descriptions of Seumas (Harry) Dobbyn as "a tall well-built and attractive man . . . [with] a great love for traditional Irish song and dance . . . very practical, never boring and with a great sense of humour" are eerily similar to portrayals of Craig Dobbin. Harry Dobbyn achieved notoriety through his association with Eamonn de Valera and his participation in the 1916 Easter Sunday Rebellion in Dublin. It was Dobbyn who made soap impressions of the jail keys that enabled de Valera, Sean McHarry and others to escape prison and eventually succeed in their efforts to create the Republic. For his part in the plot, Dobbyn was punished with solitary confinement.

Several Dobbins joined the Irish diaspora to escape recurring waves of famine and set off for Newfoundland. Some historians believe that the Irish emigration from Waterford to St. John's represented the largest number of people travelling on a point-to-point basis between Europe and the New World in the nineteenth century.

Subsistence on the Rock was often as difficult and trying as life in Ireland. The immigrants soon discovered they had traded the soft air and emerald fields of their home country for harsh nor'easters and untillable land without freeing themselves from the dominance of England. For many years, the English banned marriage among Irish settlers in Newfoundland, and long-term settlement was discouraged; the Irish were required to sign agreements to remain on the island for only a fixed period before returning.

The Waterford Dobbins appear to have rejected fishing as a means of earning a living. By the early 1930s various branches of the family were operating businesses in and around St. John's, and two men, sharing the familiar sobriquet applied to Irishmen, achieved notable success. "Black Horse Paddy" acquired his title as the agent for imported Black Horse beer. "Foxy Paddy" was named not for any perceived cunning but for his shock of red hair.

Foxy Paddy Dobbin entered the lumber supply business with F. M. O'Leary Ltd., where he rose to become manager of the firm's building supplies division. In a move repeated later by his sons, Foxy

Paddy ultimately rejected the idea of working for someone else and launched his own firm dealing in lumber and hardware. From all accounts he did reasonably well, assisted to one degree or another by his seven sons, four daughters and wife Rita. His legendary optimism, a quality passed on to his children in varying quantities, helped him overcome the usual challenges encountered by an independent businessman. "My dad might sell a thousand board feet of lumber," Craig Dobbin recalled years later, "and make maybe twenty-five dollars on the deal. But he'd count the profit taking the order and count it again in his head when he delivered it."

Given the social and economic state of St. John's through the 1930s, Paddy Dobbin's irrepressible optimism was admirable, perhaps even essential. A collapse of world fisheries markets following the First World War depressed cod prices dramatically, and they had barely begun to recover when the Great Depression arrived. There may have been more dismal places to live than Depression-era Newfoundland, but few locations suffered more seemingly endless economic setbacks.

Two events enhanced and altered Newfoundland over the next twenty years, and both deeply influenced Craig Dobbin. The first was the 1941 decision by the United States, as part of the Lend-Lease agreement between Britain and the U.S., to employ Newfoundland as a major military base. The construction of Fort Pepperell and other military facilities within Newfoundland and Labrador injected a jolt of prosperity into the region. It also introduced a brash, American-made free-enterprise attitude with an egalitarian bent. Anyone, the Yanks believed, could become successful and wealthy with sufficient determination, energy and ideas, a concept sharply contrasting with Newfoundland's British-dominated and St. John's–based approach. Not everyone bought into the American philosophy, but some scrappy young folks did. A small core of family groups, their identities more closely linked to Newcastle than to Newfoundland, had held sway over the colony's economy for generations. These Water Street merchants spoke and socialized mainly with each other, and native Newfoundlanders grew accustomed to playing the role of employees rather than employers. Success in business, they surmised, depended more on family name than on education, ambition and ability, an attitude many maintain was encouraged by the Catholic church hierarchy, who were traditionally pro-establishment.

Within a few months of Washington's decision, hundreds of young men with Yankee drawls were supervising million-dollar construction projects and building roads, barracks, aircraft hangars and recreational facilities. Family names and social status meant nothing to the impatient Yanks, who called on locals to assist them. If you showed up on time and did your job, you were paid well. If you demonstrated qualities of leadership and exceptional abilities, you were awarded extra responsibility and earned more pay. This was something of a revelation to a people who for generations had toiled in a class-based society. Some saw little reason to alter their actions, recognizing how tenacious the old structure would be, but a few, like Craig Dobbin, felt the message power their ambition.

The second shift in the colony's status occurred with Newfoundland's 1949 entry into confederation with Canada. The Americans remained in Newfoundland through the 1950s, and in Labrador far beyond that, but their influence was diluted somewhat by the expanding public-sector employment funded by Ottawa. Both social services and personal income grew enormously with Ottawa's attempt to bring the new province's living standards in line with the rest of Canada.

In less than a generation, Newfoundland moved from a Dickensian economic oligarchy towards a class-based model and into a social structure based in large part on the injection of public funds. A canny Newfoundlander coming of age during this period might be attracted to the idea of partnering with government programs to build private wealth, spurred by the American-imported "can-do" attitude.

Limits remained, however. According to Newfoundland ex-pats such as journalist Jim Roache, "For most of us in the 1960s and beyond who truly wanted to succeed, we had to either leave or settle for being a clerk on Water Street or [taking] a job in construction. Talk about a glass ceiling—to many Newfoundlanders, this one was concrete."

Craig Laurence Dobbin had no intention of spending his working years as a Water Street clerk, nor of abandoning the Rock—not at the outset, at least. And if construction was the route to riches, he would follow it not as a labourer setting out in the back of a truck each morning at dawn but as the person who determined where the truck would go and what the labourers would do when they got there.

Paddy and Rita Dobbin's third son, he arrived on September 13, 1935, a Friday and a bad-luck day in the dark period between the advent of the Great Depression and the launch of the Second World War. Craig matured through the arrival of the Americans and the often contentious debate about Newfoundland entering Confederation. Shaped and inspired by both events, he grew up in a home environment of hard work, strong family identity and deep religious affiliation.

All members of Foxy Dobbin's family were expected to spend every available hour working in the large white-framed house on Kingsbridge Road or the nearby lumberyard. Little time was available for sports. While Craig's school chums spent afterclass hours playing hockey, football or baseball, he and his brothers were kept busy assisting in the family business. Sport was frivolity; business was survival. In Craig's case, this may not have represented much of a loss. Despite his physical size—he grew taller and more physically dominant than any of his siblings—Craig Dobbin demonstrated little athletic talent as a youth.

There was always time, however, for religion among the Dobbins. In fact, each morning began with the family travelling to church for mass. Nothing could disturb this ritual, including lack of sleep.

"Every kid wanted to sit behind the old man," Craig's brother Derm Dobbin recalls, "because if you were sitting in front of his pew and he noticed you nodding off during the service, he would reach across and cuff your ear."

Their Catholicism intertwined with Irish culture, the Dobbin children grew up with three allegiances: to Newfoundland, to Ireland and later, in a manner almost secondary, to Canada. The Irish identity thrived in the family's soul. Everyone who arrived from the Dobbin ancestral land found a warm reception at the large house, where the drinks, conversation, music and laughter flowed easily.

Paddy Dobbin may have dominated the business and spiritual side of the Dobbins' life, but mother Rita, referred to as the Queen, was the unchallenged ruler at home. She was not a large woman, but her booming voice commanded respect, as did her ability to consume quantities of Jameson and a cutting wit characteristic of Irish Newfoundlanders. "For the love of Jesus, get down off the cross," she once bellowed at Craig, interrupting his complaints about his business and personal life. "Somebody else can use the wood!"

All of the children were loved in a rough and ready manner, but the future roles for daughters and sons were clearly defined. Girls were expected to perform domestic duties, seek a relatively undemanding short-term career, wed a good Catholic boy, and produce babies. Boys were obliged to marry a good Catholic girl and work hard enough to feed all the hungry mouths of the children they produced while providing generous support to the church.

It is the stuff of legends, this tale of a family of abundant children, limited luxuries, abiding faith, hard work, religious conviction, and an affection for Irish whiskey and Irish music. The lessons were well learned. The eldest son, Patrick, earned a medical degree, while other Dobbin sons achieved outstanding success in business, and their sisters sought careers in nursing and stenography.

Beyond being popular among his friends, Craig's years at St. Bonaventure College were not marked by distinction. "St. Bon's" adhered to the notion that adolescent boys were, if not an invention of the devil, perpetually influenced by Satan, and the best way of countering that influence was through frequent corporal punishment. As an adult, Craig Dobbin recalled every teacher at St. Bons who punched, slapped or kicked him into appreciation for the gentle nature of Christ. There was one exception. Brother Augustus Fidelis Brennan chose a different means of dealing with Craig and others, rejecting physical blows in favour of gentle words. During Dobbin's most successful years as a businessman, he would remember and reward Brother Brennan for his tender nature.

Although he attended Bishop Feild, the Anglican school rival of Catholic St. Bonaventure (and an important locale for author Wayne Johnston's novel *The Colony of Unrequited Dreams*), Craig's neighbour Bob Cole became a friend. The two boys often scoured ditches, culverts and back alleys for liquor and soft drink bottles for their two pennies' deposit. Cole later became a sports commentator, serving for several years as the voice of CBC-TV's *Hockey Night in Canada*, and he and Craig remained close friends through their long careers.

After graduating from St. Bon's, Craig Dobbin abandoned book-based education and scavenging pennies in pursuit of serious lessons and bigger earnings. This represented a break from his parents' expectations. Of all Foxy Dobbin's sons, Craig was the only one who did not enrol in college or university. Patrick was sent by Paddy Dobbin at considerable expense to Ireland to obtain his medical degree. Basil earned an engineering degree from Dalhousie, and Barney became a government mediator in PEI. Derm originally planned a law career but determined that working as a contractor alongside his brother Craig would be more rewarding.

Craig's first full-time job after school was at a nearby USAF base as a voucher clerk, where he enjoyed the income but resented taking orders. It was there he learned the shipwrecks at the bottom of St. John's harbour represented an untapped mine of scrap brass and bronze, and along with his partners he formed Aquasalvage to recover the metal. The enterprise involved no glamour and little profit, but it was a beginning of sorts. Dobbin's close call at the bottom of the harbour was enough to steer him back to land, where he began marketing and delivering lumber. This required a reliable pickup truck, something Dobbin did not have and could not afford to purchase, so he converted his old car into a lumber conveyance by knocking out the windshield and back window, then setting the joists and two-by-fours beside him, at times around him, their ends protruding over the hood in front and beyond the trunk at the rear.

Years later, Craig Dobbin reflected on the determination that drove him to succeed as an entrepreneur. "I got tired of seeing companies from elsewhere come into St. John's and take away our business," he explained. "I wanted to build a company that came out of Newfoundland and went everywhere in the world to do business, just to even things up."

His timing enabled him to ride a wave of entrepreneurial spirit rising out of the Atlantic provinces in the mid-twentieth century. Central Canada, particularly Ontario, saw itself as the industrial engine of the country, the locus of manufacturing and finance, and indeed it was. But the economies of Ontario and Quebec in the 1950s were based on managerial skills, not entrepreneurial risks. The large mining, steel-making, automotive, farm equipment and appliance manufacturing corporations had been launched a generation or two earlier, and many had since been acquired by U.S.-based firms. Much industry on the Canadian mainland was already trundling down the road towards branch-plant status. In that climate, injecting your last dime into an unproven or previously non-existent industry was a risk to be avoided. Things were decidedly different in Newfoundland.

"Craig and the rest of us are the product of changing environments in Newfoundland," suggests Frank Ryan, a major developer in the St. John's area who was a close friend of Dobbin's. "We were the first generation to mature after confederation with Canada, and all the changes that took place in 1949 and afterwards affected us, especially those of us who decided to become businesspeople."

If you wanted to purchase clothing, furniture, jewellery or a loan prior to Confederation, you sought out an Englishman. If you needed fish or someone to work in the mines, you looked for an Irish surname. Derm Dobbin, a successful developer in his own right, relates the tale of an Irish Newfoundlander in the 1950s who entered the Water Street office of an English businessman known simply as Mr. Joe. "Would you be having an opening for me, Mr. Joe?" the Newfoundlander asked, twisting his cap in his hands as he spoke. "Yes, I have," Mr. Joe replied. "The door behind you. Be sure to close it on your way out."

"Any idea of an Irish Catholic setting out on his own to become a successful businessman was unheard of," Frank Ryan points out, "because he couldn't do it without help from the English, and there was no relationship between the Irish and the English. The Americans . . . were here for almost twenty years, and that's when the English influence weakened. For the first time in our history, room was made in the business world for Irish Newfoundlanders, and many of them assumed an American 'can-do' attitude. Not an English or a Canadian approach to business, but an American one. That's what made the difference."

What began happening east of Gaspé at that time has only recently has been recognized and assessed. New businesses were born in Canada's Atlantic region, frequently achieving success on a remarkable scale. The names of these midcentury Maritime-based entrepreneurs remain prominent today, thanks in part to their refusal to sell or merge their corporate offspring with big-money interests, especially those south of the border. They include the McCain brothers, whose firm dispenses frozen potatoes from Nova Scotia around the world; the Sobey family, whose supermarkets compete briskly with their central Canada competitors; the Irvings, whose dominance of the petroleum industry in the Atlantic provinces is unmatched in North America; Ken Rowe, whose Halifax-based IMP Group International employs 3,500 people to operate airlines, manage hotels and manufacture products ranging from surgical supplies to rubber boots; Harry Steele, who rose from shovelling gravel in Deer Lake to create one of the country's most successful media-based conglomerates; John Risley, whose Clearwater Seafoods achieves almost half a billion dollars in annual sales throughout the globe; John Bragg, whose rural Nova Scotia firm Oxford Frozen Foods is the world's largest producer and processor of blueberries; and Ron Joyce, who left his Nova Scotia home to define the North American coffee-and-doughnut industry with Tim Hortons.

None of them achieved success more ostentatiously than Craig Dobbin. Throughout his life Dobbin appeared to embrace financial risk, betting all of his chips as freely as any Las Vegas high-roller. He did avoid physical risk after his close call in St. John's harbour, but after 1958 he had other responsibilities besides his own survival.

In that year he married Eleanor Penney, a dark-eyed beauty introduced to him by Craig's sister Maureen. One of a family of six from the Burin Peninsula, the arm of land extending south into Placentia Bay, Eleanor had come to St. John's in pursuit of a nursing career, one of only three vocations generally available to Newfoundland women in the 1950s (the others were teaching and stenography). Nurses were called by their surnames; Eleanor became Nurse Penney in the hospital, and as Craig's wife she was simply Penney.

Penney had all the qualities that Craig's upbringing had taught him to search for in a mate. Warm, attractive and even-tempered, she delighted in domestic duties. As Craig's career progressed and he invited associates and political buddies home for food, drink and celebration, Penney remained in the kitchen, preparing meals for the men talking business in the parlour. She continued to work as a nurse between the arrivals of five children over the first six years of their marriage: Joanne, the first-born, was followed by Mark, David, Carolyn and Craig Junior. While her husband pursued business with a determination bordering on obsession, it was Penney who prepared the children's dinners, helped them with their homework, tucked them into their beds and kissed them good night.

Penney anchored the family in a manner that Irish-Newfoundland mothers have been doing for generations. The affection she generated in her sons and daughters, while equally deep and abiding, differed from their feelings for their father. Craig was the hard-edged, grinning, give-'em-hell persona who persuaded his children they could achieve any goal if they worked hard enough. Penney was the person whose soft lap you crawled into when your finger was cut or your feelings were hurt, the one who surprised you with cookies and milk, the mother who was more comfortable making pies in the kitchen than sipping cocktails at a reception. Her world was her home and her family; pretense and artifice failed to interest her, especially the kind encountered at social functions. Penney remained her own woman, warm and giving but with a determination to follow her own values. She ignored her husband's suggestions to colour her prematurely white hair to make her appear younger, and when Craig bought her a mink coat she thanked him politely, hung the garment in a closet, and never wore it.

During the family's early years, with Penney's periodic nursing income funding her husband's often overreaching ambitions, the two complemented each other perfectly. As Craig Dobbin began his rise to heights no other Newfoundlander and few businessmen of any origin were able to achieve, cracks would appear in the marriage, a too-familiar story.

CRAIG DOBBIN ABANDONED the idea of marketing building products. Nobody was making much money in that business, including his father, who had closed his operation. The big opportunities lay not in selling lumber and hardware but in using them to build homes, then selling *those*. Growing prosperity in and around St. John's during the 1960s was creating a demand for houses, and Craig Dobbin stumbled upon a critical fact: not only could he sell a house before it was completed, but he and his family could reside in it until the deal was done. The profit you earned from selling your house enabled you to build a larger house, which you lived in while completing it. You sold that house as quickly as possible, pocketing an even larger profit, and on and on.

Canada Mortgage and Housing Corporation (CMHC) sweetened the pot by offering mortgages covering 130 per cent of new homes: build a $10,000 house and receive a CMHC mortgage on the property of $13,000, leaving $3,000 to fund another project. And if the house happened to be your domicile of record, the extra profit was tax-free. The mathematics were simple and the appeal was irresistible. Craig Dobbin became a builder and developer.

Accounts of Dobbin's skill as a hands-on house builder vary with the source. Most agree that he never displayed the attributes of a master carpenter, but recall that he could at least swing a hammer. Brother Derm, who should know, has a different memory. Craig, Derm claims, might swing a hammer, "but the nail wouldn't go in." It didn't have to. Thanks to the CMHC mortgage deal and the tax-free profit on selling his own house out from under him, Dobbin parlayed his profit with each sale and hired all the hammer-swinging tradesmen he needed.

For much of the 1960s the Dobbins were local itinerants, moving from one home to another, each new address located in a better part of town and displaying a larger, more expensive home. All the homes had one thing in common: none was completed while the family occupied it, and each was sold for enough profit to finance the next house. The family would make way for a new owner by moving into the next partially completed home, which already would be on the market. Son Mark recalls that in one house he and his siblings needed a ladder to reach their second-floor bedrooms because Craig had yet to install stairs, and their morning wake-up calls often came in the person of workers installing drywall, plumbing or electrical outlets on the floors below. Their father would already be at work by then, assessing new building lots, arranging financial deals, negotiating with sub-trades, and carting supplies from the lumber dealer.

House building brought Craig Dobbin more than his first taste of financial success. It taught him the wisdom of hiring workers who could perform a given task better than he could. In constructing houses, this was relatively easy to achieve. He was no plumber, no carpenter, no electrician, so he chose the best in these job functions and put them to work. Later, determining specific talents and selecting those with extraordinary abilities in other fields would prove more challenging; it is easier, after all, to gauge a worker's ability as a carpenter than as a business strategist. In most cases, though, Craig Dobbin's ability to evaluate undeveloped talent proved superb; the ability to encourage the employee who possessed that talent and provide him or her with the freedom to apply it was responsible for much of his business success.

As a builder and developer, Dobbin looked for every edge available. Finding a parcel of land on Wicklow Street, at that time part of the northern fringe of St. John's, he noted the property's price was substantially lower than that of similar lots located just a block or two away. For good reason: the expensive building lots were flat and square, with plenty of topsoil for easy excavation; the Wicklow Street lots were irregular and extended up a slope broken by stony outcroppings, making it impossible to construct a standard-design structure on them. Craig Dobbin bought the lots at bargain prices and built homes that flowed up the slope and between the stones. He sold them for a larger profit margin thanks to the low cost of the building lots.

Edges were found in other places, especially in relationships with people who could influence decisions in his favour. The St. John's lawyer who represented CMHC in the province would be in a conflict of interest were he to represent Craig Dobbin Ltd. in a financial deal. But there were other ways, Craig Dobbin suggested, to gut a cod. A local butcher named Sandy Foster, an acquaintance of both men, provided Dobbin with a sufficient arm's-length distance to funnel mortgage money from CMHC through him and into the coffers of Craig Dobbin Ltd. The prologue to one agreement declared it was a contract between Craig Dobbin Ltd. "and Sandy Foster, hereafter to be known as The Butcher." No one appears to have criticized the arrangement, and no evidence exists that Dobbin, Foster or the lawyer did anything untoward. But the benefits were obvious.

Cultivating such relationships may sound devious, but the motive behind Dobbin's friendship was never apparent to the target of his attention. He possessed a natural charm, an affinity for people that layered his business ambition. "When he talked with you in social situations," one business acquaintance recalls, "he was focussed totally on you. He wasn't looking over your shoulder or around the room, searching for someone more important. He was really interested in what you were saying. Everyone sensed this about the man and was drawn to him."

Throughout his career, Dobbin would be praised for the acuity of his vision, his ability to crunch and juggle numbers, and above all his determination to succeed. No attribute, however, played a bigger role in his success than his talent for building trust and affection among those he dealt with on a personal or a business level. This trait was not always applied when he encountered cash flow problems, though, a perpetual situation during his earliest years in business. Some of those who dealt with Dobbin then continue to grumble about his delay in settling debts, especially those related to his investments. "He'd buy on margin," one notable Toronto-based financier complains, "and if the stock went south the broker had a hell of a time collecting."

When cold, hard cash wasn't involved, Dobbin's warm and freely dispensed charm brought him unexpected rewards. An early example occurred in 1966, when he was invited to join the local homebuilders association one month before the organization's annual election of officers. Despite being the newest member of the group, Dobbin easily won the presidency and began making changes immediately. "The homebuilders had met for years in a room over a Chinese restaurant on Harvey Road," recalls Frank Ryan. "Not the most prestigious place in town to gather. Craig's first decision as president was to declare they would start meeting at the Hotel Newfoundland where the board of trade and other groups met, a more suitable location for people who were changing the face of the city."

A few months later the president of the national homebuilders association, a Quebecer named Jean-Yves Gelinas, paid his annual visit to the St. John's chapter, and he quickly became both an admirer and a friend of Dobbin's. The meeting began a long relationship between the two men and a strong affinity, on Dobbin's part, with Quebec. Some suggest that Dobbin responded to the alienation of the Québécois from the rest of Canada, seeing in this situation a parallel with the treatment of Newfoundlanders by mainlanders. Others believe it was more a matter of similar lifestyles and values, an emphasis on *joie de vivre* reflected in the Irish culture that Dobbin inherited. Whatever its origins, Craig Dobbin valued and pursued his relationship with Quebec throughout his career.

Dobbin was doing well with houses, but each project demanded special attention, and the return was limited by the market price of single family homes. If he could develop multiple residences in one project, he realized—apartment buildings with dozens of units— the profit would be far more rewarding. The potential was apparent. Small, square frame houses lined the streets of St. John's leading up from the harbour, but apartment blocks, though burgeoning elsewhere in Canadian cities, were nowhere to be found. The demand was there but the supply was not, thanks to an unusual city tax code that discouraged apartment developers.

Houses paid municipal taxes in the usual manner—a mill rate based on fixed property values. Apartment blocks, however, were taxed not by mill rate but on 20 per cent of the gross rent paid by their residents. Developers of apartment units renting at $100 monthly would see $20 vanish off the top before they covered building costs, heating, maintenance and other expenses. The tax was an easily administered and profitable money grab for the city, but it discouraged developers from investing in apartments despite a pent-up demand. The tax could be absorbed if the building costs were controlled, Dobbin believed. More important, with pressure in the right places, the tax just might be rescinded in the future. When that happened, every apartment building owner in town would see an immediate bonus dropped into his or her lap. Dobbin determined to be among them.

He made a down payment on a stretch of undeveloped land along Torbay Road, near his father's now-closed building supply business. Using a basic four-storey walk-up apartment building design, and funded by CMHC 130 per cent mortgages, he sank everything he owned into a complex of eleven buildings incorporating almost 500 units in total, labelling the development Hillview Terrace. Each $9,000 apartment unit was mortgaged for $11,700, leaving Dobbin a $2,700 cushion. Multiplied by a hundred or so units, it made dollar bills dance before Dobbin's eyes—this was a very good business to be in.

On the advice of Jean-Yves Gelinas, Dobbin hired a Montreal project foreman named Michel Montaruli to supervise the construction. Within a day or two of arriving in St. John's with his family, Montaruli regretted his decision. Dobbin wanted the apartments completed and ready for tenants within eight months, an enormous challenge made more difficult by a shortage of trained carpenters in the area. Instead of throwing up his hands and retreating, however, Montaruli assigned the available carpenters to perform special, limited tasks: one group cut beams to length, another worked on cutting angles, others erected the materials and a fourth group installed doors and windows. To supervise the journeymen house builders, Montaruli imported experienced workers from Montreal, and for several weeks the Irish-tinged Newfoundland chatter was accompanied by orders delivered in heavily accented Québécois English.

It was a risky venture, and Craig Dobbin stood to lose everything, including the family home on Sussex Place. But thanks to Montaruli's management skills, residents began moving into Hillview Terrace, the first privately funded apartment complex in St. John's, within seven months. Dobbin was more pleased than he could express, and from that day forward every building development bearing his name was managed by Michel Montaruli.

With time the 20 per cent apartment tax was dropped, but the development's success failed to solve all the cash-flow problems at Craig Dobbin Ltd. On more than one occasion Dobbin's only source of cash was the coin-operated laundry machines in the basement of each building, and he would visit regularly to open the washers and dryers and scoop up the nickels, dimes and quarters. The coins were used to meet a payroll, cover a utility bill, or enable Penney to buy groceries. Dobbin duelled with banks and financial backers, often appearing about to slip beneath the surface yet somehow staying afloat.

The financial strain took its toll on both Dobbin's temper and his immediate environment. Derm Dobbin recalls visiting his brother at Craig's office during this period. "First thing I noticed," Derm remembers, "was the wall behind his desk. Some places were covered in brown splatters and others had deep dents in the drywall. 'What's happened to your wall?' I asked Craig, and he said it was nothing, ignore it." Some time into their meeting, Craig took a telephone call from his banker, who was clearly pressuring him for payment on a loan. As Derm watched, Craig grew more and more agitated, until he slammed down the receiver, picked up the telephone, and hurled it at the wall, where it added a new dent among the others. "Sometimes," Craig smiled back at his brother, "I have a cup of coffee in my hand instead."

Dobbin succeeded in holding on to his real estate developments, but the building restrictions and financial conservatism that prevailed in St. John's limited his field. He would have to go elsewhere to realize the success he craved. To the mainland, he thought, perhaps to Quebec, where they appreciated entrepreneurs with vision and ambition, and where his friend Jean-Yves Gelinas promised opportunity. In 1968, Craig, Penney and the children moved to Montreal.

Opportunity indeed awaited. After successfully building and selling houses in Montreal, Craig launched a major development in Aylmer, Quebec, across the river from Ottawa. With Gelinas as an equal partner he formed Omega Investments Ltd., which soon became a builder and developer of Kmart store locations throughout eastern Canada and into the U.S. as far south as Virginia. His profitable association with Gelinas proved the first of many for Dobbin and his multiple ventures. "There was always a French connection between Craig Dobbin and his business," one associate comments, "all the way through his career, right up to the end."

Dobbin referred to the Kmart stores as barns—massive, high-ceilinged structures designed with little grace and built on tight budgets. Profits on the developments were slim, and Kmart lived up to its reputation for being a tough negotiator and penny-pinching tenant. The stores, built to Kmart specifications, were leased to the firm by Omega and often used to anchor strip malls. The strip mall tenants generated better profit for Dobbin than the giant discount operator did, often marking the only profit he earned.

Kmart began demanding ever more difficult lease terms, especially in markets such as St. John's where the opportunity to rent the structure to another tenant when the lease expired was minimal. Any effort by Omega to raise the lease payments, reflecting increased costs and taxes, proved futile. In the end, the Kmart experience was most valuable as a lesson in hardball negotiating, a lesson that Craig Dobbin applied through the balance of his business career.

Dobbin's association with Jean-Yves Gelinas prompted another move for his family, this time to Ottawa, where he continued to pursue development opportunities. But Ottawa wasn't Quebec. More important, it wasn't Newfoundland, either. In 1970 the Dobbin family returned to St. John's, settling into a cosy home that included, among other features, an indoor swimming pool.

Thanks to Omega, Craig Dobbin was now a multimillionaire, on paper at least. He had honed his negotiating and business skills immeasurably since the days of carting lumber in a windowless car to construction sites. His ambition was hardly satisfied, however, and he believed his biggest opportunity for success lay not on the cut-throat mainland but in his hometown, among people he knew and trusted. That would prove true, but not from developments. Unexpectedly, Craig Dobbin's fortune would grow out of his love of fishing for salmon in remote wilderness rivers.

2

Craig hated air conditioning, just hated it. When he built a
new office building for himself and the company, he agreed to install
air conditioning and then complained about the sealed windows.
One day he wanted fresh air so badly he kicked out a window, put
his foot right through it, and a breeze came blowing in from the
harbour. "That's better," he grinned, and went back to work. It's the
Prince Charles Building on Torbay Road, and if you look carefully,
one of the corner offices has a window you can open, the only one in the
building. That was Craig's office. That's the one he kicked out.

KEITH STANFORD, president, Craig Dobbin Ltd.

TO MAINLANDERS, THE APPEAL of operating a global or even a national business out of Newfoundland is not immediately apparent. The big money and the powerful contacts needed for corporate expansion are on Bay Street, not Duckworth Street. St. John's may be a historic and interesting little city, the business heavyweights shrug, but nightclubs are non-existent, good restaurants are few and far between, the labour pool is limited, the ability to lure senior executives is minimal, and you can forget about direct flights to and from New York, London, Zurich or anywhere else in Europe or Asia.

Craig Dobbin had heard it all, as has every entrepreneur in the Atlantic provinces. Like them, he ignored the comments. He was a child of Newfoundland and would remain one. He also planned to be among the wealthiest of the island province's offspring.

Dobbin would never be content as a developer. For a while, however, that's the role he played. All of his efforts into the early 1970s were related to land development, managed under the growing herd of companies and partnerships he owned, or at least dominated. He created Dobbin Properties as an umbrella firm and Titleist Mortgage Company Ltd. to handle financing, forming the Bond Hotel Company Ltd. to add a downtown hostelry to the mix.

Through it all, he exhibited a shrewdness innate in those who possess it and inaccessible to those who don't. In the mid-1970s the city of St. John's decided to expropriate and demolish a block of decrepit buildings along Queen's Road, leaving a vacant lot. No one was interested in the property; the city was developing along the waterfront and west into the suburbs of Mount Pearl and Paradise. But midtown property always retains its value, Dobbin believed, and with some tough negotiating Dobbin Properties acquired the land for a few thousand dollars. He held onto the property for several years, planning to donate it to the city as an important site, perhaps for parkland. Before he could do so, however, the city of St. John's expropriated the property again at a reported price of $1 million, intending it for commercial development. Dobbin shrugged and accepted the cash. Frank Ryan and Craig's brother Basil, partners in Cabot Development Corporation, added their own parcel of land to it, and at the behest of municipal politicians they developed the St. John's City Centre, including a major hotel on the site in the mid-1980s.

Other encounters with political officials proved more rewarding in lessons learned than in profits gained. In 1971, Dobbin's Omega Investments saw an opportunity to meet a housing shortage in Sydney, Nova Scotia, by constructing an extensive tract of new homes. As usual, Dobbin maximized his prospects by avoiding unions. Things went well until Dobbin's project manager reported from Sydney that he couldn't locate enough non-union workers to complete the houses on schedule. "I know a few in Newfoundland," Dobbin replied, and within a week 150 non-union carpenters, masons, roofers, plumbers and electricians arrived and began clambering over the building site.

The reaction from Sydney union leaders was explosive. Every unionized construction worker in the area, an estimated 10,000, walked off the job and stormed the offices of local politicians, demanding that the interlopers be sent packing. The Nova Scotia government launched a royal commission to investigate the impact of non-unionized out-of-province workers on the economy, and Premier Gerald Regan summoned Dobbin to his office. Regan made his point rather directly.

"He said, 'Look now, man, you're driving down the road at the proper speed limit'," Craig Dobbin recalled years later, "'and there's a guy coming at you in a tractor trailer and he's drunk and he's wandering all over the highway. Now, if I were you, I'd get off the highway.' I got the message that I should sell the project and get out of town." With the provincial government acting as broker, a local firm was persuaded to meet Dobbin's price, take over the project, and develop it with unionized workers following local guidelines. "We sold the development at a profit," Dobbin recalled. "Made a little money on the deal." And the new owners? A sly smile. "They went broke within three months."

Not all of Dobbin's decisions proved profitable. Some time later, he began developing a large tract of houses in New Brunswick, and only after committing himself and his company to the project did he realize the area was already saturated with housing. Prices dropped sharply, and new houses were sitting empty. Pulling out of the deal cost him $5 million, one of a series of events that nudged him and his firm towards bankruptcy. He often approached the brink but never tipped over the edge.

None of his financial troubles dampened his enthusiasm or sullied his image as a deal-maker. Through the first half of the 1970s, Craig Dobbin was a major presence throughout Newfoundland and much of Atlantic Canada, acquiring land, developing residential and commercial properties, and making contacts with influential business and government leaders. Among those he met and impressed were then-Premier Frank Moores, whose engaging personality and frenetic lifestyle meshed with Craig's, and Moores's minister of lands and development, John Crosbie. In the beginning, Crosbie was circumspect about dealing with Dobbin, for fear of conflict of interest charges being tossed his way by reporters and political opponents. Dobbin's charm and his care to avoid discussing any aspect of business in Crosbie's presence won the curmudgeonly politician over, and the two became lifelong friends.

"Craig had a flamboyance about him that you don't see in most businessmen," Crosbie comments. "He loved being in the public eye. Most businessmen, especially those dealing with government, prefer to keep their head down so nobody knows what the hell they're up to. Not Craig. He never hid his light under a bushel. He did and said whatever he wanted. You don't encounter businessmen like him these days, or back then either."

Behind an innate charm that affected men and women with equal impact, Dobbin concealed a degree of business acumen as developed as that of any Harvard MBA graduate. Of course, no MBA course would ever countenance the degree of risk that he practised from his earliest stages as a businessman, leveraging every dollar to the limit. From time to time, however, his charm backfired. He once sent the St. John's Residential Tenancy Board a Christmas gift of a few cases of his favourite whiskey. They sent the gift back, accompanied by a curtly worded note charging that his gift represented an effort to compromise the group's independence and integrity, a gesture they would never tolerate. Dobbin shrugged, tossed the note aside and said, "So I'll drink it myself."

Dobbin possessed the rare knack of never being intimidated by anyone he encountered, and never intentionally intimidating anyone who met him. Separating this skill from his business interests was impossible, though no evidence exists that he seriously attempted to do so. Many people with the power to influence Dobbin's business interests assumed that he sought them out because he enjoyed their

27

company, and on one level they were correct. On another level, they had been assessed according to the interests of Craig Dobbin Ltd. Dobbin never saw contradiction or insincerity in this approach. You worked with people whose company you enjoyed, he believed, and you enjoyed the company of those who worked alongside you.

Throughout his life, Dobbin followed no definitive political philosophy, claiming he had ties to people, not parties. He proved it over the years, criticizing Tories and Grits with equal vigour and castigating Premier Clyde Wells while supporting the provincial and federal forays of Wells's fellow Liberal Brian Tobin.

Dobbin's camaraderie with friends in high places stirred criticism from time to time. In the mid-1970s, a storm of controversy was launched when his fishing buddy Frank Moores agreed that the province would lease office space from a building Dobbin planned to construct. Depending on the terms of the lease, the deal might actually have benefited the province; it most certainly would have benefited Craig Dobbin Ltd. At any rate, the arrangement contravened the public tendering act, and when a member of Moores's government resigned over the issue the idea was quietly withdrawn.

"Craig Dobbin is the kind of fellow," provincial politician Steve Neary observed when the dust from this particular kafuffle had settled, "who will either wind up as Newfoundland's most prominent millionaire or he will end up with the seat out of his pants."

THE SUCCESS OF Craig Dobbin Ltd. and Dobbin Properties provided enough cash flow, wildly fluctuating as it might be ("You'd hear he was practically broke today and the next day you'd read that he just closed a deal for a million-dollar profit," one friend recalls), for Dobbin to indulge himself playing golf and fly-fishing for salmon in the wild, remote rivers of Newfoundland and Labrador. Both activities provided much-needed relaxation, not to mention opportunities to create and develop relationships with politicians, financiers and business colleagues.

Dobbin became a first-rate golfer, capable of driving the ball 250 yards off the tee and eager to play any course he encountered with any partner available. It was salmon fishing, however, that provided the most recreational pleasure, and many friends who joined him for a weekend note how his personality changed as soon as he was standing in a salmon pool, clad in his hip waders and preparing to drop a fly in the shadow of a rock outcropping where the biggest, most wary fish lurked. His face would relax, the furrows would fade, and the smile would widen.

Leasing land near Hopedale in Labrador and Long Harbour in Newfoundland, Dobbin built fishing camps in each area and headed there at every opportunity, often in the company of Frank Moores. Adlatuk, purchased from the U.S. military, which had used it as a recreational facility, was his favourite. The landscape was remote and rugged, and the clear waters adjoining the camp teemed with salmon. In the beginning, both camps were declared off-limits to women. Dobbin and his cohorts spent the evening playing cards and drinking whiskey until well past midnight. On many occasions, musicians and entertainers arrived from St. John's, and the night air carried songs and laughter out across the rocks, streams and pools of the dark landscape. The following morning, the first man at the river's edge or the salmon pool was invariably Craig Dobbin, eager to hook a big one in the dawn light when the waters were calm and the fish were hungry.

By 1976 Dobbin had the contacts, the wherewithal and the determination to establish the remarkable career that would become legendary. Money to satisfy banks and creditors may have been a problem from time to time, but there were always enough funds for a vacation with his family or a trek into the fishing camps by chartered float plane. And for a round of golf with his friend from St. Bonaventure school days, Bob Cole.

"We were playing golf at Bally Hally here in St. John's one day," Cole remembers. "Craig was saying how much he loved the fishing camp and how difficult it was to get there. Just as he was saying this, we heard the sound of a helicopter approaching. It flew directly over the course. Craig looked up as it passed and said, 'Now, if I had one of those things I could drop right into a fishing camp, no trouble at all.' And for the rest of the game he had this distant look on his face, as though he were deciding how to make it work, how to get his hands on a helicopter for the sole purpose of spending more time at his fishing camps."

The helicopter soaring over the golf course was not Craig Dobbin's first awareness of a chopper as a means of reaching remote locales. Frank Moores, responsible for inspiring Dobbin's love of fishing the unharnessed rivers of interior Newfoundland and Labrador, commandeered government helicopters as though they were his personal fleet of commuting vehicles. Craig Dobbin never forgot the thrill of the first ride Moores arranged for him, saying the helicopter ride made him feel like a bird, a great floating bird that could venture anywhere it chose. But the appearance of the helicopter over Bally Hally just as he was describing the pleasure of wilderness fishing may have seemed an omen to him. It was at least an impetus. Within a few weeks, Dobbin had spent $85,000 on a Bell JetRanger helicopter that was capable of carrying him and three friends, plus the pilot, a distance of 600 kilometres at 200 kilometres per hour. From that day forward, every flight in a helicopter heightened his love for the machines. "It's like being a god," Dobbin described the experience. "There's nothing like it. The power of being up there, the vista."

The JetRanger was a toy at first, an opportunity for Dobbin to invite friends, often impulsively, to take off for a weekend of salmon fishing or an aerial tour of the Newfoundland landscape or a jaunt to the offshore French islands of Saint-Pierre and Miquelon for lunch.

He expressed no interest in obtaining his own helicopter pilot's licence, an arduous process that would cut deeply into the time needed to manage his business. This was probably a wise decision; the intense focus and strict adherence to rules needed when piloting any aircraft, but especially a helicopter, would have frustrated him enormously. Instead, he hired a full-time pilot to chauffeur the chopper, a move that added another layer of expense. Dobbin soon discovered that the annual maintenance costs of a helicopter roughly equalled its initial purchase price. In effect, it was like purchasing a new helicopter every year he retained the same machine.

Confronted with such a drain on their cash flow, most businesspeople would either shrug and absorb it or heed the advice of their accountant and pass the toy along to someone else. Dobbin, in a move mirrored at every stage of his career, did neither. The aircraft, he believed, could be altered from a consumer of cash to a creator of cash by chartering it. Of course, if he were to be serious about the business he needed more than one aircraft; in other words, he would respond to the cost of operating a single helicopter by adding the expense of buying and operating three or four of them. Additional JetRangers were purchased in short order, and in 1977 Sealand Helicopters, 100 per cent owned by Craig Dobbin, was launched.

Many observers have suggested that the birth and subsequent success of Sealand was a stroke of Irish luck. True, the launch of Sealand and its growth into the Canadian Helicopter Company (CHC) happened to coincide with the development of Newfoundland's offshore petroleum industry, but it would be foolish to suggest that Dobbin did not foresee the business potential from the beginning. Sealand was not initially designed to be a major player in the province's oil and gas production, and JetRangers were not ideal machines to meet the needs of the petroleum giants; they were too small, too slow and too subject to being grounded in bad weather conditions, making aerial surveys, photography and chartered flights their main applications. There was money to be made from these markets, but not *big* money. That opportunity lay elsewhere.

No industry was more cash-rich than the petroleum industry, which was gearing up for exploration and production in Newfoundland's offshore oil fields. He would shift Sealand into a firm dedicated to meeting the industry's need for helicopters, Dobbin decided. But they had to be the right kind of helicopters, he realized, flown by the right kind of pilots and backed by the right kind of management.

"It didn't take a genius to see how big the offshore oil business was going to be for Newfoundland," Patrick O'Callaghan points out. President and CEO of a large St. John's catering firm, O'Callaghan became fast friends with Dobbin around that time. "The first contract I got with the offshore oil companies was $1.7 million a year just to feed the workers on one rig. We all thought we were in heaven."

Offshore oil and gas production is almost totally dependent on safe, efficient helicopter service to transport personnel, and to a limited extent equipment and materials, between the mainland and platforms, between multiple platforms, and even between ships. The equation is simple and inviolate: without helicopters large enough to carry a dozen or so personnel, advanced enough to overcome virtually any weather conditions, flown by pilots skilled enough to alight on a platform the size of a suburban front lawn in the heart of a North Sea storm, efficient offshore oil production would be impossible.

There were applications beyond the oil fields for helicopter services in Newfoundland and Labrador. In fact, it is difficult to think of any place that could benefit more from the access-easy qualities of the craft. The province has no rail service and few paved roads, and much of its geography is too rugged to justify massive investment in a transportation infrastructure. With inland shipping facilities virtually non-existent, access by air remains the only prospect for much of Newfoundland and Labrador's industrial development. But that access can't be provided by fixed-wing aircraft, with their need for expensive airports.

A well-managed Newfoundland-based helicopter service, Dobbin knew, would open up possibilities in exploration and development that had not existed before. He may have entered the helicopter business industry on something of a lark, but over time he built more than a massive service firm based in Newfoundland; he constructed a means of generating wider interest in the province's resources and helping to alter Newfoundland's have-not status. Helicopters had been providing entry to the region's rugged interior for years, but Sealand was the first home-grown operation to provide both access to its land resources and air service to its offshore petroleum industry.

The move involved substantial economic risk. Operating a fleet of helicopters—maximizing their time in the air to minimize their enormous fixed expense and riding out the cyclical nature of the resource industry—is made more costly by the maintenance demands of the aircraft. A jet-powered helicopter is basically a flying furnace surrounded by several thousand parts, each subject to high levels of stress and all of them essential to the whirlybird remaining safely airborne. Helicopter owners cannot wait for a part to wear out before discarding it. Maintenance procedures often dictate that components be replaced within a fixed number of hours of service to the point where, after a few years, the oldest things on the helicopter are probably the serial number plate and the pilot.

From the beginning, however, Dobbin recognized an aspect of helicopters that partially balanced their high capital costs and expensive maintenance. Unlike most equipment associated with the petroleum industry, helicopters are multi-functional assets. The mechanical ability and pilot skill that enable a large helicopter to fly in bad weather conditions, and to land and take off in an open space not much wider than the radius of its main rotor, are qualities highly valued in applications beyond servicing offshore oil rigs. Search-and-rescue functions, medivac operations, aerial survey work, cinematography, tourism and other ventures all benefit from the availability of professionally managed and flown helicopters. In addition, the availability of medium- and large-sized helicopters with all-weather navigating ability is severely limited. One investment advisor familiar with the industry estimates there are fewer than 1,200 helicopters in the entire world capable of carrying ten or more people. The combination of extensive applications and limited numbers reduces depreciation concerns for quality helicopters. "In the twenty-seven years I've been in the business," said the CEO of a U.S. competitor to Craig Dobbin's business, "I don't think I have ever sold a helicopter at a book loss."

Dobbin grasped the significance of these facts early. He also understood that, by servicing the production side of the petroleum industry rather than its exploration activities, his company would be immune to the market gyrations caused by fluctuating prices and geopolitical events. While helicopters can play a crucial role in the exploration for new oil deposits, this aspect of the industry involves substantial upfront costs and faces high odds against success; any drop in oil prices results in severe cutbacks. Once a production facility is operating, however, it becomes to a large degree inured to any rise and fall in prices. Craig Dobbin shaped and managed his helicopter companies to service production facilities first, creating a relatively stable floor of business volume.

These strategies reassured him in situations where others unfamiliar with the industry grew concerned. They also fuelled his defiant drive to realize his dream. The engine that propels all entrepreneurs to keep rolling the dice and doubling the bet at every opportunity is the belief that they cannot fail. Many, of course, do. The fact that Craig Dobbin succeeded to an astonishing level, in spite of the physical and monetary barriers along the way, remains at the core of the legend that surrounds him.

BUILDING APARTMENTS, KMARTS and strip malls provides few opportunities for learning how to manage a helicopter service business. In 1977, when Dobbin first leased space for Sealand Helicopters in a cavernous hangar on the edge of St. John's airport, he appeared to be a relatively wealthy man dabbling with a fleet of expensive toys. In one respect, this was true. Sealand's helicopters did allow Dobbin and his friends to reach almost any location in Newfoundland and Labrador for a weekend of fishing and fun. On that basis, some might have suspected that the helicopters would eventually lose their appeal and be set aside.

Not in this case. The helicopters became an animated version of Dobbin's property developments, something to manage into a business as broad as his vision and ambition. He couldn't fly a helicopter, but he was never skillful at cutting and assembling a perfectly true roof truss, either. It didn't matter. The world was filled with people who possessed these abilities. They were indispensable, but at the end of the day their chief concerns lay elsewhere.

Few of them woke at two in the morning and rose out of bed to scribble thoughts about a new market to be exploited or a new means of financing debt and generating cash. Few of them fully appreciated the Chinese wisdom that crisis equals opportunity. Few of them, if suddenly finding themselves in possession of a million dollars in cash, would look around immediately for the means to turn it into two million dollars or, what the hell, ten million. And few of them could do all of this while having the time of their lives drinking and playing cards until two in the morning and then showing up for work before dawn, revelling in the anxiety and the action.

Craig Dobbin did all of these things. He did them, as he freely acknowledged on many occasions, by relying on talented people with skills that were beyond him. Like hammering a nail straight into a two by four, or flying a helicopter, or knowing how to maintain it.

Sealand's first fleet of JetRangers were utility machines suitable for limited duties such as ferrying vips and engineers, delivering essential parts to manufacturers, providing transportation for wildlife managers, and serving as air ambulances. For several years this latter chore had been assigned to Universal Helicopters Ltd., a Newfoundland division of Okanagan Helicopters. Okanagan, headquartered in B.C., was the only real competition to Sealand. The province had ruled that only Newfoundland-based industries would qualify to bid for contracts, so Okanagan sidestepped the regulation with Universal Helicopters, which was nominally headquartered there. Universal provided good service at reasonable rates, and its government contract was renewed each year without a tender being called.

Dobbin noted that Universal was operating Sikorsky s-61 machines, by this time a twenty-year-old design (also the basis of Canada's notorious Sea King helicopters, still in use today). Newer machines would be faster, more comfortable, more fuel efficient and more flexible in their operations. With this advantage, plus his determination to shave his margins to the bone, Dobbin set out to dislodge Universal and establish Sealand as the dominant player along Canada's east coast. He began pressuring Premier Frank Moores and various provincial cabinet members, insisting that Sealand be invited to submit a bid on the next appropriate public tender until the province agreed. Having persuaded them to open the door, Dobbin was not going to miss the chance of walking through it, and Sealand easily outbid Universal/Okanagan, claiming a steady if barely profitable piece of the industry. "There was no money in the contract for us," Dobbin declared years later, "but it got us into the business and gave us a platform to expand."

Winning the provincial contract also created hurdles to overcome in the future. One of those was the severe criticism of the Moores-Dobbin friendship batted around within and beyond the legislature. Some critics declared that Moores had agreed to swing government contracts to Sealand and his affable fishing buddy, locking out competition. The charges were biting enough that Dobbin avoided pitching Sealand's services to the province on several occasions to avoid complaints of cronyism. It also severely annoyed an Okanagan shareholder named John Lecky, a man who was far removed from Dobbin in heritage and style yet would play a major role, usually as an adversary, in Dobbin's future business dealings.

SEALAND TOOK DELIVERY of eight Bell LongRanger helicopters in 1979, bringing its fleet size to twenty-six. A medium-sized craft, the LongRanger had been created by attaching a JetRanger power plant to a larger fuselage, providing more comfort for more passengers, more room for bulky cargo and, with its wide double doors, greater ease in loading and unloading. It was in a LongRanger that Dobbin invited three friends to join him in August 1979 for a weekend fishing trip to St. Alban's, about 250 kilometres west of St. John's. The guests included Mose Morgan, president of Memorial University; Jim Walsh, manager of the Royal Bank branch where Sealand's accounts were located; and Walsh's boss Robert "Red" Everett, the bank's regional manager. It would be a two-step journey, the four men flying first north to Clarenville, then changing to another Long-Ranger for the balance of the flight to St. Alban's.

On schedule at 8:30 a.m. on Friday, August 10, 1979, the four men landed in the parking lot of Clarenville's Holiday Inn. The pilot of the second LongRanger, Tim Neuss, helped transfer their gear to his aircraft, and within a few minutes they lifted off for the second leg of their journey. Not far into the trip, however, the Allison turbojet engine powering the LongRanger died and the craft began to descend.

Pilots of fixed-wing aircraft often decry helicopters, considering them too complex to be reliable. When power is lost in a helicopter, however, the risk of injury is decidedly lower than in a standard aircraft, because the disabled helicopter can be made to act like an oversized Frisbee. Disconnecting the main rotor from the engine enables autorotation, and the craft settles relatively gently to the ground, the spinning rotor slowing the drop. Pilot Tim Neuss followed this procedure but soon realized they were dropping directly towards a high-voltage power line running between two steeply sloped hills.

Avoiding the lines required him to steer the craft rather than let it descend vertically, and the attempt sent the helicopter slipping sideways. It crashed heavily into a massive outcropping of rock.

Jim Walsh was killed instantly. Neuss was severely injured. Mose Morgan and Red Everett suffered serious injuries, as did Craig Dobbin, whose sternum was crushed and whose scalp was almost torn from his skull.

Despite his injury, Dobbin persuaded everyone to remain where they were. Ripping off his shirt and wrapping it around his head to stem the flow of blood, he set off for help. He remembered having seen a railway line south of their location, and he stumbled towards it. Reaching the line, he had the presence of mind to drag a log across the tracks, marking the spot where he emerged from the woods. Then, almost blinded by blood, and with pain from his chest marking every breath, he headed towards the sound of chainsaws somewhere to the west.

Eventually he encountered a group of lumbermen. They were aghast at the sight of the large man lurching towards them, his head wrapped in a blood-soaked cloth, telling them to get help and hurry, damn it, men were dying back there. Rescuers were dispatched. Thanks to Craig's care in marking the entry from the railroad tracks, the surviving men were quickly located, carried out of the bush and flown to hospital.

Tim Neuss clung to life for a week before succumbing. Morgan, Everett and Dobbin eventually recovered. Craig was the first to be released from hospital, and he spent the next few days questioning his decision to become involved with helicopters. Two men he had known and cared for were dead because of his decision to take a helicopter flight. These things never happened in housing construction, where most injuries were limited to a hammer blow on an errant thumb. Should he give it up and let others make a living from these complex, unpredictable machines?

He voiced his concerns to his eldest son Mark, then an MBA student at Dalhousie University. "Dad," Mark replied, "if you're that concerned about safety and about being sure nobody else is hurt in a helicopter crash, maybe you're the only guy who should be running things. Because you know what can happen, and how bad it can be."

His persuasion worked. The following day Dobbin rode with a Sealand pilot, ordering him to perform as many air acrobatics as the pilot could handle and the craft could stand. Upon landing, he was more convinced than ever: helicopters represented an essential service to the industrial growth of Newfoundland and the world. He loved the thrill of flying, and he loved watching a vision become reality. He was already in the business, and he was damned if he would give it up, even after enduring tragedy.

A few months later, a provincial inquiry determined that the crash had been caused by the helicopter's engine failure, not by poor maintenance or pilot error. The Allison engine aboard Bell helicopters was subject to coking, an excessive and unpredictable build-up of carbon. Similar instances had been reported and were being addressed by the manufacturer. Sealand bore no responsibility for the disaster.

FROM THE BEGINNING, Craig Dobbin recognized that the helicopter pilots who handled small machines generating a few hundred dollars an hour in revenue could adapt to the larger machines, whose hourly rate soared to thousands of dollars. It was one reason he had moved up to the larger LongRanger machines. "Small helicopters are all over the world, like flies," according to one former helicopter services executive, "but they're not making much money. The real money in this business is made from big helicopters, not from small two- and four-passenger craft."

Craig Dobbin didn't need years of experience to appreciate this point. He needed bigger machines, and he planned to use them in his pitch for contracts. Only large helicopters equipped with state-of-the-art navigation and control systems would meet the demands of the offshore petroleum industry, the largest potential market in the region. True, the capital cost for the larger machines rose significantly, but this was merely the price of becoming a bigger, more successful player. Spending millions on large helicopters with greater range and payload, as well as the ability to fly in weather that grounded smaller craft, was the natural way to build the company.

Sources of financing were a challenge, one that Dobbin met through his charm, his resolve and his personal contacts. Here a little bit of Irish luck did help from time to time. The first break for Dobbin came from a man who over the years had become as close to him as a brother.

Back in 1969, Dobbin had learned that the Canadian armed forces were planning to build sixty houses to accommodate servicemen and their families at Gander. With many of his CMHC-funded apartments in the region sitting empty, Dobbin arranged a meeting with the base commander to pitch the flats as an economical alternative. After listening to his pitch the commander raised his eyebrows and told Dobbin he knew about the apartments. They were so damn cramped, the commander noted, that residing in them would be "like living inside a Salvation Army drum." Dobbin roared with laughter at the description and spent the rest of the day in the commander's company, trading stories and discussing business and politics. He never gained a lease from his pitch, but he acquired Commander Harry Steele as a lifelong pal. As much as anyone Dobbin ever encountered, Steele served as his confidant, mentor, ally and comrade in the years that followed, though it is almost impossible to imagine two more contrasting personalities.

Born in Musgrave Harbour on the shore of the Labrador Sea, Harry Steele spent the first year of his working life shovelling gravel to build roads, and the next twenty-four as an officer in the Royal Canadian Navy. After retiring from the navy in 1974, he applied his leadership abilities to business. Steele's first major achievement evolved from an investment in Eastern Provincial Airways. In time he became the company's majority shareholder, and he orchestrated its sale to Canadian Pacific Airlines for a $20-million profit.

Meanwhile, opportunities were opening in the province's off-shore oil industry. Okanagan, the country's largest helicopter services firm, made a pitch to service the first producing well in the Hibernia field, but their bid was undercut by a new firm launched by a Newfoundland businessman determined to cash in on the bonanza. Unfortunately, the businessman did not own a helicopter, planning to obtain an s-61 aircraft under lease to Okanagan from Sikorsky. When Okanagan refused to release the machine, the deal was stymied. As a solution, Okanagan bought out the owner, launched a new firm called Universal Helicopters, transferred the s-61 lease to Universal, and recruited Harry Steele to run the company, granting him a seat on Okanagan's board.

Forming Newfoundland Capital Corporation in 1980, Steele directed the publicly traded company towards investments in transportation and communications. By 2000, Newfoundland Capital owned and operated four hotels in Newfoundland and Labrador and more than seventy radio and television stations from Deer Lake, Newfoundland, to Elkford, British Columbia. Most were located in small communities, although Steele added a smattering of larger locations such as Ottawa, Winnipeg and Edmonton. Newcap's operations may not be players in the giant competitive markets of Toronto, Montreal and Vancouver, but that's just the way Harry Steele likes it. Steele's business acumen has produced a steadily expanding core of assets, a comfortable margin of profit, and the elevation of his status, according to *Canadian Business* magazine, into one of the twenty most powerful business people in Canada.

Aside from their modest beginnings, Craig Dobbin and Harry Steele could hardly have been more different. Steele, by his own description, is frugal; Craig Dobbin, by general consensus, was flamboyant. Harry avoids the limelight; Craig thrived in it. Harry drives a seven-year-old Chrysler; Craig Dobbin once spent $600,000 on a Rolls-Royce that accumulated barely 7,000 kilometres before being sold for a third of its original cost. Yet it is unlikely that any two businessmen in Canada were as closely linked through the heights of their careers.

Their relationship was cemented in 1980 when Dobbin became involved in yet another quest for investment money. That year, Steele was contacted by Alan Bristow, a former Royal Navy helicopter pilot who had launched a helicopter service dubbed Air Whaling Ltd., renamed Bristow Helicopters several years later. The firm, located in Surrey, England, was a major participant in the U.K.'s offshore petroleum industry, primarily in the North Sea. With activity stirring in Newfoundland, Bristow saw the potential to expand into the North American market. Knowing Harry Steele's business success and military background, Bristow approached Steele with a direct offer. "We have similar backgrounds," Bristow said in a telephone call. "We're both former naval officers, and I want you to be my partner in launching a helicopter service over there."

"I learned a long time ago that you can't dance with everybody," Steele comments today, "and I had a history with Okanagan. When Bristow called I told him I wasn't interested in a partnership."

Nevertheless, Bristow and Steele met in Steele's Albatross Hotel in Gander a few days later. "Bristow was pretty flashy," Harry Steele says. "He arrived with a pouch full of expensive cigars and did a lot of big talking. I told him again that my association with Okanagan ruled out any partnership. Then I said, 'There's a guy down in St. John's named Craig Dobbin who has a helicopter company. Maybe you should go talk to him.' And he did."

On his way to Britain to negotiate with Bristow, Dobbin flew out of Gander, staying overnight at Harry Steele's Gander hotel and popping into Steele's office the next morning for a quick farewell. He had barely enough time before his flight to meet with Robert Foster, a Toronto-based financier whose company Capital Canada engaged in the placement of private funds for corporations. When Dobbin expressed concerns about the prospects of reaching a deal with Bristow, Foster handed Dobbin a card and suggested Capital Canada might be able to provide the funds.

Robert Foster's personality and style contrasted as much with Craig Dobbin's as Dobbin's did with Harry Steele's. Foster was and remains quintessential Bay Street, formally educated, highly connected and so impeccably groomed he might have stepped out of a display window at Holt Renfrew. Dobbin reflected his roots as a blue-collar son of Newfoundland, lacking both polish and pretension. "He was wearing a pair of blue shorts and looked like he was on his way to go fishing, totally relaxed," Foster says, describing the day he first met Dobbin at the Albatross. "I assume he chose a more formal wardrobe for his flight. But that was my first image of him, and I had never met anyone with more raw energy and a more positive outlook than Craig Dobbin."

Foster was not entirely a stranger to Newfoundland business and politics. At the time he met Craig Dobbin, he was a friend of Tory cabinet minister John Crosbie and a principal fundraiser for Crosbie's campaign to seize the leadership of the federal Progressive Conservative party from Joe Clark. (Crosbie to Brian Mulroney.) Another member of Crosbie's team was Craig's brother Bas, who was becoming a major player in the property development game in Newfoundland.

Alan Bristow and Craig Dobbin needed each other, Bristow for Dobbin's toehold in the Newfoundland market and Dobbin for Bristow's investment potential. It should have been a win-win situation, but within a few months of striking a deal the two men were shouting at each other, then not speaking at all. Eventually, each would sue the other. By the time the dust cleared—Craig Dobbin reportedly won a $500,000 settlement—neither man needed nor could tolerate the other.

When Dobbin's deal with Bristow collapsed, he remembered the smooth Bay Street moneyman he had met in Gander. After meeting with Dobbin again and reviewing the proposal, Foster arranged $5 million in financing for Sealand through Manulife Insurance, placing himself and a Manulife representative on Sealand's board of directors. It would be the first of many Foster-Dobbin deals, and the launch of a long and mutually beneficial relationship.

3

Craig became famous for his motto: When things get tough,
you get bigger. And he really believed it. When things got tight
financially he looked around for something to buy or some way
to expand. That was his solution to almost everything.
SYLVAIN ALLARD, president and CEO, CHC Helicopters Ltd.

IN 1977, ITS FIRST full year of operation, Sealand Helicopters
earned $784,000 in gross revenue from provincial government
contracts and charters. Barely four years later Sealand recorded
more than $7.5 million in revenue. The fact that it also suffered a
net loss of $500,000 was a minor concern, especially when the com-
pany almost doubled its income to $13 million the following year.
Now Craig Dobbin set his sights on the biggest potential money-
maker of all.

Within a year of Sealand's launch, the discovery of enormous
petroleum reserves at Hibernia on Newfoundland's Grand Banks
had been confirmed. The resulting interest in the province's offshore
petroleum developments represented massive potential for profit. In
other applications, helicopters were primarily a convenience, a means
of cutting travel time. When it came to servicing offshore drilling and
production platforms, however, they were a necessity. And who had
deeper pockets than the multinational petroleum companies?

Barriers existed to joining the international petroleum club as
a significant player, and one of them was the need to dislodge Uni-
versal/Okanagan, well established in offshore work for the industry.

Dobbin could undercut their pricing, as he had to obtain the provincial contracts, but this was a more complex situation. He did not have Frank Moores's guidance this time, and the primary issue with the petroleum companies was more than price. No oil company executive would risk the loss of personnel and production to a bunch of inexperienced pilots in exchange for saving a few hundred thousand dollars in transportation fees. There was also the question of the aircraft used to transport workers and equipment between the mainland and the offshore drilling rigs. Sealand's LongRanger machines weren't up to the job in capacity, comfort or communications. To become a serious bidder, Sealand would require a fleet of helicopters similar to Okanagan's aging Sikorsky s-61s. To chase the contracts Dobbin would have to upgrade his fleet. But instead of the economical option of buying or leasing his own Sikorskys, he chose a strategy that became a hallmark for both the remarkable successes and the various crises the company encountered over the next twenty years.

The rational, reduced-risk, MBA-based approach would have been to minimize the firm's capital outlay. Other craft were available, including larger Bell helicopters than the LongRangers currently in the Sealand fleet. Sealand had a record with Bell and a good negotiating position. Why not exploit it?

But the Sikorskys were old technology, and the Bells were limited in size and application. The finest large helicopter in the world, capable of carrying up to twenty-three workers clad in survival suits over the North Atlantic in safety and comfort, was the new AS 332 Super Puma built by European manufacturer Aerospatiale (today Eurocopter). Originally designed for military use, the AS 332 incorporated a number of design features that enhanced its reliability, including run-dry transmissions, redundant electrical and hydraulic systems, thermal de-icing of the main rotor blades, and an advanced radar system providing all-weather flight capabilities. With a maximum speed of more than 300 kilometres per hour, each

Super Puma could carry its passengers 370 kilometres, making it a near-ideal craft to supply offshore oil platforms.

Forget used Sikorskys or new medium-sized LongRangers, Craig Dobbin decided. They were half-measures. To get the job done right he would order a fleet of Super Pumas, immediately identifying Sealand as a serious player in the industry. It was a bold, almost foolhardy move. The Super Pumas were among the most expensive craft available, each carrying a purchase price of $6 million, or about half the company's annual gross revenue at that point. He would have to float their purchase at a time when interest rates hovered at record levels of 16 to 18 per cent. What's more, the Super Pumas were unproven in the North American market; they looked good on paper, but no one was anxious to test-fly the machines in the tightly scheduled and highly competitive offshore petroleum industry. No one, that is, except Craig Dobbin.

On the upside, Dobbin's pioneering move provided leverage in his negotiations to purchase the Super Pumas. Aerospatiale needed a breakthrough in the North American market, dominated by home-grown competitors Bell and Sikorsky. Aerospatiale were prepared to accommodate the first serious purchaser of Super Pumas with attractive deals, and they did, after Sealand received an injection of capital from Louisiana-based Petroleum Helicopters. Cash acquired in exchange for 22 per cent equity in Sealand enabled Dobbin to place a down payment on a fleet of Super Pumas for delivery in 1982.

Persuading Mobil, Gulf Oil, Chevron and Petro-Canada to trust Sealand for their offshore transportation took more than new equipment. No Sealand crew had flown the routes to offshore rigs, and no Sealand pilots had settled the 9,000-kilogram craft onto a platform in the wake of a January nor'easter. Dobbin's solution was to recruit the best of Universal/Okanagan's crews, offering them higher salaries and the opportunity to fly newer, more responsive Super Pumas. It worked. As with the provincial government contracts, Universal/ Okanagan were undercut by the newest guy in the air, and Sealand became the means of air travel between the offshore rigs and the mainland.

Craig Dobbin's heart was no longer in bricks and mortar assets. The dynamics of helicopter operations seized his attention. Helicopters lifted off from the ground and vanished across far horizons, sometimes to other continents. They were complex and demanding, almost alive, and their potential was still being developed. Real estate was fixed, immobile, dull in comparison. Anybody could do a land survey, obtain building permits, erect buildings and fill them with merchandise and people. How many people could turn a fleet of helicopters into clattering, high-speed money machines, travelling, as Sealand's soon were, across eastern Canada and well inside the Arctic Circle?

The shift from real estate to helicopters was achieved thanks to traits that Dobbin acknowledged several times in his career, those that mark all successful CEOS no matter what industry they serve. The traits are to hire carefully, assign responsibility widely, and avoid micro-managing wherever possible. Dobbin knew little about piloting helicopters and even less about servicing them. These were not his functions. "I'm not an expert on anything," he explained. "Whatever the job, whatever the challenge, somebody out there can do it better than I can. True entrepreneurs surround themselves with professional managers who share their vision and put form around it. Not only can you not do it all yourself, it's not necessary, and it doesn't make sense. I believe in being a good casting director of people who work together and share together."

The "casting director" analogy was appropriate but inadequate. Craig Dobbin was not only capable of selecting staff and employees with exceptional skills; he could also detect untapped talent and encourage its development, as he did in 1982 with a young French-Canadian helicopter pilot named Sylvain Allard.

Allard had received his helicopter flight instruction at Chicoutimi, Quebec, under a provincial training program. Qualified for

47

small craft, he wanted the chance to fly large helicopters and perhaps cash in on the growth of the offshore oil industry in eastern Canada. A friend who was flying with Sealand suggested Allard visit the firm's Gander office and submit a job application. Allard contacted Sealand to alert them to his interest, but just as he was leaving for an anticipated job interview he received a telephone call from Sealand's chief pilot, who informed him that no positions with Sealand were available. Allard, the chief pilot suggested, should stay home. Sealand would keep his application on file, and if an opening came up in the future...

"I had already booked my flight," Sylvain Allard recalls, "and I thought, what the heck, I'll go anyway. It was April 1982, and we landed at Gander in a roaring blizzard. I tracked down the chief pilot, who was surprised to see me and said, 'As long as you're here we might as well take a ride and I can check you out.' And off we went in a JetRanger to deliver firewood to a fishing camp at Devil's Lake."

The weather was bad all the way up the coast, but Sylvain impressed the chief pilot with his flying skills, especially his ability to land precisely and gently. "We got the sling of firewood unloaded and were getting ready to take off when this big guy comes out of one of the buildings and waves us inside, out of the wind and snow, to have some tea with him. It was Craig Dobbin, of course."

Allard wasn't entirely comfortable with the invitation. He hadn't expected a test flight, let alone an interview with Sealand's owner. Besides, as Allard puts it, "My English back then wasn't so good. But as soon as Craig learned I was from Montreal he told me how much he loved the city. He started dropping French words into the conversation and pretty soon we both felt right at home."

Dobbin turned to his chief pilot. "Do you have a job for this guy?" he asked, jabbing a thumb in Allard's direction.

The pilot said no, they had all the pilots they needed at the moment.

"Well, I've worked with a lot of Quebec people in my day, and they're all good employees," Dobbin replied. "Find him a job." Craig Dobbin had just hired a future CEO of his company and the man who, second to Dobbin himself, is credited with building CHC into a global entity.

AS THINGS EVOLVED, Sealand's Newfoundland location and fleet of Super Puma helicopters failed to provide the company with permanent access to the riches of the offshore oil industry. The initial contracts, picked up at the expense of Okanagan, were permitted to expire by the petroleum giants, who turned elsewhere for helicopter services. According to Harry Steele, the problem was personal; management at the multinational oil companies working offshore disliked Craig Dobbin. "Craig never flew to the platforms," Steele points out, "and he never got involved in that aspect of their business the way others did, the way his own top people did in later years. So he never really cashed in on the business the way he should have." The cancelled contracts no longer mattered when Hibernia development was delayed due to federal and provincial squabbling over offshore rights, a dispute whose echoes reverberate today.

Interest rates on loans and leases reached record heights during Sealand's early years, exceeding 20 per cent annually before settling into double digits for some time. Carrying the enormous debt imposed on the company by the purchase of the Super Puma helicopters, Dobbin searched elsewhere in the world for opportunities. He appointed his son Mark, fresh from a year's experience with Louisiana-based Petroleum Helicopters, as international marketing manager for Sealand and dispatched him to South America. To his credit, the younger Dobbin succeeded in obtaining contracts from oil exploration firms in Colombia, Brazil and Trinidad-Tobago. Many involved working in locations under periodic attack from guerrilla forces and, in the case of one contract, stickhandling around government bureaucracy.

Occidental Petroleum was attempting to construct an 800-kilo-metre pipeline through dense jungle in Colombia, running from Canon Limon, near the Venezuelan border, to the port of Covenas on the Atlantic coast. On several occasions guerrillas destroyed sections of the completed pipeline with explosives and threatened to kidnap workers. With a contract from Occidental to provide helicopters capable of ferrying men and equipment into remote locales, Sealand sent several Super Pumas south. Lacking entry permits, however, the company was forced to park the helicopters at Aruba, where they sat for weeks waiting for bureaucrats to process the permits.

"Dad was going ballistic," says Mark Dobbin, who was shepherd-ing the contract. "We desperately needed cash from that contract to stay afloat, and here we were spending money we couldn't afford to keep the crews and aircraft in Aruba." Pleas from Sealand to expe-dite the permits generated little more than smiles and shrugs from Colombian officials.

It took a disaster of historic proportions to end the crisis. In mid-November 1985 the volcano Nevado del Ruiz erupted for the first time in nearly 150 years, spewing ash and lava from its 5,000-metre summit. Towns and villages were buried beneath ash and mud, and rescue efforts were hampered by fallen bridges and impass-able roads. Literally overnight the impasse over entry permits van-ished. Instead of barring the Sealand choppers, Colombia pleaded for them to assist in search-and-rescue operations, and for two weeks Sealand craft and crews worked around the clock delivering food and tents to survivors in remote villages and ferrying others to safety. Even with these efforts, assisted by contributions from other countries, thousands of Colombians lost their lives in the eruption.

With their humanitarian duties completed and their helicopters within Colombian borders, Sealand was able to fulfill its contract. Colombia's military held the guerrillas at bay while Sealand ferried disassembled drill rigs and other materials deep into the jungle, and Sealand's performance under these demanding conditions helped build the company's international reputation, opening doors to new opportunities around the globe.

Other barriers to obtaining contracts in South America were more direct, involving plain brown envelopes filled with small pieces of green-backed paper bearing portraits of U.S. presidents. Craig Dobbin was upfront about this aspect of his business, explaining that he needed partners "to get the appropriate licence for us, get the appropriate visas for our personnel, provide us with co-pilots, clear our products and inventories through customs and, if there was any graft involved, to pay the graft," although he despised this aspect of the business.

Expanded business did not translate into expanded profits, however, and on several occasions Dobbin was forced to dip into the coffers of his real estate arm Omega Investments to meet Sealand's payroll. When Omega itself was unable to play the role of cash cow for Sealand, Dobbin established a four-day work week for Sealand employees, reducing their salary by 20 per cent and encouraging them to draw unemployment insurance benefits for the fifth day of each week, almost restoring their original salary levels.

Sean Tucker, a Sealand pilot (and nephew of Craig Dobbin), recalls occasions when Dobbin gathered pilots and maintenance staff together in the company's hangar at St. John's airport to announce, "Boys, I can't make the payroll this week. If you hang on I'll do my best to see that you get paid next week, and I'll catch up then."

"Each time it happened," Tucker remembers, "the response was, 'That's all right, Mr. Dobbin. Do the best you can.' It was an amazing example of the loyalty and affection everyone had for him. And he was as good as his word. Everybody got paid eventually."

From time to time, Dobbin stretched that loyalty to its limit. One year while reviewing Sealand's expenses and projected income, he determined that the only route to survival lay in everyone absorbing a 10 per cent cut in salary, and he instructed CEO Al Soutar to sell the idea to the staff. When Soutar managed to do it, with minimal grumbling from employees, Dobbin was so impressed with his abilities that he bought Soutar a new car. For months afterwards the sight of Soutar driving his shiny BMW prompted Sealand employees to mutter, "Gee, our 10 per cent runs well, doesn't it?"

Even with the 10 per cent cut, from time to time Sealand's cash situation was insufficient to keep the company afloat. Bob Dunne, a childhood friend of the Dobbin clan who managed the Sealand hangar in the mid-1980s, recalls Dobbin being forced to lay off several of his staff, among them Dunne himself. "He gave me my severance cheque, and it was a pretty good one, too," Dunne says. "But I was the guy who made the deposit at that particular bank branch and I knew there wasn't a bunch of money there." Leaving the Sealand offices, Dunne made a prudent decision. "I beat it to the company's bank. I knew if I went there I'd get [the cheque] changed without question and without waiting around to see if she'd bounce or not. So I got her changed to cash, then went up the road to my own bank and deposited it."

The next day, Dobbin called Dunne back to the hangar and said, "Good news. I've got your job back for you."

"He asked me for his cheque back," Dunne grins, "and I told him what I did. I said I went straight to his bank and got the cash without waiting to see if the cheque would clear or not. And you know what Craig Dobbin did? He laughed and said, 'You did the right thing. That was good thinking on your part.' That's what he was like."

Dunne also recalls Dobbin rushing into his office, a cheque in his hand, and telling Dunne to jump in his car and race the cheque downtown to the power company. "The light and power company had called to say they were tired of waiting for their money and they were sending a man in a truck to the airport to shut 'er down," Dunne remembers. "I was given orders to get to the power company with a Sealand cheque before their guy in the truck got to the airport." Halfway between the airport and downtown, Dunne passed the light and power company vehicle heading in the opposite direction, and he pressed the accelerator to the floor. "I didn't get a speeding ticket from there on, but I might've," he laughs. He dashed into the utility's office with the cheque, and the company reached their technician at the hangar just as he was preparing to shut off Sealand's electric power.

Despite constant threats of bankruptcy, Dobbin kept finding new ways to expand the company, ways that demanded access to new sources of investment capital. His confidence and charm, plus a remarkable knack for grasping and assessing financial figures, helped him succeed where others would not even venture. On one occasion, he announced to a Sealand manager that he was off to New York in search of new financing. "But we're in a serious debt position," the manager reminded him. "How are you going to convince anybody in New York to give us more money?"

Dobbin grinned and replied, "A cat makes strange jumps when it's cornered." A few days later he returned with a new inflow of badly needed cash.

Paddy O'Callaghan recalls dropping in on his friend shortly after the visit of Pope John Paul to Newfoundland in 1984. The helicopter ferrying His Holiness around the province had used the Sealand helipad, and Dobbin had naturally seized the opportunity to meet and speak with the religious leader.

"He's sitting at his desk, writing a letter," O'Callaghan grins, recalling the event, "and in front of him are rosary beads and a scapular."

Dobbin explained that he was composing a letter to accompany the beads and scapular, which he was sending to the chairman of Aerospatiale, supplier of Sealand's most expensive aircraft. Sealand owed Aerospatiale several million dollars. "He gave me a set and blessed them," Dobbin told O'Callaghan, "and when I asked for another set he gave me these and blessed them too, and I'm sending them to France. Impress the hell out of them, it will."

"And I said, 'Craig, you can't give them to somebody else now,'" O'Callaghan remembers. "'That's sacrilegious, the Pope actually gave them to you.' And Craig said, 'I didn't tell him what I was going to do with them, did I?'"

It often appeared that Dobbin could not resist an opportunity to expand his business empire, no matter how many challenges that might present or how much deeper in debt it would place the company. In the early 1980s, a change in Department of Transport regulations persuaded him to launch Air Atlantic as a feeder airline in the maritime provinces for Canadian Airlines Ltd. Dobbin got Air Atlantic into operation several months ahead of its competitor Air Nova, which would serve a similar role with Air Canada. Air Atlantic enjoyed immediate access to CAL's ticket counters, baggage handlers and computer reservations system, but Air Nova was unable to secure its deal with Air Canada for some time. "In any business deal, timing is generally everything," Harry Steele observes, "and Craig's timing was perfect."

Launching and managing a scheduled airline demands substantial attention, and many entrepreneurs have built their entire careers around such an endeavour. But Dobbin never considered Air Atlantic a major component of his business. He placed it almost entirely in the hands of experienced executives such as ex-chairman and former president of Eastern Provincial Airways Keith Miller. "I don't think it was ever really on his radar screen," says Barry Clouter, who rose to become a regional manager for CHC. "I think he just loved the glamour of being in the airline business, because I know he didn't make much money from it."

Dobbin also loved the give-and-take of business, even when the occasion involved a financial conflict or a risk of bankruptcy. It was almost as though he relished the opportunity to display his fabled Dobbin charm in a mano-a-mano encounter, as he did with Steve Hudson.

Hudson, born into a Toronto blue-collar family, launched his business career as an accountant in a suburban hospital, not the most propitious start to building enormous wealth. His hospital experience taught him much about leasing in the health care industry, however, lessons he applied to his launch of Newcourt Capital. Within a remarkably short time, Newcourt grew to become the second-largest non-bank financial lending source in North America, with the boyish and exuberant Hudson at the helm.

Seeking to add several new Dash 8 aircraft to the Air Atlantic fleet, Dobbin contacted Newcourt Capital, which financed the purchase of six new aircraft for the firm. Dobbin signed a ten-year lease agreement, and some months later the Dash 8s took to the air. The $40-million contract represented the largest financing and leasing deal Newcourt had arranged to that point.

The relationship between Air Atlantic and Canadian Airlines was always shaky, and it was never more strained than in the months following delivery of the new Dash 8 fleet. In Craig Dobbin's view, Canadian wasn't feeding sufficient passenger loads to Air Atlantic, and many of the regional airline's routes were distinct money-losers. Since the new aircraft were not bringing money into Air Atlantic, Craig Dobbin was damned if any money would flow out of the company to cover lease payments.

Steve Hudson made several attempts to obtain payment from Air Atlantic, all of them ignored. With no alternatives remaining, he contacted legal authorities in Newfoundland, obtained a writ of seizure, and expected to hear that the aircraft had been repossessed. When they were not, Hudson took things into his own hands and flew to St. John's, determined to get the job done.

But he couldn't: the aircraft were always somewhere else. Everywhere, in fact, except where Hudson and his writ were. Told they were in Gander, he tried seizing them there, only to be informed the planes were now in Halifax, or perhaps Deer Lake. For three days Hudson chased down his $40-million investment. "It was winter and the weather was terrible," Hudson recalls. "Each day the wind came blowing in off the ocean, so strong that the snow was moving horizontally across the ground." Hudson seethed at the idea of spending so much time in such miserable weather while the man who owed him a substantial amount of money played cat and mouse with Hudson's own aircraft. Dobbin's strategy, Hudson gathered, was to assume that Hudson would give up his attempts to seize the aircraft and return to Toronto. Hudson promised himself he would not leave until he settled the issue.

On the third day, Hudson received a telephone call at his suite in the Hotel Newfoundland. It was Craig Dobbin. "You know," Dobbin said, "a dumb Upper Canadian will keep running around this province looking for those damn planes. But a real man will come have an Irish whiskey with me and settle it."

Later that day Dobbin welcomed Hudson into his office, retrieved a bottle of Jameson from his desk drawer and poured a glass for each of them. "Twenty minutes later we had a deal," Hudson smiles, "and from that day forward we were the best of friends. Craig just dared to dream, and he was determined that Air Atlantic would survive. My demand to be paid? It was just another hiccup to him."

Over time, no one admired Craig Dobbin and valued his companionship more than Hudson did. In 1992 a roast celebrating Hudson's upcoming marriage was held at Toronto's Skydome Hotel, with all proceeds going to charity. Most of the all-male audience comprised representatives of Canada's financial community. Dobbin, unable to attend, sent a telegram pledging $5,000 to charity but offering to double the amount if Hudson dropped his trousers and mooned the Bay Street heavyweights. Hudson agreed. The belt was unfastened and the trousers were lowered. Almost fifteen years later, Dobbin would return the gesture under different circumstances, before a somewhat different audience.

Dobbin reached further into the scheduled airline business when he purchased 18 per cent of Ontario Express, a regional operation affiliated with Canadian Airlines International. The investment made him the second-largest shareholder of Ontario Express after CAI, and qualified him for the position of chairman of the board of the airline. The experience was unprofitable for Dobbin by any measure; less than three years later CAI acquired total ownership of Ontario Express, along with Alberta-based Time Air, and Dobbin bowed out. He may have gained experience in managing a scheduled airline, but he earned no recorded profits. It didn't matter. Sealand was now the sole focus of his efforts. It was the company that would generate the most fun, the most outrageous risks, and the most money in Dobbin's bank account and pockets—more money than he ever dreamed of accumulating.

SEALAND'S FIRST CEO was Al Soutar. Soutar was a famed helicopter pioneer, and his experience and contacts in the industry enabled Dobbin to pull together a workable team of pilots, maintenance specialists, schedulers and other key team members. With his move into the offshore oil industry, though, Dobbin needed a CEO with wider abilities and experience, including budgeting and cost control. As he had with pilots, he filled the position by raiding Universal/ Okanagan.

J.C. Jones (he was christened James Canfield but has been known as J.C. since his school days) grew up in Virginia and still retains a soft southern U.S. accent. Trained as a helicopter pilot in the U.S. military, Jones served in the Vietnam war, an experience he avoids discussing. Discharged in 1970, he moved to Newfoundland to work as a pilot for Universal Helicopter. Most of Universal's work at the time was contracted by the provincial government in support of wildlife services, surveys and other functions.

Jones demonstrated enough management ability for Universal to finance his return to school to earn his MBA. With degree in hand, he moved to Okanagan's head office in Vancouver as the general manager, IFR (Instrument Flight Rules, the most demanding pilot designation), domestic division, meaning he directed virtually all of Okanagan's operations in Canada. "I knew about Craig Dobbin and Sealand," Jones recalls, "but at Okanagan we didn't pay them much mind at first. Okanagan was a giant, and Sealand was some regional operation that was never expected to grow because it took too much capital investment to acquire the big craft that could make you money. Even when Dobbin stole the Newfoundland government contract from us, the people at Okanagan didn't take him seriously. We really expected him to go away financially, sinking under all of his debt." But Dobbin didn't go away, and by the mid-1980s Sealand represented the only serious competitor to Okanagan east of Ontario. Dobbin needed Sealand to grow, and he needed someone like J.C. Jones to help grow it.

Jones and his family were settled in Vancouver, a city he loved, and Jones enjoyed working at Okanagan Helicopters. His wife, a doctor, had a thriving practice. They owned a home near the water and had no interest in returning to the east coast. "In fact," Jones says, "if you had told me an hour before I met Craig Dobbin that I would ever move back to Newfoundland, I would have bet my life savings against it."

Nevertheless, when Dobbin called Jones one Saturday morning in 1984 with an invitation to join him for lunch, Jones accepted. "We had a policy at Okanagan that you never turned down a chance to meet with a competitor if invited," Jones says, "because you never knew what he might say without intending to reveal something important. I figured I could listen to him talk, not offer much on our part, and maybe come away with something important to Okanagan."

Instead, Jones came away with an offer to join Sealand as the new CEO, replacing the retiring Al Soutar. Jones almost laughed at the idea. Leave a top-level position with giant Okanagan in Vancouver to run little Sealand back in Newfoundland? The proposal remained just as ridiculous on Monday morning when he informed Okanagan CEO Pat Aldous of the offer, assuring Aldous that he had no intention of joining Sealand.

Dobbin had stopped in Vancouver on his way to an extended trip in China, so it was several weeks before he contacted Jones again.

Jones explained to Dobbin that he enjoyed his job, he and his wife loved Vancouver, and though he was flattered by the offer he was not interested. Refusing to concede, Dobbin called several times over the next few months, attempting to persuade Jones to accept the job, even flying Jones and his wife to St. John's for a meeting. Jones continued turning down the offer until the day Dobbin called Jones at a relative's home in Winnipeg and said, "What the hell is it going to take to get you back east running Sealand?"

"I couldn't believe that he'd tracked me to Winnipeg," Jones recalls. "So I figured I'd put him off for good, I'd just get rid of him." Jones asked for twice his current salary, adding that Dobbin would have to cover all his moving expenses to Newfoundland, provide his family with an acceptable house, and have a new car waiting when he got there. "I made it as ridiculous as I could, convinced that he would give up."

Instead, Dobbin replied, "Okay, done deal. How soon can you get out here?"

Bidding goodbye to his astonished co-workers at Okanagan, Jones departed for St. John's. Within a few days of arriving at Sealand, he began doubting the wisdom of his decision. He may have wangled a good deal out of Dobbin, but its value was worthless if Sealand was unable to meet its financial obligations to him. That was a distinct possibility, since the company was having difficulty meeting its financial obligation to almost everyone else. Among Sealand's most vocal creditors was Aerospatiale, awaiting payments for its fleet of multimillion-dollar Super Pumas plus spare parts and servicing equipment in Sealand's possession. The chances of settling the debt quickly were minimal. Sealand's revenue was about $20 million annually, but overhead costs were absorbing so much of its income that little was left over. Much of Jones's effort, he soon realized, would consist of juggling one dollar in the bank with every three or four dollars the company owed. Sealand's immense debt was disconcerting to him and every staff member aware of the situation. But not to Craig Dobbin.

"I learned that Craig's management style was based on gambling," Jones explains. "I had earned my MBA, which equips you to manage and reduce risk. That's important, but the process sucks all the entrepreneurial spirit out of you. Craig never had a formal business education. He admired people who did, but he didn't trust or didn't appreciate some aspects of it. He was always working like a man at the very edge of a cliff. One strong gust of wind would blow him over the brink. The other managers and I, we were always trying to get him to pull back from the edge and give us a little manoeuvring room. But as soon as we did, he'd take us back again with some scheme or deal. He was never really comfortable unless he was right on the edge."

Jones found himself spending as much time managing Craig Dobbin—or attempting to manage him—as he spent handling the company's business affairs. "Over and over again, I would say, 'Craig, if we do this idea of yours we will be rolling the dice, and we stand to lose the whole kit and caboodle. If it fails, we close up.' Craig would just grin at me and say, 'J.C., we're fuckin' doin' it!'"

Sealand's banks, along with Manulife Insurance, a major source of capital for Dobbin, initially were encouraged by the arrival of Jones in the president's chair. Jones had managerial experience and was clearly more conservative in his approach to business than the flamboyant Dobbin. "The banks would call me in for a chat," Jones recalls, "and say, 'Now here are the things we'd like you to change over there at Sealand to protect your job and our investment.' And I would go back to Craig and tell him what the money boys wanted, and he would laugh and say, 'Carry on, J.C. No need to change a thing.'"

Cutting expenses to balance the books wasn't Dobbin's style. In fact, the concept wasn't in his genes. Determined to gain maximum fun *and* profit from business, he refused to surrender one in favour of the other, especially when the fun involved all those expensive whirlybirds at the hangar.

In Craig Dobbin's view, he wasn't just running a helicopter company. He was the owner of a fleet of expensive toys ready to carry him and a group of friends aloft or to amuse him whenever he needed a lift, physical or emotional. Recognizing the enormous capital and operating costs associated with the aircraft, helicopter companies place tight restrictions on who can access them and for what purpose, eliminating non-revenue–producing flights. "Every time one of your helicopters takes off," one company executive said, "you want to hear it making a buck or two with every beat of the rotor," adding, "In well-run helicopter companies, God can't get a free ride if He's not paying."

But Craig Dobbin could and did take all the free rides he wanted, to the dismay of J.C. Jones. It wasn't just the Chairman's liberal use of the helicopters to carry him and various friends to lunches or weekend fishing trips that drained Sealand's cash flow; it was also Dobbin's excessive generosity to anyone he chose to enjoy his largesse. "Guys would show up at the hangar and tell me, 'Craig said I could have a helicopter to go fishing,'" J.C. Jones says, "and we would check and Craig would say, 'Sure, take him up to Long Harbour or somewhere for the day.' And these people would come back with a nice salmon in their creel and all of us would know it was a $10,000 fish."

Jones kept raising the issue with Dobbin, pointing out that free trips represented a substantial leak from the company's revenue stream. Finally he laid it out with all the strength and conviction he could muster. Controlling this single expense, Jones lectured, would represent a major step in the company rising out of its debt position. "J.C., that's just what I need to hear," Dobbin replied, slapping Jones on the back. "You get on top of this and tighten it up for me." Jones asked Dobbin if he was serious; Dobbin assured him that he was damn serious.

Quickly rounding up all the Sealand pilots, Jones announced there would be no further free helicopter service for anyone. "Only two ways can you take one of our choppers off the ground," he ordered. "If it's a real revenue-producing flight under a contract, or if my signature is on the flight request. Got it?" The pilots got it.

That weekend, Jones was working in his garden when he looked up at the sound of a CHC helicopter passing overhead. Recalling no scheduled flight that day, he checked the log on Monday morning to see that the craft had been flown by Sealand's chief pilot. Jones encountered the pilot and asked, out of curiosity, the purpose of the flight. An emergency call from a client? A post-maintenance test?

"The pilot, who I knew adored Craig, started pawing the ground with his foot and looking around, trying not to answer me," Jones says. "All he said was, 'I had to go somewhere,' and I kept asking him where, what was he doing? Finally, he admitted Dobbin had called, telling the pilot he wanted to go flying and swearing the pilot to secrecy, saying, 'For God's sake, don't let J.C. hear about this!' So there was the Chairman in conspiracy with his own people to keep me in the dark because I was trying to save the company money."

DOBBIN BECAME ADEPT at both negotiating good deals and manoeuvring his way past obstacles. These skills were, in many ways, his two best management talents.

Borden Osmak, a senior vice-president with Scotiabank, quickly grew to admire Dobbin for his negotiating style. "He'd walk in like he just walked off the farm," Osmak says, "dressed in a proper suit and tie and all of that, but he definitely wasn't Bay Street. He was what he was, a guy who believed in himself and wouldn't take no for an answer. He'd keep trying, keep coming back at you to get the deal done." One Dobbin quality made a deep impression on the banking executive. "He was always respectful of your opinions," Osmak recalls. "He would never say, 'You're full of crap, goodbye!'"

Craig Dobbin proved as skillful a negotiator with helicopter companies as he was with banks and financiers. Bell Helicopter considered Dobbin outstanding in this respect. "The president of Bell told me that Craig Dobbin was the best negotiator he had ever seen," Harry Steele says, "because Craig was always ready to double the bet on the last roll of the dice. The people at Bell admired him for that."

The people at Aerospatiale had a different view. For several months the company had tolerated Sealand's neglect of its debt in exchange for Sealand's showcasing its Super Puma fleet in North America. U.S. helicopter firms had long favoured domestic manufacturers, notably Sikorsky and Bell. The Super Pumas were foreign and highly advanced. How reliable could they be, and how good was French engineering and quality control? Whenever those questions arose, Aerospatiale pointed to Sealand's success in servicing oil platforms off the coast of Atlantic Canada, high in the Arctic and down in the South American jungle. There was a limit to Aerospatiale's tolerance, however.

In 1985 yet another crisis arose to challenge Craig Dobbin's determination to succeed. In a perfect storm of adversity, offshore petroleum exploration and production around the world plummeted, and the federal government cancelled a package of incentive programs. Both events occurred just after Sealand placed an order committing it to accept delivery of six new Super Puma craft from Aerospatiale and purchase an additional six in the near future. Almost overnight, too many helicopter service operations began chasing too few contracts, creating an unprecedented buyer's market. Less than two years earlier, Sealand was winning bids of $240,000 per month to supply one Super Puma and crew; now they were being asked to provide the same service at $99,000, with a second Super Puma as backup.

Cutting costs everywhere to keep the company afloat, Dobbin reduced and delayed the firm's payments for the Super Pumas. Some time after J.C. Jones assumed the presidency of Sealand, the European company appointed a new management team for its North American operations, working out of Grand Prairie, Texas. One of the tasks assigned to the new team was to clean up overdue accounts receivables, and it didn't take long for them to identify Sealand as the biggest, most blatant offender. In the opinion of the new Aerospatiale group, who were anxious to please their French bosses, Sealand wasn't a means of promoting Super Pumas in North

America; it was a deadbeat outfit located in some remote corner of Canada that refused to pay its bills.

Responding to a direct summons, Dobbin and Jones travelled south to Aerospatiale's North American office, expecting to negotiate terms for future payments in a businesslike atmosphere. Instead, they encountered a herd of hostile executives and angry lawyers determined to wring money from Sealand with all the finesse of a Texas posse in pursuit of outlaws.

"They talked to us like we were a couple of schoolboys catching hell in the principal's office," Jones remembers. "They weren't polite, they weren't accommodating, they weren't even businesslike. They considered us a couple of dummies from Canada who owed them money and weren't paying them." One lawyer repeatedly challenged Jones, growing ruder with every effort Jones made to explain the situation. Referring to Jones and Dobbin as idiots and crooks, the lawyer interrupted every utterance from Jones with a fresh insult and accusation.

All attempts to present Sealand's case were made by Jones. Craig Dobbin sat quiet and unsmiling. He let the Sealand president absorb the verbal abuse during several minutes of Aerospatiale's harangue, then interrupted another of the lawyer's diatribes by standing up and raising his hand. "I've had it up to here with you people," he said when the lawyer sputtered to silence. "You want your helicopters back, here's where they are." He began waving his arms, directing the Aerospatiale's team towards appropriate points of the compass. "There are three parked deep in the Amazon jungle, two more up on Baffin Island, two in St. John's and three in Africa. You want 'em, you go and get 'em. But I'm cutting off the insurance on them, bringing my pilots home, moving the helicopters out of the hangars, and you can forget about maintenance. So go get your helicopters. We're going home. Let's go, J.C." Without even a glance back, Dobbin stalked out of the board room, J.C. Jones at his heels.

As they rode in a taxi back to their hotel, Jones believed Sealand was about to be forced into bankruptcy. Craig Dobbin, however, was more sanguine. "Look," he said to J.C. when they were settled in their hotel, a glass of Jameson in his hand, "we can't pay them now and we won't be able to pay them for a while. Someday, sure. But not right away. So let's not try to hand them some bullshit story about giving us another break or promising to be good little boys and go back home and work on our cash flow. Because it ain't gonna work. Not with that crew."

In Dobbin's eyes, the risk of Aerospatiale shutting down Sealand was nil. The machines were about to sit uninsured and unprotected in locations around the world without pilots to ferry them to France or Texas. The prospect of Aerospatiale selling the machines at better than fire-sale prices to anyone else within a short time was not good; in exchange for taking Sealand's debts off its books, Aerospatiale would acquire an inventory of a dozen used machines, perhaps with operational problems and with no immediate buyers. Dobbin's decision to walk was hardly risk-free, however. Without the Super Pumas, Sealand was certain to lose its offshore petroleum contracts, and Aerospatiale could apply sufficient legal pressure to shut down Sealand entirely if it chose.

That evening, while J.C. Jones fretted over his decision to leave the relative comfort and quiet of Okanagan for the crisis atmosphere and limited future of Sealand, Craig Dobbin slept soundly in the next room.

Early the next morning, the Aerospatiale team called Dobbin's hotel room to politely suggest that he and Jones drop by to discuss resolving the problem in a way that would benefit both parties. Dobbin beamed with confidence. Jones sighed with relief. "When we walked in that second day, they treated us like respectable folks," Jones says. "And the lawyer just sat there taking notes and saying nothing."

The second meeting proceeded in the manner Jones had expected all along. Aerospatiale understood that Sealand's current cash position prevented the firm from settling everything to the helicopter company's satisfaction, they said, and Sealand agreed that it couldn't ignore Aerospatiale's concern about continuing to provide parts and support without payment, especially when so much money remained outstanding for the purchase of the Super Pumas. The two sides agreed on a plan of repayment that met both their needs, and Sealand continued its operations.

It was classic Craig Dobbin, this rolling the dice with everything on the table, and he would repeat the action over and over again in the coming years.

WITH THE AEROSPATIALE financing crisis out of the picture for a time, Jones began searching for new business opportunities, new sources of income to reduce Sealand's massive debt. He quickly targeted an operation considered by industry observers to be the most professional helicopter service in the world.

In the mid-1980s, Ontario was by far the most prosperous of Canadian provinces, its wealth reflected in the extent of medical services provided by the Ontario Health Insurance Plan (OHIP). Among OHIP's most impressive benefits was its air ambulance service, an essential aspect of medical care considering the province's immense size and wide distribution of communities. In addition to the program transporting critically ill or injured patients to hospitals, an increasing portion of its budget was allocated towards carrying organs for transplant between donors and recipients. This latter function was best served by fixed-wing aircraft, small executive jets capable of travelling at near-supersonic speeds between large cities. Helicopters were slower—most cruise at 250 kilometres per hour— but their ability to take off and land almost anywhere made them ideal for patient transportation.

The province, in the flush of building what it believed would be the most comprehensive health services system in the world, had enough money to set exceptional standards. Ontario operated helicopter air ambulance centres in Toronto, Sudbury and Thunder Bay, contracting the work to two private suppliers. Toronto Helicopters Ltd. held contracts for the Toronto and Sudbury locations;

Okanagan Helicopters, Jones's former employer, serviced the Thunder Bay area.

OHIP air ambulances were often compared with Rolls-Royce automobiles. Sikorsky s-76 Spirit models had been converted from executive transport craft into air ambulances, and they were the first of their kind to incorporate satellite-assisted navigation systems as well as other amenities. Despite the high capital cost of the aircraft, both Okanagan and Toronto Helicopters generated impressive profits from the OHIP contracts, and when efforts by other helicopter companies to dislodge them failed time and again, rumours began circulating. The contracts tended to be renewed without competitive tenders being solicited, competitors noted, with some agreements extending over seven years. Suspicions grew that Okanagan and Toronto Helicopters shared an arrangement that each would not encroach on the other's territory, and that neither company would cut pricing below its apparently lucrative level. Meanwhile, the province's air ambulance expenses soared, enriching the coffers of both firms.

J.C. Jones, from his time at Okanagan, knew just how profitable the OHIP contract could be, and when he outlined the situation to Craig Dobbin, the response was immediate. "Go get it," Dobbin ordered Jones. "Get that contract for us."

The appeal to Dobbin may have been more than an opportunity to add to Sealand's bottom line. It might have been personal. Dobbin's winning the offshore oil contract from Okanagan a few years earlier had deeply angered one of Okanagan's larger shareholders, John Lecky. Since that time, Lecky had acquired control of Okanagan, and Craig Dobbin may have enjoyed the chance to challenge him again, the son of a St. John's lumber dealer matching wits with the Cambridge-educated sophisticate who was heir to the Mac-Millan Bloedel fortune. Many businesspeople, including Harry Steele and Robert Foster, liked and admired Lecky. Craig Dobbin did not. "John Lecky inherited a billion dollars," Dobbin once noted, "and it's become his hobby to blow it all away."

Lecky had achieved much beyond the good fortune of his birth, including winning a silver medal in rowing at the 1960 Olympics; he later served on the executive committee of the 1988 Calgary Winter Olympics. While gaining experience as an investment analyst with Richardson Greenshields, he recognized the investment opportunity of Okanagan Helicopters and began accumulating shares, seizing control of the company in a hostile takeover. Choosing to focus on larger helicopters with greater profit potential, he sold off Universal, with its fleet of smaller craft, to Harry Steele. In Steele's opinion, Lecky had earned his stripes as a shrewd investor and political manoeuvrer.

But John Lecky had never scavenged for scrap metal on the bottom of St. John's harbour, never hauled lumber in an old car with its windows removed, never sold an unfinished home out from under his family to finance his next project, never raided coin-operated laundry units to meet the week's payroll. Craig Dobbin had done all of this and more to survive, and in his eyes they negated Lecky's achievements.

"Craig Dobbin just didn't like John Lecky very much," J.C. Jones remembers, "and I had a sense the feeling was mutual." Harry Steele can attest to that. "I remember being at the airport to meet Craig and John Lecky, who had flown into Halifax on the same flight," Steele recalls, "and when they got off the plane they were furious at each other. Turns out they got into such an argument during the trip that it almost turned into a fist fight."

Jones's experience with Okanagan enabled him to draft a proposal to OHIP that addressed the province's every objective for and concern about its air ambulance service. Sealand, Jones submitted, could perform the duties of both Okanagan and Toronto Helicopters at a more attractive price. The price was so much less than existing contracts that it would justify the province breaking its seven-year agreement with the two Sealand competitors. The province remained unimpressed, however. "They told us they preferred using the older Sikorsky craft over our new Super Pumas," Jones says. "We told them fine, we'll get Sikorskys and adapt them, but then they questioned the experience of our pilots in handling the Sikorskys, which was ridiculous, of course."

After spending time and effort on the OHIP pitch, Jones was dispirited when he broke news of the province's rejection to Craig Dobbin, expecting the Sealand owner to abandon the idea. Dobbin, however, had a different response. "The hell with the contract," he grinned. "Let's buy the buggers out and we'll get the contract that way! We'll start with Toronto."

Buy them? Jones thought. What a crazy idea. Toronto Helicopters was comparable to Sealand in size, providing craft and pilots for a wide range of services beyond the OHIP contract. It was also a very profitable company. What's more, John Lecky had been attempting to purchase Toronto from company president Len Rutledge for some time; each effort was turned down flat. Why should Rutledge look with favour on Sealand's offer?

One of Craig Dobbin's most popular aphorisms was "Never take no for an answer," and he instructed Jones to contact Rutledge, set up a meeting and arrange a deal. To Jones's surprise, Rutledge's response to his request for a meeting was, "Sure, let's talk."

Within a few days, Jones was on his way to meet with Rutledge at his firm's office in Buttonville Airport, northeast of Toronto. Rutledge greeted him warmly, then set the first rule. Before negotiations began for Sealand to acquire his company, Rutledge wanted a guaranteed non-refundable deposit of $500,000. No matter how the negotiations proceeded and whether or not a purchase deal was reached, Rutledge would pocket the $500,000. Rutledge also set a negotiating deadline. If a deal was not reached within ninety days of Rutledge receiving the deposit, discussions would be cut off and Rutledge would retain the half-million dollars.

Jones's ebullience sank. He had no idea what other demands Rutledge might raise beyond the terms of the deposit, or even if

Rutledge was sole owner of all his company's shares, as he claimed. If this were a poker game, which it resembled in some ways, Sealand was losing $500,000 to the house before the cards were dealt. That was only half the problem of doing the deal. The other half was even more daunting: Sealand did not have $500,000 in cash at its disposal, nor any prospects of acquiring it. As J.C. Jones puts it, "We didn't have a pot to piss in." Jones relayed none of this to Rutledge. Instead, he promised to present Rutledge's opening terms to Craig Dobbin.

On the return flight to Newfoundland, Jones assumed the deal was dead before it was born. Rutledge was not prepared to accept empty promises. He had told Jones, in effect, that when the $500,000 was deposited in Rutledge's account, they would talk. Until then, nothing was going to happen.

In St. John's, Jones broke the news to Dobbin, who pondered the situation for a moment, then shrugged and said, "So pay him the half-million out of our operating line," meaning the million-dollar credit arrangement Sealand had with TD Bank to cover the firm's day-to-day expenses.

Jones protested they couldn't do that. TD granted the credit to pay for salaries, rent, fuel and other expenses, not to spend it on acquisitions. The bank would never approve giving half of Sealand's entire line of credit to Rutledge just to open negotiations. Besides, reducing their access to available cash by 50 per cent would leave Sealand in a difficult position when it came to paying its bills.

Dobbin's response was familiar to Jones by now. "Screw the bankers," he said. "Let's do it."

Jones transferred the half-million dollars to Rutledge's account. That likely surprised Rutledge, but not nearly as much as it surprised TD Bank. "The bankers went ballistic when they found out," according to Jones, "absolutely ballistic. They threatened to cut us off, close our accounts, not honour our cheques, the whole deal." In the end the bank did nothing, perhaps because Dobbin had reportedly been the bank's first corporate customer when they opened their operations in Newfoundland in 1962. With a new $500,000 debt to the bank, Dobbin began working on a deal to acquire Rutledge's firm, turning to Robert Foster's Capital Canada for assistance.

To Foster, the purchase of Toronto Helicopters by Dobbin's teetering-near-the-edge Sealand Helicopters made a good deal of sense. "Toronto Helicopters was very profitable, which meant it was paying a lot of taxes," Foster points out, "and one way you value a company is against its aftertax income which, in this case, reduced its value to the seller." Meanwhile, Sealand was losing money and recording substantial depreciation costs against its fleet of Super Puma aircraft, enabling Sealand to shelter Toronto's enormous income free of tax.

Foster tapped BT Canada, the local arm of Bankers Trust in New York, as a funding source, and on behalf of Sealand he began negotiations with Len Rutledge to purchase Toronto Helicopters. According to Foster, the negotiations grew complicated because of Rutledge's apparently endless demands. "We would reach an agreement and get ready to sign off," Foster says, "and Len would say, 'Oh, there's one more thing,' and we'd have to deal with that." Rutledge kept raising issues each time Foster believed they had a deal until, within a day or two of the final deadline, he said again to Foster, "Oh, there's just one more thing."

"Len," Foster replied, "I'll do this 'one more thing,' but if there's anything else I'm going to advise Craig Dobbin to just walk away and forget everything." The "one more thing" this time turned out to be the purchase of Rutledge's Mercedes-Benz. Foster agreed, and negotiations were completed. Sealand was about to purchase its larger rival, leaving Sealand with a sweat-generating 27:1 debt-to-equity ratio.

The ink was still wet on Foster's brokered deal, and just one day remained before the negotiating deadline expired, when J.C. Jones and Rutledge met with Bankers Trust to sign the financing arrangements. To this point, two vice-presidents of BT Canada had monitored and approved the proposal without any serious concerns, and things had been settled with little more than a handshake. For the signing ceremony, the two local Bankers Trust VPS were joined by a lawyer from the New York office. The lawyer had taken no part in the discussions up to this point, and he quickly made his position clear to Jones. "This is a bad deal," he barked as soon as he sat down. "We don't like it, and we're not going to do it."

Nothing Jones offered could sway the lawyer from his position. Finally, the New York man offered to provide the money at an interest rate two full percentage points above the agreed-upon level. In a take-it-or-leave-it offer, Bankers Trust was employing a strategy designed to improve its own profits by hiding details of its agreement during preliminary discussions, cornering Sealand until it could not afford to kill the deal. The hardball-playing New York lawyer, Jones suspected, had ridden into town determined to fleece the trusting, slow-moving Canadians.*

Jones turned to the Canadian vice-presidents of Bankers Trust, reminding them that they had given their word on the terms of the deal and had represented the bank's position during weeks of discussion. Sealand had invested an enormous amount of time and money to this stage, based on BT's assurances. "You can't change the rules on the one-yard line," he insisted. The vice-presidents remained silent. "They wouldn't even look at me," Jones says. "Meanwhile, Len Rutledge is at the other end of the table grinning from ear to ear,

---

* Events suggest this may have been the case. A few years later, Bankers Trust was successfully sued by Procter & Gamble and Gibson Greetings. Both firms charged that representatives of BT intentionally withheld and obfuscated details of a financing agreement to conceal their company's excessive profits. The trial and its results garnered much notoriety when the court heard audiotapes of Bankers Trust representatives gleefully boasting that their clients would never understand all the ramifications of the agreements. The court agreed that "the treatment of P&G [by Bankers Trust] was not an isolated incident or a 'garden-variety fraud,' but rather part of a pattern of mail, wire, and securities fraud spanning a number of years and involving multiple victims."

counting the half-million dollars he was about to make for essentially doing nothing."

The action of Bankers Trust, Jones believed, was akin to extortion, costing Sealand millions of dollars more than anticipated. But there was no backing out. He agreed to the higher interest rate, new terms were drafted, an agreement was signed, and the deal was completed. Craig Dobbin was furious over the actions of Bankers Trust, of course. In retrospect, however, the purchase of Toronto Helicopters proved a major step in transforming the company into a global powerhouse.

With Toronto Helicopters rolled into Sealand and its cash flow solving many of Sealand's liquidity concerns, Craig Dobbin's eyes brightened at the prospect of the next step in expanding his company, this one even more audacious.

One morning shortly after the deal to purchase Toronto Helicopters was completed, Craig Dobbin strolled into Robert Foster's Toronto office. "Robert," he said, "I want you to get on a plane, fly to Calgary and buy Okanagan Helicopters for me."

"But Craig," Foster replied, "you don't have any money."

Dobbin shrugged and said, "That's your problem."

4

Every minute with Craig Dobbin was better than
an hour with the rest of the world—and certainly more fun.
HARRY STEELE, chairman, Newfoundland Capital Corporation

ROBERT FOSTER GRASPED THE logic of Craig Dobbin's plan to buy Okanagan Helicopters, even though Sealand's bank account was empty. As a member of Sealand's board of directors, he knew the effects cutthroat competition was having on Sealand and Okanagan. Both sides were practically giving their work away, and neither was generating much profit. Together, the two companies would generate synergies, the obligatory axiom in the lexicon of mergers.

The challenge of obtaining the substantial amount of cash required to pull off such a deal was dwarfed by two other factors. One was relative size. With almost 600 employees and 125 helicopters, Okanagan was three times larger than Sealand, suggesting Jonah swallowing the whale instead of vice versa. The other was the widely acknowledged fact that Craig Dobbin and John Lecky, Okanagan's owner, despised each other. "Those two men were like a mongoose and a cobra," Foster recalls. Foster was fond of Lecky, but J.C. Jones disliked the Okanagan owner, considering him erratic, moody and something of a snob.

Jones, who was stunned when Dobbin suggested purchasing Okanagan, pointed out the vast differences in size, experience

74

and complexity of structure between Sealand and its takeover target. Sealand, Jones suggested, lacked more than the money to buy Okanagan. It lacked the expertise to manage a company engaged in diverse industries, with offices and clients scattered across the country. Most people looking carefully at the two companies would have agreed; this was not a plausible deal.

Okanagan Helicopters was more than the largest firm of its kind in Canada; it was among the largest in the world. It possessed a heritage and tradition that qualified it as the first helicopter service in the country. Launched shortly after the Second World War by three ex-RCAF officers, pilots Carl Agar and Barney Bent and engineer Alf Stringer, its initial business plan was to spray pesticides on fruit orchards in and around Penticton. After investing $50,000 to purchase a basic Bell 47 helicopter and maintenance equipment, the owners launched a test flight to impress local farmers. Unfortunately, the test revealed that the machine was efficient at coating not only the orchards with pesticides but everything and everybody else in the vicinity. Pinpoint spraying of orchards was out of the question. The fledgling company was saved from bankruptcy when the B.C. forestry service hired it to spray a bug-infested region of the Kootenays and mosquito-breeding pockets of water created by the 1948 flood of the Fraser Valley.

Growing steadily, Okanagan was soon ferrying personnel and equipment related to topographical studies of the province's mountainous interior, and transporting workers and equipment to Alcan Aluminum's massive Kitimat project. It also initiated the Canadian Helicopter School of Advanced Flight Training, teaching pilots the technique of flying in mountainous terrain. The program grew to be so highly regarded that the Penticton school welcomed students from the United States Army, Navy and Air Force as well as the Canadian Coast Guard. By 1987 Okanagan's reputation was impeccable, and its revenue substantial. The company was John Lecky's pride and joy, and he operated it with the same degree of taste and style he sought in his personal life. Selling his creation to an east-coast rival whom he clearly disliked appeared unlikely.

It took the combined efforts of Robert Foster and Harry Steele to persuade Lecky even to meet with Dobbin. He agreed with some reluctance, insisting that he and Dobbin reside in separate Calgary hotels during negotiations.

"I want to buy your company," Dobbin said when he and Lecky finally got together. As direct as that.

Lecky grinned as though Dobbin had just told him a mildly amusing story. "The way I hear it," he replied, "you can't write a cheque for more than a dollar without having it bounce."

Dobbin replied he was serious and asked Lecky to name a price.

"Twenty-five million dollars cash," Lecky said. Then, taking a page out of Len Rutledge's playbook, he added: "Before we get started, I want a non-refundable deposit of one million dollars paid personally to me, and there is a sixty-day deadline for completing the deal. How does that sound?"

If Lecky expected Dobbin to turn pale at the terms, he was disappointed. Assuring Lecky he would hear from him within a few days, Dobbin returned home to liquidate as many of his assets as it took to accumulate the million dollars. Whatever asset he owned that wasn't mortgaged to the hilt and could find an eager buyer was put on the block. Craig Dobbin was pushing every poker chip he had into the centre of the table.

A week after meeting Lecky, Dobbin dispatched a certified cheque for one million dollars to the Okanagan owner. "Let's get it done," Dobbin said in a follow-up phone call.

Senior executives and most of Okanagan's staff grew outraged when they heard Lecky was negotiating the sale of their company to Craig Dobbin. Okanagan was a piece of Canadian aviation history, a model of good management and fiscal responsibility, highly regarded around the world. Dobbin's Sealand Helicopters teetered from one financial crisis to another, directed by an upstart whose major business achievement had been building hundreds of cheap cookie-cutter apartments. How could John Lecky, the blueblood aristocrat, consider dealing with a rascal like Dobbin?

Lecky, with Craig Dobbin's million-dollar deposit in his bank account, suggested his employees relax. The people at Sealand, he assured his staff, were a bunch of clowns. They wouldn't be able to raise the money, he promised, and eventually they would return to Newfoundland, tails between their legs, leaving Okanagan to carry on as usual. He felt especially confident because he had set stringent conditions for the negotiating process, making things as difficult for Dobbin as possible. "I don't want them sneaking around here while we're going through these motions," Lecky reportedly said. In fact, no one from Sealand would be permitted to speak to Okanagan staff or employees, nor could they set foot on Okanagan property without Lecky's permission.

Robert Foster made his pitch to potential investors based in part on the performance of recently acquired Toronto Helicopters. The addition to Sealand was an established, well-run organization whose steady cash flow promised to alleviate Sealand's fiscal problems. Adding Okanagan would make Sealand a healthy operation capable of riding out future financial difficulties. The response from Bay Street investors was decidedly cool; as J.C. Jones put it, "Everywhere we went we got sand kicked in our faces."

Undaunted, Foster abandoned the plan to raise money through private sources and decided on a public offering of shares. Among the investment firms he approached was McLeod Young Weir, now ScotiaMcLeod. The story, as McLeod Young Weir understood it, was different from the tale absorbed by previous money sources. In McLeod Young Weir's interpretation, the merging of Sealand/ Toronto with Okanagan created a virtual monopoly for helicopter services in Canada, especially in the burgeoning and profitable offshore oil industry. Nobody else would be in a position to bid against the new firm, and it would take enormous financial investment for a new competitor to enter the market. Craig Dobbin had foreseen the same advantage, of course, but selling the concept of creating a monopoly in an industry is a dangerous thing to do. McLeod Young Weir didn't need to be sold; they got the message on their own. Joined by Richardson Greenshields, with Robert Foster's Capital Canada acting as fiscal agent, an IPO was underwritten to fund a newly formed corporation named CHC (Canadian Helicopter Company) Helicopters.

Only when it appeared that Sealand would defy the odds and actually generate the funds did Lecky permit Sealand negotiators to speak with Okanagan's president Pat Aldous, along with the firm's CFO. The discussion with the two Okanagan executives was critical. "We had to keep this thing together," Jones explains. "The last thing we needed was a mutiny, with these guys getting up and bolting from the company. Sealand lacked the depth of personnel to go in and run things if Okanagan's top people were going out one door as we were coming in another."

Hurdles needed to be jumped. Pat Aldous had assumed that he would remain CEO of Okanagan as an independent corporation. No, Dobbin informed him, the two companies would be merged into one. In that case, Aldous proposed, he should be named CEO of the new company, since he held the top post in Okanagan. Again, no; J.C. Jones, who just a few years earlier had reported to Aldous, would serve as Aldous's new boss. "Craig Dobbin was loyal to me," Jones said. "He believed you went home from the dance with the person you came with."

A public offering of shares in CHC Helicopters was made on October 12, 1987. With assets totalling more than $100 million and a projected working capital of $33 million, the IPO targeted $30 million, including $15 million in convertible debentures and $15 million in common shares. Manulife provided an additional $500,000 in working capital. Common shares would be listed on the Toronto and Montreal exchanges, and debentures traded over the counter. The proceeds, according to the prospectus, would be used to purchase 51 per cent of Okanagan and repay outstanding debts. The remaining 49 per cent of Okanagan would be held by United Helicopters, which was in turn 49 per cent owned by Bristow Helicopter Group. The offering was soon oversold, and Dobbin paid cash on the barrelhead for Okanagan.

To John Lecky, the unthinkable had occurred. Canada's largest, oldest and most respected helicopter company was in the clutches of an Irish upstart from Newfoundland, a man whose very name elevated Lecky's blood pressure. Lecky's future foray into air travel would prove disastrous, when his Canada 3000 airline attempted to extend itself from a profitable charter operation into a global scheduled airline, slipping into a pool of red ink when air travel volume collapsed after September 11, 2001.

Craig Dobbin now operated what was by far the largest helicopter company in Canada and one of the five biggest companies of its kind in the world. At the end of September 1987, CHC's accounts payable had been averaging almost twelve months in arrears. Shell Oil was threatening to cancel Dobbin's personal and corporate credit, refusing to provide further products or services until the outstanding debts owed by him and Sealand were settled. By October 15, Sealand/CHC's accounts payable had dropped to near zero, and Craig Dobbin's personal bank balance was nudging $20 million.

On Monday, October 19, 1987, stock markets around the world suffered their largest one-day decline in history, shaking the faith of investors the world over. Many took years to fully recover their losses. CHC's IPO was the last in Canada before Black Monday, and shares of the company that had been snatched up at $10 dropped within a week to $2.50. Had the IPO been delayed by two weeks, it clearly would have failed. John Lecky would have retained his company and the one million dollars, and Craig Dobbin would have withdrawn to St. John's, devoting his time to paying down the massive mortgages on everything he owned. But the luck of the Irish kicked in. Instead, Dobbin's credit was up to AAA, and his prospects were brighter than ever.

HURDLES HAD BEEN surmounted, but bumps remained along the road. Okanagan president Pat Aldous remained unwilling to accept former underling J.C. Jones as his new boss. Resigning, Aldous launched Alpine Helicopters, which engaged in applications that included forestry work, seismic evaluation, air ambulance, cinematography, heli-skiing and tourism. Most Okanagan staff accepted the change, though, and while disputes between Sealand/CHC and Okanagan people arose from time to time, they were easily dealt with.

The dominant size of CHC enabled Dobbin to extend the company's clout in the industry and acquire more competitors. By the end of 1987, CHC had gathered fuel distributor Aero Flight Holdings Ltd. under its corporate wing, along with Offshore Helicopter Technologies Ltd., operator of a flight simulator facility in St. John's. Early the following year CHC spent $9.7 million to purchase Ranger Helicopters Canada, highly regarded for its geological services, then topped off its acquisitions with Quebec-based Viking Helicopters in early 1989. Second only to CHC in size within Canada, Viking was Quebec-based, providing Dobbin and CHC with a solid blanket of services across Canada. The once regional Sealand reigned supreme over helicopter services in Canada as CHC, with annual revenues approaching $100 million and Craig Dobbin being hailed as a genius financial strategist.

John Lecky did not share this view. Barely a month after the successful IPO of CHC that enabled Dobbin to acquire Okanagan, Lecky could not resist sticking his oar in Dobbin's water. In a letter to the CHC chairman dated November 11, 1987, Lecky, who held no position within either CHC or his former company, attacked Dobbin's policy of restricting the board's access to company managers. In doing so, he disparaged his former vice-president J.C. Jones, suggesting that "directors should hear from those who are actually hands-on running the business or they will be deluded. This means operating management, not head office personnel. The president and CFO are simply not qualified to coordinate effectively a head office operation." Later in his letter, he extended his rather haughty critique of Dobbin's decision to retain Jones: "The principle of rewarding loyalty rather than addressing the best interests of the business, i.e., ... the preference of J.C. Jones over Pat Aldous is a bad signal to the bulk of the staff who are much wiser than one might choose to think ... Unfortunately, the commercial luxury of running a school for senior management is not permitted in the current or foreseeable state of the helicopter market."

While the operator of any newly acquired corporation welcomed the acquired wisdom of the previous owner, Dobbin was taken aback by Lecky's unsolicited advice, phrased as though Lecky and not Craig Dobbin were determining the shape and direction of CHC. Lecky's directives were especially caustic with regard to his claim that Dobbin was "running a school for senior management" rather than an internationally acclaimed corporation. Among Lecky's suggestions: Remove J.C. Jones from the president and COO position; direct the CEO (Dobbin) to run CHC through a committee consisting of the operating heads of the company's subsidiaries; and abandon St. John's as a head office location and coordinate all functions out of the Okanagan office in Vancouver, "where high-grade systems and capacity now exist." Finally, Lecky predicted that the firm's 1987 actual and 1988 forecast financial targets would not be met and said Dobbin should admit that "the attrition of qualified managers is obviously a material factor in this underachievement." The latter comment referred specifically to the resignation of Pat Aldous, former Okanagan president.

Had Craig Dobbin acquiesced to all of Lecky's proposals, it would have been tantamount to handing the CHC throne to his predecessor at Okanagan. Whatever initial reaction he may have had to Lecky's condescending note, his written response was calm and businesslike, noting among other facts that Aldous "was never in the running to be president of CHC. In fact, we made every effort to retain Pat in a viable productive position within CHC. He could not accept working for either me or J.C. Jones as J.C. had been his subordinate in years past." Dobbin also claimed that Aldous disagreed with various changes Dobbin and Jones were proposing for the operation of Okanagan within CHC. "For these reasons," Dobbin concluded, "it was obvious that we could not work together and Pat chose to resign."

Friction between new owners and existing managers of newly acquired divisions is almost *de rigueur* during the initial transition phase. Whatever Aldous's reasons for resigning and Dobbin's motive for designating Jones as president and COO, this exchange between Lecky and Dobbin was motivated as much by the open hostility as by any differences in management style.

Problems with Craig Dobbin's management were raised by other board members as well, most of them rooted in Dobbin's hell-for-leather methods. For years he had made decisions, both personal and business-oriented, in his role as sole proprietor of his multiple ventures. Now chairman and majority shareholder of a publicly traded company, he was expected to appreciate the concerns of the company's minority shareholders and respect the opinions of his board of directors. But Craig Dobbin had not risen from humble origins to the most elegant boardrooms of Bay Street by following other peoples' rules. He was unwilling, and possibly unable, to change his style just because the company he directed boasted several thousand owners instead of him alone.

Dobbin's approach generated unease in one member of the board who was associated with a major Canadian financing firm. Barely six months after the IPO that launched CHC, this man wrote in confidence to two other board members:

At our [board] meeting last Thursday we reiterated many specific issues but there are two broad categories that I personally find most offensive.

The first is Craig's belief that he can still run CHC as a private company, one that he controls unilaterally. At the April 25th board meeting we had long discussions on the issue of relocating the [former Okanagan] corporate office from Toronto to St. John's, corporate realignment, diversifications, etc. Because there was such a wide diversification of opinions between Craig and the board we decided to call in management consultants to review the entire situation. Within one month of our meeting Craig has taken it upon himself to consolidate the corporate office in St. John's. From a business standpoint, I am convinced this is madness. In the first six months of the current fiscal year 70 percent of revenue was being generated by Okanagan.

The second major issue that I find deeply disturbing is the question of Craig's personal financial conduct with company funds. At the board meeting it came out that this was also a concern to the audit committee of which I am not a member. Thus steps were taken that would supposedly tighten up the situation. I am not convinced in my own mind that Craig has yet to get the message.

The question now becomes, where do we go from here? It is not an easy issue to lay out or to propose solutions. However, I will put forth a couple of suggestions. The first is to leave Craig as chairman just to deal with long-term strategic planning issues. Any recommendations he may come up with must have full board approval. As far as the organization below Craig, we can have management consultants study the company. Our president J.C. Jones may or may not be capable of having his role expanded as president and coo.

Concerning my second major issue, Craig's personal expense account, strict controls must be implemented with the preauthorization for cash and travel expenses by an audit committee member. Upon return he should submit an expense account that is fully itemized and only those expenses backed by valid receipts will be reimbursed if approved by an audit committee member.

In summary I am going to have complete satisfaction in my own mind that my major concerns are being addressed or else I will have no choice but to tender my resignation from the board. Craig may get cavalier about senior executives leaving but he does not have that luxury with this board. I don't doubt that he can rustle up six or eight warm bodies to constitute a board. I would contend, however, that if myself and one or two other board members tendered our resignations CHC would be virtually cut off from future financing in the Canadian investment community. Unless you both get complete satisfaction that Craig understands the gravity of the situation we should call, at the earliest possible date, a full meeting of the board *in Toronto* [sic] to discuss how we next proceed.

It is unclear whether or not Craig Dobbin ever saw this complete document, but he apparently was made aware of its tone and contents. Whatever the validity of the writer's complaints, his attitude and proposals would likely have inspired a shower of coffee cups and telephones against the wall of Dobbin's office. Management consultants? Dobbin might have demanded. What management consultant would have proposed the spectacular growth of Sealand, made in the face of constant threats and demands from banks and financiers? What consultants would have advised him to build CHC in the first place and expand the company to create the board seat this incipient rebel occupied? Had Dobbin retained management consultants in the past, CHC would be flying tourists over the Narrows of St. John's harbour and government VIPs off to fishing junkets instead of functioning as one of the largest firms serving the global petroleum market.

And what was "madness" about retaining the company's head-quarters in Newfoundland? Did Canada's business community believe major decisions could be made only within six blocks of King and Bay streets? CHC had been built by people with Newfoundland roots, Newfoundland values and Newfoundland pride, and any effort to eradicate that quality in the company had nothing to do with good business sense and everything to do with Toronto hubris. The threat of recruiting a herd of dissatisfied board members to walk away and deny CHC future financing from the nabobs of Hogtown was not even worth discussing.

As for Craig Dobbin tugging at his forelock while carrying itemized expense vouchers to some mealy-mouthed bookkeeper, in hopes of being reimbursed for every beer and burger he consumed . . . well, it wasn't going to happen. The grumbling financier resigned from the board, the CHC head office remained in St. John's, and Craig Dobbin continued to run things Craig Dobbin's way. As opportunities presented themselves over the next several years, he replaced various mainland board members with the likes of Frank Moores, John Crosbie, Brian Tobin and other Newfoundlanders who believed they were as capable of running an international corporation as anyone west of Fundy.

Nothing could soothe the long-standing acrimony between John Lecky and Craig Dobbin. The antipathy between the two men burst out in a new flurry of accusations against the CHC chairman by the former Okanagan owner.

Among the details of the contract covering the purchase of Okanagan had been an agreement that CHC would return to Edmalec, Lecky's private holding company, an anticipated $2 million in prepaid taxes from Revenue Canada. With Okanagan in his back pocket, Dobbin obtained a legal assessment suggesting that Lecky had no greater claim to the money than CHC did. On that basis, Dobbin ignored Lecky's demands for payment, prompting a scathing letter from the former Okanagan Helicopters owner to Pat Callahan, CHC vice-president of finance, on December 23, 1988.

After complaining about CHC's failure, in his opinion, to abide by the purchase agreement regarding the $2 million and other tax matters, Lecky concluded: "This matter is not only aggravating but will involve professional costs and cannot help but reflect poorly on yourself and CHC. For my part I have done nothing to induce such behaviour which I feel is scurrilous and totally unwarranted. I expect you to redeem the [$2 million] note in full as promised to me at Canada Trust St. John's office by Friday, December 30th. Such expectancy is no more than a reliance on your given word as a professional financial officer and the reputation for so doing is your own stock in trade."

Dobbin did not immediately return the $2 million, preferring to negotiate, perhaps as a means of annoying Lecky. If that were the case, he succeeded, based on Lecky's letter to him after an agreement was reached two months later:

> The settlement reached yesterday virtually mirrors that which was offered to you over one month ago. If anything, the terms were somewhat less favourable to you. In order to achieve this result I incurred needless legal costs and aggravation. You have a long history of upsetting people and causing pain when you momentarily have the advantage and can act the bully. Do you do this for pleasure or because you cannot help yourself? What goes around comes around and it can make life a lonely affair.
> *Yours sincerely,*
> JOHN

John Lecky had his own motive for suggesting that Craig Dobbin might someday pay for his shenanigans, and though Dobbin faced a number of challenges in the years to come, loneliness would not be one of them. It is unlikely that any CEO of a major corporation generated more loyalty among his employees, attracted more friends ranging from Inuit villagers in Labrador to former prime ministers and presidents, or had more hellraising fun than Craig Laurence Dobbin. "We called him the Wild Colonial Boy," Robert Foster recalls.

"Craig could go through more good whiskey and more games of cards than anyone I know," explains Bob Glass, a Dobbin golfing buddy and card-playing friend. "Craig could stay up until two in the morning and be into his office before six. If he had been partying with employees and they staggered in around eight or nine o'clock, he'd say, 'Where the hell have you been? I've been working here for three hours already!'"

It was the same at the legendary parties that took place at Dobbin's fishing camps at Long Harbour, Newfoundland, and Adlatuk, Labrador. Arriving in CHC helicopters, the men engaged in fly-fishing for salmon, consumed large quantities of whiskey, held extended and often raucous card games, and managed to survive on minimal sleep. The days Dobbin spent at his fishing camps with cronies were clearly among the most joyful of his life.

Sean Tucker, Dobbin's nephew and a proficient helicopter pilot in his own right, related a profound experience he had with Craig Dobbin one weekend at Long Harbour. "I was playing bartender on that trip," Tucker explains. "I was mixing and serving Bloody Caesars for him while he relaxed in a chair on the riverbank. As the sun started to set he decided he wanted to fish a little more that day, so he pulled on his hip waders, grabbed his pole and headed for the water, me tailing along behind. He was in the river, wearing a heavy sweater with those hip waders, and I saw him slip and fall. All I could see above the water was the back of his head."

Tucker jumped into the pool and seized the back of Dobbin's sweater, preventing him from sliding into deeper water. Given Dobbin's heft and Tucker's slim physique, it took the efforts of both men to stand Dobbin upright.

"I managed to get his head out of the water," Tucker says, "and when he got his feet on solid footing he stood up, opened his eyes, turned to me and said, 'When I go, that's the way I want it to be.'"

5

*I consider myself a stage manager, somebody who can
spot talented people, put them to work and let them do their job.*
CRAIG DOBBIN

IN CHOOSING THE FIRST board of directors for the publicly traded
CHC, Dobbin drew on experience within the helicopter services
industry and connections with his ongoing financial sources. In
addition to J.C. Jones, the first board included Bryan Collins, managing director of Bristow Helicopter; Peter Dey, a partner with the
law firm of Osler Hoskin & Harcourt; Robert Foster of Capital Canada; Donald Parkinson, VP of Canadian investments, Manufacturers Life Insurance Company; and David Sobey, scion of the family
who controlled the highly successful Nova Scotia–based grocery
chain. With variations, this group constituted the core of the board
for the next several years.

His selection of J.C. Jones to step into the president and COO position was both strategic and timely—strategic because Jones brought
depth of experience and an unflappable manner to an organization
that required both to balance Dobbin's impetuous nature; timely
because Jones provided insight into Okanagan that enabled CHC to
absorb the firm, its systems and its equipment more quickly and with
less difficulty than might otherwise have been encountered.*

---

* In another example of the endless animosity between Dobbin and John Lecky, in 1987 Lecky
brought legal action against Jones, charging that Jones had taken "large quantities of clas-
sified corporate information" with him when he left Okanagan for Sealand in 1984. Dobbin
and Jones challenged Lecky, calling his actions "malicious prosecution." The court eventually
granted Jones an absolute discharge.

Dobbin's apparently impulsive decision to hire Quebec-based pilot Sylvain Allard after meeting him by accident had proved unusually prescient. Allard had soon become Sealand's chief pilot, performing with such proficiency that Dobbin assigned him the role of base manager for Sealand's contract with Occidental Petroleum. From its operations centre in Cucuta, near the Venezuelan border, Allard and other Sealand pilots flew over the Colombian jungle and set down in locations where antigovernment guerrillas regularly attacked pipeline workers. Some helicopter companies in the region lost their craft to guerrilla action. Insurgents once tried to commandeer a Sealand craft, but Sealand encountered fewer problems than other helicopter firms servicing the project. According to one source, this was the result of two factors: Sealand's Canadian identity (its competitors were U.S. firms) and the piloting and management skills of Sylvain Allard.

Many pilots avoided being selected to ferry the Chairman because his presence made them nervous. Others, Sylvain Allard among them, enjoyed the pressure and were prepared to take periodic criticism from the Chairman of their abilities. Craig Dobbin grew familiar with the personalities and ambitions of a number of these pilots, often engaging them in conversation about business and management, moving those with special talents into supervisory positions. Of them all, Allard became a favourite.

"Being with him every summer, when we'd fly back and forth to the fishing camps," Allard recalls, "made me his confidant on some things. I would know before any of the other pilots what aircraft he was going to buy, where he was going to pitch for new business, and so on. We'd toss ideas back and forth during the flight."

On one trip, Dobbin asked if Allard wanted to do anything else besides fly helicopters. "I loved flying," Allard says, remembering the conversation, "but every pilot fears that someday he'll lose his medical clearance and end up with nothing to do." Even relatively young pilots can be grounded if they develop a heart flutter, high blood pressure or one of a dozen different ailments, leaving them on the ground with few useful skills. Allard's backup plan was to acquire management training that would keep him in the industry if and when his licence was lifted due to medical reasons.

Dobbin, upon learning of Allard's aspiration, promoted him to eastern operations manager in place of a former U.S. military officer. Sylvain's warm, responsive manner was in sharp contrast to the intense, by-the-book approach of the military man, and he proved an effective supervisor, improving staff morale and profit performance.

The acquisition of Quebec-based Viking Helicopters presented Dobbin with a serious challenge. Significant labour unrest had dogged Viking for some time, and the company's sixty-plus helicopter pilots, upset about the treatment they had received under Viking management, appeared ready to unionize. The prospect of CHC becoming subject to the dictates of intransigent unions was unacceptable to Dobbin. When he investigated the pilots' principal concerns, he discovered most were directed against the current Viking president. Dobbin replaced him with Sylvain Allard, who knew many of the Viking pilots personally. Allard's presence and his Québécois heritage quickly disarmed pilots who had been advocating a union.

Dobbin decided to operate Viking as a separate entity within the company, providing Allard with an opportunity to develop and demonstrate his managerial abilities free from constant head-office scrutiny. Shortly after assuming the Viking president's chair, Allard enrolled in the Executive MBA course at Concordia University, winning recognition as a Gold Medallist graduate. Among those attending the graduation ceremony in Montreal, beaming as proudly as if Allard were one of his own children, was Craig Dobbin. By this time, Dobbin knew Sylvain Allard would eventually fill the role of CEO.

"Sylvain is a crackerjack," Harry Steele notes. "He was great with the oil companies, whose middle management didn't care for Craig Dobbin that much. The two people who built the company's business with the big oil companies for Craig Dobbin were Sylvain Allard and Christine Baird."

THE CAREER SUCCESS of Christine Baird is illustrative of both Dobbin's insight into an employee's potential and his ability to exploit that potential for his own and the subject's benefit. Hired as secretary to Sealand's then-president Al Soutar, Baird impressed J.C. Jones when he arrived to fill Soutar's role. "I was doing a lot of travelling at the time," Jones says, "and I would call back to the office to check on things, see if this helicopter had been serviced on time or that flight had left as scheduled. When I would ask to speak to the ops manager or the service manager, Christine would say, 'What do you want to know?' I would tell her, and she would have the answer right there at her fingertips. In my opinion, and this includes everybody, vice-presidents and all, she was the sharpest person in the CHC building. An amazing woman."

"I had humble beginnings," Christine Baird explains in an accent that carries an inflection more suggestive of a Newfoundland outport than of the executive suite she now occupies. "I joined the company as a secretary, taking dictation and typing, but I wasn't working directly for Craig Dobbin." No matter how much executive talent she possessed, Baird did not at first escape the traditional chores assigned to women in a male-dominated organization, especially one dedicated to flying aircraft through storms to offshore oil platforms. "I was called upon to prepare lunch for the Chairman, and sometimes for people the Chairman was entertaining," she recalls without rancour.

One day some years after she joined Sealand, Dobbin asked Baird to contact a low-level manager to perform some function. "He's not available," she replied, explaining why. Dobbin thought for a moment, then instructed her to call another staff member to do the job. Christine raised her eyebrows. "I think I can do the job better than him," she suggested, and Dobbin without hesitation replied, "Then do it."

Baird performed the chore with such success that Dobbin began assigning progressively more demanding tasks to her. Soon all international logistics at CHC, from obtaining work permits and visas to registering aircraft in foreign countries and arranging to have them ferried to the other side of the world, became the responsibility of the former stenographer. Within a short time she was appointed special projects manager, moving later to sharing ops manager duties with Sylvain Allard and eventually settling into the role of commercial manager.

Of all CHC executives, past and present, none generates more open admiration from her peers than Christine Baird. "She handled all international marketing for the company during the 1990s," one former CHC executive says, shaking his head. "Here's this attractive young woman travelling by herself to some very nasty places in the world, including the most dangerous regions of Africa and Azerbaijan, places you and I might not go in a group, and she's all alone. Christine would enter government offices in countries where women were not permitted to vote or drive cars and negotiate deals with power and authority. She was able to get in-country, make the contacts, get the business and come out alive. She was absolutely tenacious, able to target key players."

Today Baird is president of CHC global operations, dealing with top executives at ExxonMobil, Royal Dutch Shell and other mammoth corporations as well as heads of state throughout Europe, South America and Asia. From her Richmond, B.C., office she manages a team of 350 employees, many of them pilots and engineers unfamiliar with being directed by a female boss. Yet she commands the respect of everyone who encounters her within and beyond the corporation. Baird's gratitude to Craig Dobbin for the opportunities and degree of support he gave her deepened through the years. Each time she appeared before the CHC board of directors to report on the activities and prospects of the firm's global division, she ended her presentation with the statement: "By the way, I love the Chairman."

KEITH STANFORD WAS never an employee of CHC, nor was he directly involved in the multiple stages of building the company over the twenty-five years he was associated with Craig Dobbin. Everyone familiar with Stanford's role, however, attributes a substantial portion of Dobbin's success to Stanford's unique talents. Newfoundlanders do not wear their heritage or their hearts on their sleeves, but their language and demeanour—Gaelic and open, devoid of any hint of intrigue—identify them with their deepest roots. Stanford expresses himself with warmth and humour, his words delivered in an accent as authentically Newfoundland as a school of cod.

Fresh out of Memorial University with a bachelor of commerce degree in 1981, Stanford passed up an opportunity to earn a chartered accountancy degree by joining Highland Holdings Ltd., an umbrella firm encompassing all of Dobbin's ventures except Sealand. Each time Dobbin launched a business he created a new corporation for it, held within Highland. The firm's portfolio included a mix of real estate holdings and non-related businesses, a grab bag of ideas launched often impulsively from Craig Dobbin's vision and ambition. Walking into Highland's office on his first day of work in December 1981, Stanford found himself in the midst of financial and administrative chaos.

Stanford may have been working for Craig Dobbin, but more than a year passed before the two men met. In the meantime, Stanford was like a firefighter trying to control a tenement blaze with a cocktail spritzer. He soon discovered that all of Dobbin's real estate holdings carried first, second and even third mortgages, at a time when annual prime lending rates floated at record levels of 18 and 20 per cent. Things were made more complex because Highland's assets extended beyond Newfoundland, reaching into Quebec, Ontario and the U.S. Within a few weeks of Stanford's arrival, his boss, the company controller, resigned in frustration, prompting the Mercantile Bank, which held most of the company's paper, to dispatch a manager from their Halifax office.

"He phoned me one day," Stanford recalls, "and ordered me to write the names of every employee in the company along with their title, their duties and their salary. I did that, and he took the paper from me and went down the list of twenty-five names, drawing a line through twenty-three of them, skipping my name and one secretary." Included on the list of highlighted names were the president, vice-president, financial analyst and sales and support staff. "He handed the paper back to me and told me he wanted to meet the people on his list the next day at nine o'clock," Stanford continues. "As soon as they showed up for work in the morning, he gave them their notice on the spot. That's why I didn't meet Craig Dobbin for a year. He basically went into hiding."

How did Stanford escape the bloodbath? "They needed a bean counter on the inside, and since I had just started, I was the cheapest bean counter in the place," Stanford laughs. Within a few days Stanford managed to convince the Mercantile representative that the job was simply too big for him and the overworked secretary to handle alone, even working twelve hours a day, six days a week. He received permission to hire an assistant, a young woman named Sherry Jennings. Like Stanford, her entire business career became linked to the various enterprises of Craig Dobbin.

They had much to do. At least once each week, a bailiff arrived with an order to foreclose on various Highland properties. Thanks to Stanford's skill at dealing with lenders and juggling cash, he managed to avoid foreclosures with the exception of two local Kmart plazas. The balance of the properties remained within Highland.

Things settled into a routine of sorts. Interest rates eased and the Mercantile Bank started trusting Stanford to manage Highland's finances, though they continued looking over his shoulder for two years. They also demanded fees for their diligence. "Mercantile was always paid first," Stanford said, "and in that first year I believe they earned about a million dollars from us, beyond the standard charges and loan interest."

It wasn't until January 1983 that Stanford finally encountered Craig Dobbin. "He walked in, stuck out his hand to me and said, 'Call me Craig,' and I did from that day on," marking Stanford as one of the few employees and business associates who didn't address him as the Chairman or Mr. Dobbin.

When Mercantile Bank finally withdrew, Stanford was free to handle Highland on his own, which was something of a mixed blessing. Dobbin's properties remained heavily mortgaged and the firm stumbled from month to month, somehow managing to remain solvent. The situation remained relatively unchanged for much of the next twenty years. "Until just a few years before he died," Keith Stanford explained, "Craig Dobbin was often asset rich and cash poor." Dobbin was also, at this stage of the game, not universally liked or trusted. "You either loved or hated the guy," Stanford said. Lenders and mortgage holders usually lined up on the obvious side of the border between affection and dislike, though others had negative views as well. "Some people asked me how I could work for that S.O.B.," Stanford says, "telling me he didn't pay his bills and had gone through many financial officers before I came along." Dobbin, Stanford would counter, was no deadbeat. "He just refused to accept the financial restrictions other people placed on him." Stanford shrugs. "He was, to be sure now, sometimes difficult and demanding."

Stanford made a critical decision after his first encounter with Dobbin: he would work hard and remain loyal to Dobbin, but he would restrict the association to business. Arguably, no one contributed more to Craig Dobbin's personal financial achievement than Keith Stanford did, yet over their twenty-five-year relationship Stanford never took part in a purely social event with his boss, despite Dobbin's many entreaties. He turned down invitations to join Dobbin and his buddies on fishing weekends in Labrador. He refused offers to fly in Dobbin's executive aircraft, with one poignant exception a week before Dobbin's death. He visited Dobbin's home only when the event was directly related to their business dealings, and he was never involved in specific deals related to Sealand or CHC, restricting himself to watching over Dobbin's personal financial status. "Keith was a Houdini," observes St. John's businessman and Dobbin confidant Paddy O'Callaghan. "Without Keith Stanford the financial wizard, there would be no Craig Dobbin the business genius."

It was Stanford who often transferred funds to Sealand from Omega Investments to pay utility bills, meet payroll needs and service the bank debt of the helicopter company. It was Stanford to whom Dobbin turned when he needed to mortgage properties in search of the $1-million deposit demanded by John Lecky before beginning negotiations for Okanagan. And it was Stanford who joined Dobbin in a good cop/bad cop routine when negotiating with the banks, alternating roles according to Dobbin's prearranged strategy. "One time Craig would go in full of sweetness, promises and commitments," Stanford says, "then send me in to demand terms and conditions in our favour. The next time I'd be the nice guy to win them over before Craig would storm in and tighten the screws as much as he could."

The banks never lost their trust in Stanford, nor their expectation that he would keep Dobbin's financial affairs in line. If Craig Dobbin was a riverboat gambler playing every game of chance in the house, Keith Stanford was a Calvinist preacher standing quietly in a corner, clenching coins within his tight fist. Dobbin's bankers and creditors learned to trust Stanford's assurances, and for several years Craig Dobbin's file at the St. John's branch of the TD Bank carried the notation: "The day that Keith Stanford is no longer in the employ of Dobbin's firm, call the loan."

Craig Dobbin relied on Keith Stanford for more than financial guidance. Dobbin had invested in a small computer that he believed would improve the firm's general management capability. It was the mid-1980s, and the explosion of computer applications for business and personal use had begun, spurred by the introduction of Apple and IBM PCs. Sold on the ability of computers to address a range of management challenges, Dobbin invested more than $50,000 in a small mainframe system and expected it to solve his management problems. It failed to, for various reasons, and over several months Dobbin's rage at the infernal machine grew. He ceased payments on the system, insisting he would not pay for something that failed to live up to its promise, ignoring the vendor's threats of a lawsuit. Dobbin's anger and frustration grew, until one winter's day in 1984 he yanked the system's connections from the wall, seized the computer in his oversized arms and carried it to a loading dock, where he dropped it into the snow.

Soon after, Stanford and Dobbin arrived to negotiate settlement terms with the computer vendor, who was suing for payment. "Where is the computer now?" a lawyer asked Dobbin, who replied that it was at the corner of Torbay Road and Highland Drive. "In the Bally Rou building?" the lawyer assumed, and Dobbin barked, "No, in a snowbank."

The more Stanford met Dobbin's demands, the more Dobbin asked of him. The demands grew substantially in Dobbin's later years when, in contrast with his previous attitude, Craig Dobbin became almost obsessed with tracking changes in his liquidity. During this period, Stanford's duties included providing a daily review of Dobbin's assets, showing changes in market valuations and cash on hand from the previous day. "The report had to be on his desk by nine in the morning," Stanford remembers. "If it wasn't there by ten after nine my telephone would ring and I would hear Craig's voice bellow, 'Where the hell is my daily report?' But this was rare. It was usually there for him."

Over time, Stanford gained the ability to anticipate Dobbin's questions and prepare himself to give the appropriate answer. Few things disturbed Dobbin in his business dealings more than a staff member unprepared with a response. In some ways he preferred an ultimately wrong answer, if the error were honest and understandable, than no answer at all. "I don't know" became a banished term in Dobbin's presence.

Keith Stanford's talent for knowing what information the Chairman would need long before he requested it became something of a legend within CHC. Stanford kept details of relevant business matters in an overstuffed briefcase. One day, called into a meeting at which several CHC managers were present, Dobbin began firing questions at him. With each question Stanford would respond, "I have it right here," withdraw a document from his briefcase and hand it to the Chairman, much to the amazement of the helicopter people present. Finally, one of them called across the table at Stanford, "Would you happen to have an operations manual for a Sikorsky S-76? You've got damn near everything else in there!"

Dobbin's respect for Stanford became enormous, and he expressed it in various ways. In 2004, while liquidating many of his long-held properties in Newfoundland, Dobbin decided to retain one of his original apartment buildings on LaMarchant Road in St. John's. Built in 1967 as the Bellevue Terrace Apartments, the building had undergone various changes over the years and was serving as a low-rent residence when Dobbin informed Stanford he wanted the complex converted to a hotel. Dobbin wasn't interested in making a lot of money from the hotel business. "Basically," explains Stanford, "he wanted a place to hang out."

Despite Stanford's protestations that they knew nothing about running hotels, Dobbin pressed on. He relocated the tenants, renovated the rooms and lobby, and instructed Stanford to hire an advertising agency to suggest names for the new enterprise. Six months later, Stanford submitted the agency's proposal. Dobbin rejected them all. Then he smiled and said, "I think I'll name it after you. I'll call it the Stanford Hotel."

Stanford protested again. The Stanford name, he informed Dobbin, belonged to a well-established chain of hotels in the southwestern U.S. whose owners would claim copyright infringement. Dobbin shrugged. "If they complain, we'll call it something else," he replied. For two years the Stanford Hotel, its name derived not from a large international corporation but from a would-be accountant who worked unheralded out of a small office on Torbay Road, served as a popular accommodation for tourists and businesspeople in St. John's. Naming the hotel was one means Craig Dobbin used to express his appreciation for Stanford's accounting magic. Other means arrived in Dobbin's last will and testament.

Craig Dobbin always trusted Keith Stanford to provide accurate information on demand, even when the news was bad. "It's been a good week," Dobbin might comment to his personal secretary late on a Friday afternoon. Then his face would cloud over and he'd say, "Get Keith Stanford on the phone and ask him for my financial summary. That'll fuck up my weekend."

THE WOMAN DOBBIN would grumble to about Stanford ruining his weekend was Candace Moakler who, against all odds, served as his personal secretary for more than twenty years.

"The first week on the job," she recalls, describing the pressure of working under Dobbin, "I went home and cried my eyes out every night in anticipation of a blow-up the next day. He was a man of little patience and would rather hear a wrong answer from you than no answer at all." Like Keith Stanford, Moakler learned how to anticipate Dobbin's demands and be prepared with the answer he needed before he requested it. "The secret to keeping him happy," she suggests, "was to stay one step ahead of him."

Moakler, who carries herself with the easy openness common among Newfoundlanders, provided Dobbin with information to support his salutary style. "He would tell me who he was meeting with later in the day," she recalls, "sometimes a CHC employee, sometimes a client or politician, and ask me about them. I would mention perhaps that he and his wife were expecting a child shortly, that they had just purchased a new home, and that his hobby was woodworking. And I would hear Mr. Dobbin greet the man later, saying, 'I hear you and your wife are expecting a child. Gonna be happy in your new house, I'll bet,' and maybe mention something about carpentry, and the other fellow would be floored, simply floored."

One of Candace Moakler's duties was to don a headset patched into Dobbin's office telephone and transcribe all of Dobbin's conversations with business associates, storing them in her computer and producing hard copies as needed. Keith Stanford and others aware of this arrangement learned to call Dobbin on his cellphone if they wanted total privacy. Clients and suppliers not aware of Moakler's passive participation in their dealings with Dobbin would be startled, whenever the topic turned to personal matters or subjects for which he did not want a written record, to hear Dobbin bark into his mouthpiece, "Candace, get off the line." At that point she would gently disconnect her headphones.

At other times, Moakler would inwardly cringe as the individual Dobbin was speaking with, unaware of her authorized eavesdropping, raised some untoward topic. She remembers monitoring a telephone call from an auditor who, after several minutes of discussing complex and mundane financial details, launched into an off-colour story. "It was the raunchiest, dirtiest joke you could imagine," Moakler laughs in recollection. "The auditor was a perfect gentleman who knew I monitored calls, but in the middle of his report it slipped his mind." When the howls of laughter from Dobbin and his caller had faded, Dobbin said, "What did you think of that one, Candace?" An embarrassed silence on the other end was broken when the auditor muttered "Oh my God!" He apologized to Candace not only at that moment but every time they encountered each other from that day forward.

None of Dobbin's associates claimed he was an easy man to work for, yet he managed to achieve remarkable loyalty among employees at every level. A good deal of this was due to his personal charm. He managed not only to spot potential in individuals but also to endear himself to them with various devices, including nicknames.

Barry Clouter began his career with Eastern Provincial Airways in the early 1970s when it was owned by Harry Steele. As an EPA district sales manager, Clouter frequently called on Dobbin, seeking business as Dobbin's preferred air carrier for his business trips.

Later, during a fishing excursion to Grey River, Dobbin encountered Clouter operating a canning machine, processing salmon deep in the bush. For some reason Dobbin considered the sight amusing. From that day forward Clouter was always "Canner" to Dobbin, who later hired him for a sales management position. Eventually he promoted Clouter to CHC regional director of North and South America, responsible for the company's business from Ellesmere Island to Tierra del Fuego.

Like others plucked from lower positions and assigned major responsibilities, "Canner" Clouter proved outstanding in his job and grew deeply devoted to Craig Dobbin, though the Chairman demonstrated unusual methods of making management decisions from time to time. "I remember when all of us regional directors were gathered in Christine Baird's office for a performance review," Clouter says. "Craig was down at his Florida home, where he had video conferencing equipment installed. None of us regional people had had an especially good quarter, so we were prepared to be challenged. He watches us all stroll into the room where the video pickup was, and we can see his face on the screen. 'How are you, Canner?' he calls out before I have a chance to sit down. I tell him I'm well and he asks me what year I was born. I say, 'I was born in 1946, Mr. Dobbin.' 'Forty-six?' he says. 'Well, that's the return I want to see on your contracts from now on, Canner. Forty-six per cent. Don't forget.' He went around the room, challenging every regional director, and he knew the returns they were getting from their clients better than they did. What's really impressive about this is, it was maybe four months before he died, and he was still on top of things."

CLAYTON PARSONS RETURNED to his hometown of St. John's in 1979 in search of work, any kind of work, after serving in the Canadian Armed Forces for seventeen years. A friend referred Parsons to Sealand, where he was hired by Al Soutar to manage the stores of equipment and parts. Learning of Parson's military background, Dobbin labelled the new employee "Old Soldier." Over the years

Dobbin grew impressed with Parson's military bearing and positive attitude, repeatedly assigning "Old Soldier" to procure and transport vital helicopter parts literally anywhere in the world. Eventually he handed Parsons the title of special projects manager.

On one occasion, Dobbin instructed Parsons to get a main rotor blade for a Super Puma from St. John's to Ecuador within forty-eight hours. FedEx and its competitors had yet to achieve the unlimited global delivery service common today, making this more challenging than it may appear. The rotor blade, which measured eight metres in length, required special packaging and handling, and no chartered air transports were available. Parsons made arrangements to accompany the blade to Frankfurt on Air Canada, fly with it from there to Paris on Air France, and transfer to an overnight flight to Quito on Avianca Airlines. When Craig Dobbin called the day after handing Parsons the task, he was amazed to learn that both Parsons and the rotor blade were on the shipping dock in Ecuador.

Following that success, Clayton Parsons became the focus of various tales concerning "Old Soldier." They included the time Parsons reportedly worked thirty-six hours straight to relocate CHC, including aircraft, spare parts, maintenance equipment, furnishings and more, from one hangar to another on short notice. On another occasion a blizzard shut down the entire city of St. John's, including the airport, but Clayton Parsons was at his desk promptly at 8:00 a.m., prepared to put in a full day's work. "He is the embodiment of one of my favourite sayings," Dobbin said in praising Parsons. "To Clayton and to me, failure is not an option." Dobbin repeatedly challenged his employees at every level with a "Just get it done" attitude. Those who succeeded, as Clayton Parsons did, found themselves within Dobbin's warm inner circle, free to move as far up the corporate ladder as they chose.

DOBBIN DISCOVERED ANOTHER hidden talent and created another nickname when, shortly after moving into his showplace home at Beachy Cove, he hired a groundskeeper named Terry Young. Young, who had been performing odd jobs at a plant nursery in nearby Portugal Cove, soon encountered the impatient optimism of his new boss. While strolling around the extensive grounds at Beachy Cove one morning, Dobbin told Young, already referred to by Dobbin as "Big Guy," that he wanted a particular landscaping feature installed. When Young suggested he was unable to do the chore, Dobbin angrily informed him never to use the word "can't" in his presence. Young discovered he was capable of the task after all.

Among the responsibilities Young assumed was managing the enormous fish pond at Dobbin's Beachy Cove home, a 450-square-metre pool fed by ocean water and stocked with cod and lobster. Dobbin's idea of installing a pond from which he could enjoy fresh cod whenever it appealed to him was inspired by a comment from his friend and business associate Cabot Martin. Martin, a history and archaeology buff, was describing how the Romans kept live fish in tidal ponds, pulling them out whenever they fancied a meal of fresh fish. "Can I do that?" Dobbin asked. "What's involved?"

Martin, who had been discussing Dobbin's potential investment in an aquaculture project (which later became Sea Forest Plantation), said of course it could be done in Newfoundland.

"Send me a report on that," Dobbin said. "Tell me how it could be done at Beachy Cove."

It took some time for Martin to prepare the material. It didn't matter anyway. Three weeks later, driving through the gates at Beachy Cove, he encountered an excavation crew carving the pond and angle-drilling through rock into the ocean far below, installing pumps to circulate water through the pond. "He just cut out all the engineering," Martin recalls, "and did it his way, himself."

With the pond completed and stocked with fish, Young was instructed to catch, clean and fillet cod for the Beachy Cove kitchen whenever Dobbin wanted a feast of cod for himself or a cod dinner for a party or reception. On some occasions Young and the kitchen staff were given extremely short notice, and Young would race to the pond with either a net or fishing rod and reel. "How you caught 'em depended on when they were fed last," Young recalls. "We fed the cod every three or four days, and if it was coming up to their feeding time we'd pull 'em in easy on the rod and reel, big guys weighing up to ten or twelve pounds. But if they'd been fed the day before we'd need the net, and that was harder work." Many of Dobbin's guests consumed cod that had been swimming contentedly barely an hour earlier just a few steps from Dobbin's front door.

FOLLOWING THE COLLAPSE of his marriage to Penney in 1986, Craig Dobbin kept in close contact with his children, or contact as close as a man who was in New York today, London tomorrow and somewhere in Asia the next week could maintain. While daughters Joanne and Carolyn chose domestic and personal interests over business involvement, sons Mark, David and Craig Junior were all provided the opportunity to participate in their father's growing business empire. Of the three, Mark is generally deemed the most astute, and he has represented CHC at various levels and in various locations around the world. J.C. Jones claims that one of his duties as president of CHC was to serve as a mentor for Mark Dobbin, providing Craig's son with work experience to go along with Mark's recently acquired MBA. If so, Jones did a more than admirable job in the opinion of many.

"My father was a very bright man," says Mark, "but there were better people than him when it came to crunching numbers and better people at setting business strategy, I suppose. Sometimes the decisions he made didn't seem logical to people on the outside looking in, but he usually made them pay off."

Mark Dobbin dresses in a casual, elegant manner and speaks in well-rounded paragraphs. Tall and handsome with still-boyish features, he would appear equally at home in a Bay Street boardroom or a *Gentleman's Quarterly* fashion feature. Defining his father's management skill, Mark puts his finger on one important aspect. "In some cases, what you decide is not as important as making sure what you decide happens. If you decide, for example, to get a contract, how you get it may not be the most logical or elegant method, as long as you get it. And if you decide to be successful, as my father did—you can criticize the way he did it but you can't question the fact that he did."

Providing their children with entry into the family business is almost an obligation for entrepreneurs, especially when those children are as well qualified as Mark Dobbin. In at least one instance recalled by J.C. Jones, however, Dobbin valued loyalty to family over his rule about hiring good people and leaving them to perform on their own. "We had an older fellow, I believe he was named George or something like that, whose job was to handle the refuelling hoses at the hangar," Jones explains. "These hoses were fairly heavy and I noticed he was having a difficult time with them, so I decided we would have to let him go, and passed the word to the office."

A day later Craig Dobbin entered Jones's office and asked if it was true that old George was losing his job. Jones explained that yes, it was true, because as good a worker as George might be, the employee simply couldn't handle the physical demands of the work any more.

"Do you know George is a veteran who served overseas?" Dobbin asked.

Jones said no, he didn't know that, but if the man couldn't do the job he couldn't do the job.

"Did you know his wife is sick and bedridden?" Dobbin continued.

No, Jones didn't know that either, but they were prepared to offer George a decent severance agreement.

Dobbin leaned across Jones's desk, lowered his voice, and said, "Did you know he's my wife's cousin?"

Jones found another job for old George.

CRAIG DOBBIN'S SELECTION of his brother Derm to serve as the primary building contractor for CHC proved controversial among some people. Derm Dobbin had planned to become a lawyer until, after he'd completed his second year at law school in Ottawa, Craig persuaded him to return to St. John's for a summer job. Discovering he enjoyed the details of construction much more than the intricacies of law, Derm never returned to school and became Craig's contractor of choice for various real estate projects. He also became closer to his elder brother than anyone else in the Dobbin family, as ebullient about life and as competent in his own field as Craig was.

Through multiple developments over the years, Derm Dobbin's role in his brother's housing and apartment deals went unchallenged, in part because Derm proved a canny and responsible contractor. He continued in this role, building hangars, office facilities and other projects for CHC as the exclusive contractor. But CHC, unlike Craig Dobbin's real estate operations, was a public corporation, and such perceived nepotism raised concerns among shareholders and regulators. It also, during his tenure, made J.C. Jones uneasy. "Those of us on the management team, when Craig wasn't around, we'd look at the deals between CHC and Derm," J.C. Jones remembers, "and we'd say, 'Boy, this should have gone out for tender.' But there was never any shoddy workmanship in those buildings, and none of them have fallen down, so aside from making some folks uneasy, nothing really came of it."

THE STAFF AND executives Craig Dobbin gathered around him justified his claim that his job function was closer to casting director than to CEO. Most continue to this day in responsible positions at CHC, vital to the company's remarkable global success.

Not all of the individuals associated with Craig Dobbin and CHC's achievements over the past twenty years were on the employee list. In the view of many who knew both the business accomplishments and the social activities of Craig Dobbin—and the two were frequently entwined—the most vital contributor to his success was not an employee. She was the second woman Craig Dobbin married.

"Foxy" Paddy Dobbin with sons Craig (*right*) and Paddy Jr.,
who became a physician.

Paddy Dobbin's clan in the mid-1950s, with a tall, crewcut Craig at rear centre.

Craig Dobbin stands front and centre as newly elected president of the St. John's homebuilders association, circa 1966. To his right, in the bow tie, is friend and mentor Jean-Yves Gelinas.

Dobbin's mid-1960s Bellevue Terrace Apartments offered, among other features, "disappearing kitchens." Later the complex was converted to a hotel, named in honour of Keith Stanford.

Sprawled along Torbay Road in St. John's, the utilitarian Hillview Terrace Suites marked Dobbin's first financial success.

Keith Stanford, numbers man supreme: If he had ever left Dobbin's employ, the TD Bank would have called in its loan.

Financier Robert Foster with his wife, Julia. When Dobbin announced he wanted to purchase Okanagan Helicopters, Foster pointed out he had no money. "That's your problem," Dobbin replied.

Dobbin at the height of his power and pleasure—a sunny day,
a salmon pool and a helicopter.

George Bush Sr.'s arrival at Dobbin's Atlutuk fishing camp created a
helicopter traffic jam.

Despite their contrasting backgrounds, the bond between Dobbin and former U.S. president George Bush Sr. was strong and genuine.

Three amigos of the salmon pool: Frank Moores (*left*), Harry Steele
and Craig Dobbin.

Proud Dobbin matriarch Rita with her successful son Craig.

6

*My mother told me that, regardless of the
situation she is in, a lady is somebody who puts other
people at ease. That's Elaine Dobbin in a nutshell.*

NANCY BLUMENTHAL, senior nurse practitioner and
transplant coordinator, University of Pennsylvania Health Center

SHE WAS BORN ELAINE Frances Davis in Holyrood, on the east
shore of Newfoundland's Avalon Peninsula. Little grief marked
her life until her father, a law enforcement officer, died tragi-
cally when Elaine was eight years old. Her husband gone, Elaine's
strong-willed mother continued to operate the family-owned restaurant and bar at the southern tip of Conception Bay. Hubert Keough,
an engineer, soon began dropping in for a chance to chat up the
proprietor, his visits encouraged by the young Elaine. Keough and
Elaine's mother married soon after Elaine's eleventh birthday.

"My stepfather was a kind, gentle soul," Elaine recalls, "open,
affectionate, expressive and generous, and I was his favourite. He
spoiled me terribly."

Elaine was the fourth child in the family of six, which included a
son born of her mother's second marriage. Her mother encouraged
all of her children to obtain a university degree, but after graduating from a private Roman Catholic school, Elaine rejected the idea.
"I wanted to get out into the real world, to see things and do things,"
she says, "not sit in classrooms for another four years."

The real world welcomed her. Hired to work the front desk at the
local Holiday Inn, Elaine was recruited as a hostess for conventions

and meeting events. She was a slim, attractive blonde who learned to carry herself with assurance in every social situation. Her physical attributes and her personality opened the door to modelling assignments, and at age eighteen she qualified as Newfoundland's representative in the Miss Dominion of Canada pageant in Niagara Falls, where she won the swimsuit competition. Back in St. John's, Elaine drew attention for both her beauty and her public-speaking skills, becoming active in the rough and tumble world of Newfoundland politics. Future federal cabinet minister John Crosbie chose her to join his Crosbie Girls during his bid to oust Joey Smallwood as leader of the provincial Liberal party in 1969. A dozen attractive young women dressed in miniskirts and berets, the Crosbie Girls accompanied their namesake to various events during the leadership convention, and in Crosbie's published memoirs, *No Holds Barred*, a teenage Elaine Davis can be easily spotted beaming her smile among the others.

Modelling and beauty pageants were fun, but Elaine Davis had no intention of making a career of them. Without training or experience, she accepted a sales position at Parson's Ford & Mercury in St. John's. The first female automotive salesperson in the province, she quickly became the most successful at the dealership, attracting the attention of the owner's son, Greg Parsons. "He wooed me," she says, "in a corny way that I appreciated, like holding my hand and taking me to dinner. I fell for him pretty hard."

Married at age twenty—"much too young," she observes—by thirty years of age she found herself the mother of three active school-aged children in a marriage that appeared to hold no future for either partner. She and her children, Rob, Scott and Kellee, moved to an apartment on Pleasantville Street in St. John's, and Elaine continued her sales career. For some time she held two sales positions, with a cosmetic firm and as a representative for WonderBra. Her work took her on periodic business trips across Newfoundland and Labrador. Later she moved with her children to a small home on Walwyn Street.

Dobbin had launched Sealand and remained active in handling his real estate development enterprises, still finding the energy and time to enjoy his almost legendary social life. The Wild Colonial Boy was a familiar face in bars and nightclubs up and down the Avalon Peninsula, and across the province in Corner Brook and Gander. By all accounts Craig Dobbin became as popular with women receptive to his considerable charm as he was with men who loved whiskey, card games and salmon fishing.

The effect of Dobbin's halcyon lifestyle on his marriage was predictable. His success carried him away on frequent business trips, almost always alone. Penney preferred the comfort of her home and the company of her children, and as proud as she might have been of her husband's achievements, the couple were not as close as they had been when Dobbin had more dreams than successes, more empty accounts than assets. His children were entering adulthood and no longer needed his constant attention, leaving him free to direct it elsewhere—towards his complex business operations and his extensive social life.

"I encountered him at various social events," Elaine recalls, "and I knew of his reputation. I wasn't interested in being one of his toys, so I avoided him. He drank too much and smoked too much, and didn't pay much attention to his wardrobe. But when he looked you in the eye, shook your hand and flashed his smile on you, a lot of that didn't matter any more."

Craig Dobbin spotted the petite self-assured blonde at a political event and asked a mutual friend to introduce them. Elaine at first rebuffed him, but Craig grew more insistent. She agreed to a date or two, enjoying his attention and generosity but keeping her guard up. Her primary role in those years was being a mother to three school-aged children, followed by earning sufficient income to support them and herself. Craig Dobbin did not fit into that picture.

Eventually he did. Over time, Elaine realized his attention to her wasn't fleeting. In 1984, arriving at Gander to make a series of sales calls on behalf of WonderBra, she pulled her car into the parking lot at Harry Steele's Albatross Motel, opened her trunk, reached for her suitcase, and was brushed aside by a massive hand that seized the handle of her luggage. "I'll take that," Craig Dobbin said, surprising her by playing bellhop. Things grew serious after that.

Dobbin persuaded her to become a real estate agent, a move she initially resisted. "Selling real estate is the kind of thing people do when they can't do anything else," she protested, and Dobbin replied, "Which is exactly why you'll be very good at it." Elaine obtained her licence and joined first Century 21 and later Tony Murray Real Estate, a midsized local firm that quickly became the leasing agency for Dobbin's Omega Investments. When Omega sold off a massive parcel of its holdings, Elaine was the agent of record.

Two years after the incident in Gander, Dobbin called Elaine at her real estate office. "Guess what I did today?" he asked, and before she could answer he said, "I left home, and all I took with me was my toothbrush." Elaine told him to turn around and go straight back home. Her advice proved as futile as she knew it would.

The breakup of a family, especially one bonded in the immutable manner of Irish Catholics, is never achieved without pain, regret and residual bitterness. Craig and Penney Dobbin's was no exception, regardless of the apparent inevitability. At least one of Craig's children continues to maintain that Elaine was directly responsible for the split. Others are reluctant to saddle her with the blame.

Living with Craig confirmed some qualities of the Wild Colonial Boy that Elaine had recognized earlier. Confident, determined and convincing Craig Dobbin might have been in business and social situations, but only because he managed to hide his self-doubts. "He was very insecure because he was not well educated," Elaine says, suggesting the motive for his insistence that all of his children attend university.

Having Elaine on his arm when meeting high-level political and business contacts may have resolved some of that insecurity. "She was quite a package," J.C. Jones says. "Her looks, her figure, her wardrobe, her grooming. When Elaine entered a room all the men would stop talking just to watch her walk by. She never saw a party she couldn't host and never met a man she couldn't handle. If she were in a room full of CEOs, politicians and royalty, she would never be intimidated, because if they were male she knew their tongues were hanging out."

Craig Dobbin was a hard-drinking, hard-living entrepreneur who bulldozed his way past union restrictions, government influence and mainland disdain, and he retained the rough edges from his early years of driving makeshift trucks and diving for salvage. On days when the banks and other creditors cut him enough slack, he could claim the title of an honest-to-goodness millionaire, and Elaine grew determined to polish his image until it reflected his achievements.

"Craig was the world's worst dresser," Elaine claims. "From the day we were together permanently, I dressed him. From his underwear out, I would choose everything he wore: his shirts, his cufflinks, his tie, his suits, his shoes and socks. And he loved it. He loved the way I changed his appearance and his image. It gave him confidence, especially when he was dressing for an important meeting."

The influence cut both ways. Dobbin basked in the response of other men when he appeared at dinners and parties with a woman who glowed with glamour. He dressed Elaine as much as she dressed him. He bought her expensive jewellery and insisted she wear fashions that emphasized her face and figure. He also set down rules for her to follow. She could wear blue jeans in the country and while working in the garden, but never when travelling. Her hair must retain its rich blonde colour, and her makeup must be perfect.

Craig's influence extended into their personal life. Dorothea Jones, former wife of Sealand president J.C. Jones and a practising psychiatrist, recognized a challenge to the relationship when she noted how Craig resented the time Elaine dedicated to her three children. Elaine agrees, recalling a comment that Craig once made to her daughter, Kellee. "He told Kellee he loved her," Elaine says, "then said, 'One problem I have is that you take up too much of your mother's time.'"

To counter any perception of Craig as a domineering, controlling man, Elaine points out that he was totally open and honest about his feelings, and he demonstrated his affection for her children in various ways. The possessiveness, she suggests, was not based on any need to dominate her or her family but was a reflection of the deeply passionate feelings they retained for each other.

Her daughter, Kellee, supports that view, with a somewhat different slant. "Craig wanted Mom's time," she says, "and nobody was going to take it from him. Nobody was ever going to say to Craig Dobbin that he was not going to get what he wanted. But I don't think it was really jealousy or possessiveness. I think it was out of real need. He needed Mom more than other people realized."

Powerful and influential as he was, there were times for Dobbin to show his softer side. "Under the rough surface he was a teddy bear at heart," Kellee says, and she recalls an instance when she, her mother and Craig were spending time at Dobbin's Florida condominium.

Each morning Craig and Kellee did the local daily newspaper's crossword together, sitting at the breakfast table, a ritual both enjoyed. One evening Kellee and Craig became involved in a heated argument over Kellee's plans to wed her boyfriend, a plan that Dobbin vehemently opposed, feeling she could "do better." Voices were raised, tables were thumped, tears were shed, and Kellee fled to her room, tossing angry words over her shoulder at Dobbin, who continued to express his opinion.

The following morning Kellee was in bed, still smarting over the quarrel, when she noticed something being slowly slid beneath her bedroom door. It was that day's crossword puzzle, partially completed by Craig. He wanted to make up with his stepdaughter, and it worked. Later, when he realized just how determined Kellee was about her marriage plans, he provided a spectacular wedding for her and her fiancé, a young man he grew to appreciate.

Kellee's brother Scott, who endured his own conflicts with Craig, is more specific about his mother's role in the relationship. "Craig was half a man without Mom," he suggests without hesitation, "and when he demanded Mom's time it was out of necessity and dependency on her, not jealousy or control."

Others had similar views. "Craig and Elaine were like two plus two equalling five," Frank Ryan says, and Harry Steele adds, "They were the perfect combination. Craig Dobbin could never have achieved all that he did without Elaine, and that's a fact. She is smart as a whip and Craig knew that. She handled him in various ways and, believe me, handling Craig Dobbin was not always easy."

Elaine also knew when and how to take charge in emergencies. While visiting friends across Devil's Lake, where they were building a log cabin retreat, Craig decided he would swim home. It was a cool day in October, but ignoring Elaine's concern for his safety, he dove into the chilly water and set off. Halfway across the lake Craig found himself in trouble, and Elaine, watching him from the shore, feared he would slip beneath the water and drown. A CHC helicopter was flying nearby, but she was unable to contact the crew by radio. When the helicopter appeared overhead, Elaine employed a direct means of communication: she removed her fleece-lined sweatshirt, the only garment covering her top, and began waving it desperately in the air. The sight of a topless Elaine waving her shirt was enough—more than enough, perhaps—to capture the attention of the pilots, and they responded to her frantic gestures, setting down and assisting her husband.

The role she played in Dobbin's business negotiations was more subtle. She may not have sat around the table while offers and counter-offers were tossed back and forth, but she remained aware of the status and conditions of the deals. On almost every occasion,

Elaine accompanied her husband on foreign trips to promote the firm, seal a contract or evaluate an acquisition. He shared his plans and concerns with her, often seeking her opinion on CHC personnel and future clients or partners.

"He would ask me to sit off to the side and listen while he talked business with somebody," Elaine explains, "or have me view a videotape of a meeting. When it was over he would say, 'What did you think of so-and-so?' and I would reply that I noticed he never looked at Craig when responding to a question, or that he seemed especially tense, or that I believed he was straight up and honest. Craig would usually nod his head, telling me that he had noticed the same thing, and would feel better about making his decision, whatever it was." Her husband, Elaine notes, was tough but eminently fair in negotiating deals. "He honestly believed that the best kind of deal was the one where both sides got what they wanted. That's how he did business. He would understand what you wanted out of the deal and find a way of getting it for you, which made it easier to get what *he* wanted."

Craig's brother Derm saw Elaine's beneficial effect on Craig firsthand. "When Craig took his dog and pony show on the road in 1987, looking for money to buy Okanagan," he recalls, "they stayed for weeks at L'Hotel in Toronto. Every day it was Elaine who got him presentable to go out and make his pitch to the Bay Street boys with all the money, the ones he had to win over." The bankers and investment dealers would not have looked favourably on the earlier unkempt Craig Dobbin; they obviously approved of the tailored suit, starched shirt and silk tie of the Elaine-influenced man from St. John's.

There were skeptics, of course. In its early stages, Craig and Elaine's relationship resembled a blend of soap opera and *Playboy*-inspired fantasy: wealthy man squires younger, drop-dead-gorgeous woman around the world, dressing her in diamonds and mink, revelling in the envious looks of the powerful men they associate with. She might be a trophy girlfriend, some whispered, but she'll never be a trophy wife.

"Lots of people believed it wouldn't last," says J.C. Jones. "Craig was too old for her, and she was too good-looking for him." Someone who had known Craig all of his life makes a cooler observation. "Elaine believed she was the reason for the party," he says, not unkindly, "and she wasn't. Craig was the reason for the party. Elaine was the hostess."

Early doubts were supported by stories of Craig Dobbin remaining close to Penney and his children. "He stayed fond of Penney, as we all did," Derm Dobbin remembers, "and even with the demands on his time, he tried to be a good father to his children." Another Dobbin friend puts it more directly: "He may have fallen out of love with Penney, but he never stopped loving her, and he would never speak a word criticizing her or hear anyone else criticize her."

While Craig's brothers and sisters understood the attraction between him and Elaine, and accepted her into the fold even as they mourned Penney's absence, the Dobbin children struggled with the new arrangement. Sons Mark, David and Craig Jr., all actively involved in their father's business at various times to various degrees, perhaps appreciated the benefits Elaine brought to their father's life and found it easy to accept her. Not so their sisters, Joanne and Carolyn.

His staying close to his ex-wife and family suggested to some that Craig Dobbin was involved in the classic middle-aged fling by a wayward husband who entertains thoughts of resuming his domestic role someday. But Quebec Premier Jean Charest, who became a close friend of the couple in Dobbin's later years, has no doubts about the feelings between Craig and Elaine. "Craig loved Elaine very much," he says. "They were physically close whenever each was in the other's presence, and he would from time to time tell her that he loved her in a voice everyone could hear. When he drank too much as the evening wore on she would gently let him know, and he would set the glass or the bottle aside." Charest smiles at the memory of parties and dinners he attended with the couple. "I can close my eyes and think of sitting in their living room," he says. "They would never be seated very far apart, even at the dinner table, and several times during the evening he would reach to touch her hand. I cannot imagine Craig Dobbin without Elaine."

Guy Savard, chairman of Merrill Lynch Canada, agrees. "She was by his side all the time, everywhere," Savard says in his corner office high above René-Lévesque Boulevard in Montreal, "a very able woman."

John Crosbie goes further. "Elaine could handle Craig like nobody else," he states. "I always thought when Craig passed on she'd be the one who would run or control the company. She could do it. She's that smart and determined."

Craig Dobbin might have succeeded without Elaine at his side for the last twenty-odd years of his life, but by general consensus he would not have achieved as much without her in the role of consort, wife, hostess, social director and nurse. As one individual who knew both partners puts it, "Craig wanted much, but Elaine wanted more."

7

Craig came to a party at our home in North Hatley, Quebec, arriving in
one of his big cHC helicopters. He told the pilot to give our children a ride,
which thrilled them, of course, and for the rest of the day I think every
child in town received a free ride in the helicopter. He loved people, and
he especially loved children. It was part of his common touch.

JEAN CHAREST, premier of Quebec

RAIG DOBBIN NOW HEADED one of the world's largest helicopter service companies, performing some of the most demanding work in the field. Few tasks in civil aviation are as challenging as flying to and from oil platforms in the North Atlantic. The flights occur day after day in every season and every kind of weather, much of it bad. Many begin and end in heavy fog under instrument flight rules (IFR), meaning the helicopter pilots must depend on their instruments, not their eyes. One definition of IFR, not entirely incorrect, is "flying blind," and the journey is made across waters whose temperature hovers near zero degrees Celsius and whose waves can easily exceed ten metres in height.

CHC managed to maintain higher than acceptable safety standards for the operation and maintenance of its fleet, a policy not necessarily upheld by others. Among the helicopter companies acquired by CHC during its period of expansion through the 1990s, one was discovered to have installed off-the-shelf automotive replacement parts on several aircraft as a cost-saving measure, the components falling well below the performance standards dictated for use in helicopters. Dobbin and Jones immediately grounded the entire fleet, tore down every machine for inspection, and installed correct, approved parts where necessary. The cost was enormous, not only for the labour and parts but for business lost while the operation was dormant. It was also essential; had an unapproved part led to an incident with one of the craft, all of CHC's fleet would have come under deep suspicion and government scrutiny, staining the company's reputation with its offshore petroleum clients.

Pilots of fixed-wing aircraft often show disdain for helicopters; to them, a helicopter is essentially unstable (which it is) and decidedly more dangerous to fly (which it is not). Aside from the risk of total structural failure, which is rare, both types of aircraft are safest while travelling at cruising speed and altitude. The majority of incidents occur during takeoff and landing, procedures that a working helicopter may carry out far more frequently in a given time period than a scheduled fixed-wing aircraft. A Boeing 737, for example, may complete one takeoff and landing cycle every ten hours, and a long-distance Boeing 767 or Airbus A340 might do two cycles every twenty-four hours. In contrast, working helicopters routinely perform a full takeoff and landing cycle every five or six minutes.

This explains, in part, the statistical difference between accidents per 100,000 hours for civilian helicopters and civilian air carriers. U.S. statistics for 2005 measured 8.09 helicopter accidents per 100,000 hours in the air (the fatal accident rate was 1.48) versus an accident rate for U.S. commercial air carriers of 0.159 and a fatal accident rate of 0.011.*

The inherent stability of a fixed-wing aircraft becomes a liability when the plane needs to set down in an emergency situation. In the event of an engine failure, a helicopter can land comfortably in

* Statistics obtained from the International Helicopter Safety Symposium, Montreal, September 26–29, 2005.

an area not much larger than its own footprint (assuming no high-tension wires are in the way, as they were in the 1979 crash that cost two of Dobbin's companions their lives), thanks to autorotation. Fixed-wing aircraft require an extensive runway approached at a shallow angle, severely limiting the pilot's options in an emergency.

Still, safety remains a primary concern for petroleum companies whose contracts through the 1990s represented as much as ninety cents out of every dollar earned by CHC. While Sealand's safety record had been good, the wider range, larger size and greater responsibility of CHC demanded that the firm instigate an exceptional safety training program for both air and ground personnel. The program has become a model for the entire industry.

Along with the risk of flying to remote and challenging landing areas in changeable weather comes the economic risk associated with the business. Capital costs for large-capacity helicopters with sophisticated navigation equipment can rival that of aircraft for scheduled airlines, but maintenance costs per kilometre flown are dramatically higher than for fixed-wing craft. Industry standards require operators to track operating time and cycles for specific components and to replace the parts even if they and the machine are operating at 100 per cent efficiency. Manufacturers' guidelines dictate that aircraft such as the Super Pumas receive 3.6 hours of routine maintenance for every hour they spend in the air. This involves not only a substantial cost for maintenance crews, most of whom work overnight on helicopters assigned to offshore service, but for parts inventory as well. While revenue is potentially high, operating costs can quickly spiral out of control, and by the late 1980s Craig Dobbin was searching for a means to absorb sudden leaps in operating costs and dramatic drop-offs in revenue.

Growing aware of the need to exert more control over financial aspects of the company, and of the reality that leasing costs for new equipment were continuing to mount, Dobbin explored the concept "If you can't beat 'em, join 'em."

The idea appears to have been planted in his mind by Tony Ryan, who operated Ryanair, a highly successful though controversial discount airline based in Ireland. While Ryanair represented Ryan's highest-profile investment, his cash cow was Guinness Peat Aviation, the world's largest commercial aircraft leasing firm. Ryan, a former Aer Lingus executive, created GPA with support from the Irish national airline and the Guinness Peat Group, a London-based financial services company. GPA dealt with fixed-wing aircraft exclusively. In 1990, when Dobbin and Ryan began discussions for a joint venture, GPA placed a $17 billion order to purchase 700 new aircraft over the following ten years, an astonishing commitment.

Ryan, as colourful and controversial in many ways as Craig Dobbin, established a pattern of partnering with heavyweight personalities in his corporate structure that Dobbin may later have duplicated. Among the non-executive directors recruited by Ryan to serve on GPA's board were former Taoiseach Garret FitzGerald; former British chancellor of the exchequer Nigel Lawson; and the former chairman of ICI, Sir John Harvey-Jones, who served as GPA's chairman.

Ryan and Dobbin agreed to create GPA Helicopters Ltd., which would purchase and lease helicopters for clients around the world. Dobbin dispatched CHC president J.C. Jones and another CHC executive to negotiate the deal. With the agreements signed, it was determined that GPA Helicopters would be managed jointly by Dobbin's son Mark and Ian Young, a member of Ryan's retinue. "The idea was that Mark would become president of the new company," Jones recalls, "but once he got over there, Mark changed his mind. He had just been married and did not want to commit his family to Ireland. Tony Ryan, for some reason, took a shine to me and suggested I run the operation on my own."

Jones knew little about leasing and financing, and he faced commuting between Dublin and Vancouver. At Craig Dobbin's insistence and with encouragement from Tony Ryan, he reluctantly accepted the position, a move he almost instantly regretted. "The constant commuting was putting an impossible strain on my marriage," Jones explains, and within a year Jones and GPA Helicopters parted ways, soon followed by a similar separation between Dobbin and Ryan.

Back on this side of the Atlantic, Dobbin grew intrigued by Helicopter Welders Ltd., a Langley, B.C., firm engaged in servicing and rebuilding helicopters, and he proposed the purchase of the company to the CHC board of directors. The board was cool to the idea. In a fit of pique, Dobbin purchased it himself, changed its name to Heli-Welders of Canada, and installed the now unemployed J.C. Jones to manage it. Within a few months Heli-Welders had expanded significantly, growing from a staff of twenty-eight to sixty employees and producing substantial profits. With a degree of understandable smugness, Dobbin sold his private company to CHC and pocketed the profit.

Craig Dobbin had moved Patrick Callahan, CHC's VP of finance under Jones, into the president's chair after Jones departed for GPA, believing that a financial specialist in the top job would alleviate the firm's traditional cash flow problems. Callahan belied the common stereotype of a financial specialist as something of a milquetoast more at ease with numbers than with people. Tall and gregarious, he was as comfortable in social situations as Craig Dobbin was, and he was popular with most members of the CHC board.

Now that Dobbin appeared to have an effective steward for the company's financial assets in the COO position, he was free to apply his entrepreneurial skills to other challenges. Returning to his idea of entering the leasing business, he created Aviaco International Leasing Inc. and Furlong International Ltd., the thirty-first and thirty-second corporation launched since he founded Craig Dobbin Real Estate Ltd. back in 1963. Perhaps as a means of achieving revenge on the computer he had manhandled into a snowbank a few years later, he also founded Dobbin Data Services Ltd. as a computer resource centre.

The explosive growth of CHC might have driven others to focus on the company, its complex operation and its remaining growth potential. Instead, Dobbin seized every opportunity to expand his business holdings in whatever direction his fancy or his impulse appeared to take him. "Craig did things instinctively," Derm Dobbin explains. "His whole philosophy of business expansion was 'Ready, fire, aim!' Overall he had very good instincts, but sometimes those instincts were wrong. Like with the fish hatchery."

Craig Dobbin knew nothing about domestic fish farming, but this did not dissuade him from investing in an operation to breed and raise cod. "He had a great belief in some people," Derm Dobbin recalls, "and if someone brought him a new business venture he would react to the person and not necessarily to the idea."

Cabot Martin brought him the idea of investing in a fish hatchery. A former energy advisor to the governments of Frank Moores and Brian Peckford and a friend of Dobbin's, Martin had inaugurated Sea Forest Plantation some years earlier, and in 1990 he called on Craig Dobbin to drop money into the company. Martin saw an opportunity to supplement the dwindling cod stocks in the Grand Banks by transferring undersized cod to an aquaculture facility, where they would be fed cheap capelin and mackerel. With expectations that the young cod would double their weight within three months, the adult fish would be sold to commercial interests, filling the gap left by the loss of wild cod.

SFP had begun operations in the mid-1980s, and by 1988 had produced 350 tonnes of cod, a reasonable beginning. When a 1992 moratorium on cod removed the company's source of juvenile fish, SFP switched tactics. Now it would raise cod from fertilized eggs, release the fingerlings in Grand Banks waters and earn income from provincial government grants set up to expand the fisheries industry. Fisheries scientists quickly scuttled this idea, warning that cod raised in an aquaculture environment risked spreading disease among the existing fish stocks.

With no prospect of earnings from government, Martin turned to Craig Dobbin for assistance in developing a purely commercial operation, selling fingerlings to other commercial aquaculture operators and raising a substantial number of cod to adult size for sale through wholesalers and distributors. Dobbin responded not on the basis that the venture made good commercial sense and promised a profit, but because cod symbolized so much of the history and soul of Newfoundland. The disappearance of the cod would represent more than a loss of livelihood. It would mark the loss of everything it had been to be a Newfoundlander. It was unthinkable. Martin's proposal suggested a means of avoiding this disaster, to at least one extent.

"We were at death's door financially," Cabot Martin explains, "and when everybody was looking for ways just to survive, maybe by cutting costs or borrowing a little more, Craig's response was 'We have to grow! We have to get bigger!'"

Dobbin invested $2.5 million in Sea Forest Plantation, topped off with a small investment from brother Derm plus government grants. In total, the corporation's capital rose to more than $4 million, most of it invested in a new aquaculture facility at Jerseyside on Placentia Bay, the first commercial cod hatchery in North America.

During its first year Jerseyside was expected to produce 300,000 juvenile cod; half would be sold to independent cod farmers who had completed an SFP training program and the remainder retained by the company. Projections indicated the facility would yield more than 2 million juvenile cod once in full production, a year-round supply for local aquaculture operators. Everyone on the Avalon Peninsula grew excited at the prospect, including the provincial government of Brian Peckford.

It was not to be. After the first generation of adolescent cod had been raised and released, fire swept through the complex, destroying buildings, equipment and facilities. The cause of the fire was determined to be an electrical fault, which didn't soften the blow when Dobbin discovered that the $4-million facility had been insured for a paltry half-million dollars. Despite later attempts to entice private investors to resurrect SFP, the project was set aside. It was not entirely forgotten, however. "We were the first successful cod hatchery in the world," Martin emphasizes. "We completed a cycle of breeding cod, something no one else had done, and that makes us a Holy Grail of aquaculture." Breeding cod and similar fish in an aquaculture facility remains a goal in other countries, and researchers from as far afield as Norway and Chile visit Newfoundland to learn and adapt techniques the firm pioneered, funded by Craig Dobbin's desire to maintain a heritage.

Forming another partnership with Cabot Martin, Dobbin launched NorTek Engineering as an engineering source for petroleum companies engaged in developing offshore energy sources. In a brilliant business move, he invited Norwegian Petroleum Consultants, builders of concrete production platforms for use in offshore exploration, to take a 40 per cent interest in NorTek.

All of this activity was carried out among a host of other decisions and actions, any three of which would have taxed the energy of an average businessperson. "It was as though he got on a horse, made it gallop, and never stopped running," one individual who encountered Dobbin during this period observed. Dobbin continued to oversee Air Atlantic's operations; monitored the merger of Okanagan, Toronto, Sealand, Viking and other firms into CHC; developed his beloved fishing camps at Long Harbour and Adlatuk; built a cabin retreat at Devil's Lake; practised and improved his golf game (at one time he had a five handicap); travelled to Africa, Asia and South America regularly in pursuit of international business contracts; managed his burgeoning real estate investments; and still found time for card games with close friends.

Finally, in the midst of all this, Dobbin finished building his dream house. Actually, it was three houses on nearly three hectares of oceanfront property in Beachy Cove, looking westward to Bell

Island. Beachy Cove remains an architectural monument to Craig Dobbin and all that he valued. High above the waters of Conception Bay, the northern edge of the property drops in sheer cliffs to the ocean below, where waves crash on some of the world's oldest rocks. No more dramatic or quintessentially Newfoundland building site exists within a half-hour's drive of St. John's.

Luxurious and spacious, the main house is more suitable for hosting parties and banquets than serving as a family home. Guest suites are appropriately sumptuous, the kitchen is as elaborate as that of any Michelin-starred restaurant, the wine cellar is stocked with exceptional vintages, and the interior is a blend of wood-panelled walls and granite fireplace facings. Craig and Elaine Dobbin covered those walls with an extensive collection of Newfoundland-Canadian paintings. Favouring realism, the couple invited artists to stay at one of Beachy Cove's comfortable guest houses for months at a time, absorbing the area's rugged scenery as inspiration for works to be purchased by the Dobbins upon completion.

A lexicon of adjectives may be applied to the showplace—magnificent, opulent, imposing—but cozy is not on the list. Beachy Cove was created as a place for Craig Dobbin to celebrate the aspects of life he enjoyed most: the company of as many friends as he chose to welcome for dinners, card parties, receptions, barbecues or any event he and Elaine indulged in. He often indulged in these with great spontaneity, too; staff at Beachy Cove grew used to receiving notice of an hour or less that the Chairman was on his way with a dozen guests for lunch or dinner, and he expected them to be served a full Newfoundland repast, including baked cod, lobster, appropriate wines, the works. Two flags constantly flew above the grounds at Beachy Cove: the Canadian maple leaf flag, and the pink, white and green tri-colour flag representing Newfoundland nationalists.

It was often impossible to identify guests at Beachy Cove according to their personal or business relationships with Craig Dobbin, and there is little evidence that Dobbin himself made that distinction. He successfully melded both, a feat that meant he and many of his guests enjoyed simultaneously the benefits of relaxation and the profits of successful deal-making.

On any given weekend the guests at a Beachy Cove dinner party, reception or card-playing tournament might include Newfoundland premiers Frank Moores and Brian Tobin; federal cabinet ministers; Quebec Premier Jean Charest; provincial cabinet minister Chuck Furey, and various other government officials at all levels. From the business world Dobbin might welcome David Sobey, Merrill Lynch chairman Guy Savard, Power Corporation president Paul Desmarais, and any of a dozen bank and investment firm CEOs and chairmen. All of these guests were in a position to favourably influence Craig Dobbin's business dealings, though there is no indication that he asked for direct assistance from them, with the exception of lobbying the Newfoundland government for an opportunity to bid against Okanagan back in 1978. Nonetheless, he was frequently criticized for his associations with government officials at all levels. Among Dobbin's controversial deals was his request for a $4.2-million federal-provincial grant to set up a Newfoundland-based helicopter training facility. When opposition government members suggested CHC received the money due to Dobbin's cronyism, Dobbin called the charges rubbish, claiming that the contract went through a tendering process and that CHC actually did very little government work. The grumbling continued.

It was easy to track Craig Dobbin's activities from the earliest days of his career, thanks to his openness not only in identifying the people whose company he enjoyed but in offering his opinion of government policies, no matter what political party they emerged from. "I agree with the Conservative philosophy of believing in the private sector," Dobbin told one newspaper reporter, "but I'm free to speak my mind," and he did, loudly and frequently.

The high esteem in which he held his friends did not prevent him from being critical of their actions whenever he felt it appropriate.

He made front-page news in 1988 with scathing assessments of Premier Brian Peckford's government style. And in reality, Dobbin did not require direct access to governments in power. He did very well with people outside the legislatures. His friendship with Frank Moores after Moores left office as Newfoundland premier was especially rewarding to Dobbin. Both men enjoyed partying, especially if the Jameson flowed freely, though Moores attempted to give up alcohol with sporadic success. The Wild Colonial Boy designation might just as easily have been hung on Moores as on Dobbin. "Moores used to disappear every summer, usually with some new lady friend," John Crosbie recalls. "People would ask me 'Where's Frank?' and I'd tell them he'd gone upstream to spawn."

John Crosbie encountered Dobbin when Crosbie was serving first as provincial minister of municipal affairs and housing in Joey Smallwood's Liberal government, then finance minister under Brian Peckford and minister of mines and energy and intergovernmental affairs with Frank Moores after switching to the Progressive Conservatives. "There was a good deal in the local media at the time about Craig Dobbin being too close to various government people," Crosbie says, "so I was wary about him and kept my distance."

The Hibernia crisis of 1990 brought Dobbin and Crosbie together, and Crosbie is quick to praise Dobbin's efforts and support in the matter. True, the success of Hibernia promised great opportunities for Dobbin and CHC, but in John Crosbie's assessment Dobbin's support was fuelled as much by his love and concern for Newfoundland as for CHC's bottom line. In contrast with Dobbin's reputation as a hell-for-leather entrepreneur, his efforts on behalf of Crosbie and, by extension, Hibernia were subtly conducted behind the scenes.

Clyde Wells's opposition to the 1990 Meech Lake agreement soured the attitude of many in Brian Mulroney's ruling Progressive Conservative party towards Newfoundland and federal government support for Hibernia. Chevron Canada had struck oil in the Hibernia region of the Grand Banks in 1979, locating a substantial petroleum field in relatively shallow water. Instead of generating delight among senior levels of both governments, Hibernia ignited a storm of dispute over who actually owned the offshore rights to the field.

The National Energy Policy, introduced by the Liberals under Pierre Trudeau within a year of the initial Hibernia discovery, appeared to hand jurisdiction to the federal government, an understandably unpopular development in Newfoundland and Labrador. The election of the Mulroney government in 1984 placed Crosbie in the happy position of supporting Newfoundland's rights to royalties from Hibernia and other offshore resources, and the development began inching forward. Critical to the project was the federal government's commitment to invest $3.6 billion in guaranteed financing to the four principal oil companies seeking to exploit the reserves. Only one of them—Petro-Canada, then a Crown corporation—was a Canadian firm.

Things moved slowly in the intervening years, until Clyde Wells derailed the Meech Lake agreement and alienated federalists in Quebec. With that event, support for federal assistance to Newfoundland via Hibernia sank like a stone. Crosbie credits Craig Dobbin, among others, for assisting him in pacifying the Ottawa Conservatives, especially Mulroney, restoring federal support, and helping put Hibernia back into play.

Crosbie and his wife, Jane, were guests of Craig and Elaine in early 1992 during the time Hibernia entered another crisis. Gulf Canada, one of the four partners committed to developing Hibernia, had announced it was pulling out of the project due to internal problems, although it was obligated to continue financial support through January 1993. The remaining three partners—Mobil, Chevron and Petro-Canada—made it clear they would not proceed with Hibernia unless someone filled the gap left by Gulf's departure. The federal government represented the obvious player, but public sentiment opposed the idea, seeing it as a bailout for a traditionally have-not province whose premier had scuppered Meech Lake.

Crosbie desperately wanted to see Hibernia proceed, and he used Craig Dobbin's Florida retreat as something of an Action Central, spending much of his time there on the telephone to Mulroney, other federal cabinet members, Newfoundland cabinet ministers and oil company executives—anyone who could influence the deal. Between calls he engaged in verbal duels with various media outlets that opposed federal funding of Hibernia as a make-work project and a boondoggle.

Craig Dobbin provided more than shelter and a communications facility for Crosbie's efforts. He led a group of Newfoundland business leaders in funding a series of advertisements in *The Globe and Mail,* whose editorial staff vehemently opposed federal funding to the project. The Dobbin-inspired campaign promoted the benefits of Hibernia for all Canadians, not just residents of Newfoundland and Labrador. Dobbin also travelled to Ottawa with various representatives of Newfoundland firms to lobby on behalf of the oil field development.

When Hibernia finally became reality, most observers in Newfoundland and Labrador rightly credited John Crosbie for saving the project. Crosbie, in turn, praises Craig Dobbin for his assistance. "All through this period," Crosbie explains, "Craig was very helpful. He was prepared to go public and try to influence opinion on the mainland and elsewhere."

Craig Dobbin shared John Crosbie's antipathy for Clyde Wells and was as vociferous as Crosbie in his comments about the Newfoundland premier. Like Crosbie, Dobbin blamed Wells for the failure of Meech Lake, claiming Wells destroyed any chance Canada had for a constitutional settlement with Quebec. He also charged that the Newfoundland premier bore responsibility for the rise of the Bloc Québécois as a force in Canadian politics.

As much as the two men enjoyed each other's company and were united in their passion for their home province, Dobbin and Crosbie shared a stubborn independence, a refusal to let anyone dictate an element of their lives. The affection and respect Dobbin held for the crusty St. John's lawyer and long-time MP led to an invitation for Crosbie to join the CHC board of directors shortly after Crosbie, along with almost every other federal Conservative, lost his seat in the 1993 federal election. Crosbie's contacts and his cranky observations on everything from cheap whiskey to his nemesis Sheila Copps added colour to CHC board meetings, but for a period of less than two years. In 1995, when Craig Dobbin called a board meeting on short notice, Crosbie failed to appear, claiming he had a previous appointment. Dobbin saw things otherwise. Crosbie, he believed, simply chose to be absent, an indication that he was not taking his director's duties seriously, and Dobbin dropped his old friend from the board.

In time the wounds healed, partially as a result of the affection Crosbie and his wife, Jane, have for Elaine. The event, however, marked the limits of Craig Dobbin's fondness for anyone where business was concerned. He expected a certain level of commitment from everyone associated with CHC, an expectation that transcended friendship, as well as a person's power and longevity.

IN MANY WAYS, Craig Dobbin was a man of three cultures. He maintained and exploited his Irish roots with great pride; celebrated the glories of Newfoundland and Labrador as frequently as he decried the mishandling of its resources by various bodies; and was equally proud of being a Canadian, despite his concerns over the treatment of Newfoundland and Labrador by Ottawa.

In fact, when then-federal fisheries minister Brian Tobin decided to counter the federal government's inaction in the weeks before the 1995 Quebec referendum with a massive rally in Montreal, among the first persons he contacted was Craig Dobbin. With Dobbin's assistance, the rally gathered an estimated 150,000 Canadians from across the country in Canada Square to express their support for national unity. The event generated controversy and some doubt about its possible effectiveness, but when the referendum was defeated by barely half of 1 per cent of the vote, few people questioned its value.

Just as he never forgave Clyde Wells for the Newfoundland premier's opposition to the Meech Lake agreement, Dobbin blamed the intransigence of Wells when PEI rather than Newfoundland was chosen as the site for two CHC subsidiary operations.

When Wells assumed power in 1989, Dobbin was planning a helicopter flight training centre at St. John's airport, with funding provided by the federal and provincial governments. Later, Dobbin changed his mind in favour of launching an aircraft overhaul facility at the same location. With this decision, the provincial government insisted the operations be moved to Gander, and Dobbin agreed. Ottawa, however, rejected the idea of relocating the site and withdrew promised funding from the federal Offshore Development Fund. The move cancelled provincial support and initially meant abandoning the entire project. Then, in the kind of twist that drives private businesspeople mad when dealing with government bureaucracy, the PEI government made a bid for the same project, supported by the federally funded Atlantic Canada Opportunities Agency. ACOP agreed to dump $4 million into a business that its sister department, the Offshore Development Fund, had just rejected. Once again, Clyde Wells became the target of Dobbin's anger, this time for not pressuring Ottawa to direct federal funds to Newfoundland rather than PEI. Of course, at this point, the Newfoundland premier was unlikely to receive enough unanticipated funds from the federal government to cover the cost of polishing his shoes. Newfoundland's loss became PEI's gain.

Continuing to use Newfoundland as his primary base, Dobbin and CHC extended the company's reach whenever and wherever a business opportunity presented itself. In the early 1990s, when Hibernia still appeared doubtful and a global recession loomed, Dobbin sent Christine Baird, now CHC commercial director, to New

York in pursuit of business at the United Nations. He was specific about his goal, telling her he wanted sixty CHC helicopters working under UN contracts across the globe by the end of the year. "He had been watching CNN and CBC news," Baird says. "'Look at the people over there,' he told me, 'they're walking everywhere. They need helicopters and we have them.' So away I went."

The audacity of the idea was breathtaking, but it proved a shrewd move, in the short term at least. Baird demonstrated her mettle, building contacts among the diplomats and UN bureaucrats and receiving assignments to assist in humanitarian flights and peacekeeping efforts in Rwanda, Uganda, Mozambique and other African states, plus Kuwait, Thailand and Cambodia. Within a year, the largest fleet of civilian helicopters in the history of the United Nations, all CHC craft, were ferrying people and supplies into and across a dozen countries. The demands on CHC pilots, often operating in regions teetering on the brink of war and unrest, were significant. So were the demands on CHC's corporate structure and finances. But it was worth it. In fact, it can be argued that the UN contracts kept CHC afloat through a difficult period, one of several instances where Dobbin's hands-on response managed to swing the company away from the brink. Soon after Christine Baird's trek to New York, Dobbin reported to the CHC board, with some satisfaction, that the company had twelve aircraft in Cambodia and six in Kuwait, with another sixteen expected to be deployed in the coming weeks. On an annualized basis, Dobbin estimated, the UN contracts would be worth more than $50 million.

The UN work became incredibly complex. Moving helicopters swiftly into place in distant regions required CHC to charter Boeing 747 or Russian-built Antonov air freighters at substantial cost. Adding to the problem was the UN's tardiness in paying its bills, requiring Christine Baird to renew her visits to New York, this time not to secure contracts but to demand promised cheques. Then, more difficulties. One by one the UN began cancelling its contracts with CHC.

The helicopters came home like swallows returning to Capistrano, leaving behind a tangle of legal and financial concerns.

Other risks to the African contracts were potentially deadly to CHC crews. In April 1994, CHC pilots were caught in the Rwandan civil war and the subsequent massacre of civilians. For four days the pilots remained trapped in their hotel room in the capital city of Kigali while national and rebel forces fought in the streets below and a frantic Craig Dobbin attempted to get his employees out of the country. Finally granted permission to travel to the airport, they were told to remain there until permitted to board an evacuation flight some time in the future. Instead, they hid in a container for twenty hours before sprinting to their CHC helicopters and lifting off for relative safety in Tanzania and Somalia.

Losses due to the UN contract cancellations were substantial, though the long-range outlook appeared positive. CHC continued to struggle with cash flow demands, battling lawsuits for unpaid services from plaintiffs as wide-ranging as the St. John's School Tax Authority, a fisheries supply firm and Caldwell Partners/AMPROP International, who claimed an unpaid invoice of more than $100,000 for executive search services.

To Craig Dobbin, these demands were gnats to be brushed aside. His vision of CHC remained as clear as ever, and his ambition as vigorous. The world was easing its way out of recession, offshore petroleum exploration and production were gaining strength, and Hibernia would soon come on stream. Craig Dobbin was running one of the world's three largest helicopter service companies, surrounding himself with rich and powerful friends and settled in a mansion with a woman whose business capabilities almost matched his own. His personal net worth swung between $40 and $50 million, divided among real estate holdings and CHC assets, and his sons and daughters were providing him with grandchildren whom he adored and enjoyed as much or more than any other aspect of his life. He was also assembling an impressive list of honours and recognitions.

In July 1990, in a ceremony at its embassy in Ottawa, the government of France awarded Craig Dobbin its Médaille de L'Aéronautique in recognition of "his outstanding contribution to civil aviation." Cynics noted that Dobbin's primary contribution had been his early support of French-built Aerospatiale Super Puma helicopters for offshore petroleum missions in North America. In any event, he was only the second Canadian to receive the honour and was generally appreciative of it. Earlier that year, St. Mary's University in Halifax had granted him an honorary doctorate of science.

All of this intensified his lust for life beyond CHC and what was left of his real estate portfolio. His passion for catching salmon in the pools and streams of his two fishing camps remained as fervent as ever. His prowess with a fly rod and reel was exceptional, and he plotted his repeated duels with wily salmon as diligently as he negotiated his real estate transactions and helicopter service contracts. He also competed with his fishing companions, determined to catch bigger salmon, and more of them, than anyone else in the camp. As much as he enjoyed the company of helicopter pilots, many of whom he invited to join him with a rod at the salmon pool, word quickly spread among the flight crews: if you go fishing with the Chairman, don't catch a fish before he does, and don't catch a bigger fish. If you do, he'll be snarly with you the rest of the day.

Frank Moores, who had introduced Dobbin to both salmon fishing in Labrador and helicopters to get there, was a more skilled fisherman than Dobbin, something the Chairman could not accept. Resolved to outdo his buddy, Dobbin travelled to the U.K. in 1992 for two weeks of instruction on fly selection and casting techniques through the celebrated fishing equipment supplier Hardy & Greys Ltd., whose better casting rods sell for as much as Can$2,000.

Upon returning from "casting school," as he called it, he scheduled a trip to Long Harbour with Moores, his brother Paddy Dobbin and several others. In the helicopter on the way to the camp he boasted about all he had learned from the finest fly-fishing instructors in world. Everyone watched dutifully the next morning as Dobbin swept the rod back and forth in graceful arcs above his head—then recoiled in horror as the fly, a variety known as a Green Highlander, swung back and hooked itself through Dobbin's own eyelid. Brother Paddy, possessed of sure hands and a medical degree, managed to extricate the fly without causing serious injury. Dobbin reportedly laughed as heartily as everyone else when reminded of the day he "rose to a Green Highlander."

To be invited on one of Craig Dobbin's extended fishing excursions was to sample a highly developed form of male bonding. Time away from the water was spent trading bawdy stories, sampling barbecued meals, sipping Irish whiskey, and playing cutthroat card games. Dobbin's demeanour during these trips was as rough-edged as might be expected from a man who revelled in his masculinity. He was no loud, uncouth chauvinist, however. In the presence of women, children and grandchildren, his manner and language were playful, courteous and respectful, and he employed only the mildest of four-letter words.

During the early years at the fishing camps the participants engaged in raucous and sometimes boyish play. Over time, Dobbin introduced initiation rites for first-time visitors. Steve Hudson's initial visit to Adlatuk involved a helicopter flight over the ocean in search of an iceberg drifting down from the Arctic. When a suitable iceberg was located, the initiate was given his instructions.

"They handed me a hammer and an ice bucket," Hudson explains. "My job was to jump out of the helicopter onto the iceberg and fill the bucket with chipped ice for our drinks back at the fishing lodge."

Icebergs, Hudson discovered, are very unstable, and riding one in the North Atlantic with a Super Puma hovering a few feet over your head is like trying to keep your balance while walking across a trampoline. "It was a lot of fun for the guys in the helicopter," he says, "but not so much fun for me, trying to knock enough million-year-old ice off the berg to fill the bucket." Back in camp the ice chilled several glasses of Jameson raised in a toast to the new crew member.

Craig Dobbin thrived on the camaraderie of companions, and his circle of political friends widened beyond Canada until it encompassed the most powerful of all political entities, the president of the United States.

A recent past president, actually. Through John Crosbie and others, Craig Dobbin got to know Brian Mulroney. Mulroney, perhaps the ultimate matchmaker in Canadian politics, suggested that his friend George H.W. Bush, recently unemployed as a result of the 1992 U.S. presidential election, might enjoy a fishing expedition to Newfoundland and Labrador. Bush was as avid about fly-fishing as Craig Dobbin was, and from the outset the two men connected on a personal level that transcended their love of the sport.

"I saw this big, gregarious Irish guy with a wonderful sense of humour," Bush says, relaxing at his winter home in Houston, Texas, and recalling his first meeting with Craig Dobbin. "He made me feel right at home on the river in Labrador, and I always looked forward to fishing for Atlantic salmon with him. He was an excellent fisherman, by the way. Really knew his stuff."

The deep and affectionate bond that formed between the two men is remarkable considering the dramatic differences in their backgrounds and heritage. Bush, born into wealth and privilege as the son of a prominent U.S. senator, rose through Texas oil and upper-level political strata. Dobbin, scouring ditches as a boy for empty bottles to claim their deposit value, clawed his way to success while battling banks, creditors and competitors. Somehow, the two achieved an extraordinary level of companionship. Bush suggests that the key quality belonged to Craig Dobbin.

"He had an amazing propensity to enjoy his friends," the former U.S. president explains. "After a day of fishing we would sit around in the evening sharing perhaps a toddy or two and reminiscing. I recall how much he loved music, especially Irish singing. I just loved being around him and his guides at the camps and the friends he would bring with him for the trip. It was more than fishing. It was what the writer Dan Jenkins calls 'life its ownself.' That's what our friendship was about." Repeating an observation that others make about Dobbin, Bush was impressed by his host's warm openness. "He never tried to sort out people by rank. He was very much grassroots."

Craig Dobbin and George H.W. Bush expressed their fondness for each other in various ways. Dobbin invited the former president to his fishing camps twice a year and mounted a plaque alongside the swimming pool at Long Harbour designating it "The Presidential Pool." "He was happy as a little kid about that," Bush smiles. In return, Bush presented Craig and Elaine with a painting for their home in Florida and invited Craig to join him for a round of golf at the Augusta National course, home of the Masters tournament, where Craig Dobbin boasted he played his best game ever.

U.S. presidents, in or out of office, travel with an entourage of personal assistants, Secret Service agents and other staff, and George H.W. Bush celebrates the fact that everyone who accompanied him on his trips to Craig Dobbin's fishing camps looked forward to the experience. A few Secret Service agents were so enamoured with Dobbin's facilities and hospitality that they returned on their own for hunting and fishing in and around Long Harbour and Adlatuk.

Of the dozen or so fishing trips the former president made with Craig Dobbin, none stands out more clearly than a July 1995 visit. Travelling from the cabin at Devil's Lake to the camp at Long Harbour, the group, including Bush, Craig and Elaine Dobbin, their guests and assorted RCMP security and secret service personnel, flew in three helicopters. Encountering a fog bank, the pilots agreed that they should set down to wait for the fog to burn off. The three craft landed in an open area, and everyone disembarked to stretch their legs. "I need to take a pee," George Bush announced, and he set off towards some trees bordering the clearing. People chatted about the weather while Craig Dobbin checked on business developments over the communication system aboard one of the helicopters.

After some time, Elaine Dobbin saw Bush strolling back towards the helicopters. Glancing away for a moment, she looked back to note that he was no longer in sight. She called out that something appeared to be wrong: the ex-president seemed to have fallen and was not getting up. This was enough to launch the security staff into action. A small platoon of RCMP and Secret Service officers sprinted towards the spot where Bush had been spotted last. To their horror, they found him up to his armpits in mud, struggling to avoid slipping beneath the surface. The first to reach him, an RCMP officer, jumped without hesitation into the mud—"If he'd died in there my life would've been over too," the officer explained later—and lifted Bush onto land.

"I wouldn't be truthful if I didn't agree he was in a very serious situation," Craig Dobbin said. "It was a matter of seconds before he would have been in over his head." Everyone was deeply concerned about the close call except the near-victim himself. "He was barely rattled by it all," Dobbin added, and after a change of clothes and a hot drink at the camp the fishing excursion resumed.

George H.W. Bush genuinely enjoyed Craig and Elaine's company, and in August 2002 he extended an extraordinary invitation. While the Dobbins were visiting him that month, Bush noted that the *Harry S. Truman*, U.S. Navy's newest, most advanced aircraft carrier, was about to sail for the Persian Gulf to participate in the anticipated invasion of Iraq. Wanting to visit the ship and offer his best wishes to the crew, he invited the Dobbins to accompany him in a military helicopter, flying from a base in West Virginia to the ship's location somewhere in the Atlantic. The two-hour flight ended with the dramatic sight of the nuclear-powered ship, its flight deck covering four-and-a-half acres, steaming beneath them. In addition to its large crew, the ship carried more than eighty aircraft, including some of the armed forces' most advanced machines: F/A-18 Super Hornets, EA-6B Prowlers, S-3B Vikings, E-2C Hawkeyes, SH-60F Seahawks and C-2A Greyhounds.

The next twenty-four hours marked yet another achievement for the son of the St. John's lumber dealer. The entire ship, plus the crew of an accompanying destroyer, stood at attention in their dress whites to salute the former president and his two Canadian friends. Numbering more than 4,000, the men and women listened via ships' radio as their former commander-in-chief, flanked by the Dobbins, wished them well in their imminent combat mission.

After dinner that evening, a female officer aboard the *Truman* stepped forward to escort Elaine Dobbin to the women's quarters, a move Elaine immediately resisted. It was standard military procedure, she was informed. The ship's complement included husbands and wives, but even they were not permitted to share the same quarters aboard the vessel. Elaine was adamant. "I sleep with my husband," she insisted, refusing to budge. It took a gesture from the ship's captain to resolve the situation. Relinquishing his own quarters to the Dobbins, he spent the night elsewhere that evening; protocol was maintained, to a degree, and Elaine Dobbin's steely resolve proved triumphant.

FORMER PRESIDENT BUSH'S comment that Craig Dobbin "never tried to sort people out by rank" is supported by many in and out of Dobbin's business circle. Landing in a populated area, the big CHC helicopter Dobbin used as his personal craft would attract large groups of onlookers, many of them children, and Dobbin would instruct the CHC pilot to fly the youngsters over the community while he tended to business or visited friends. On many occasions, this required several takeoffs and landings to ensure that every child who wanted to experience the thrill of a helicopter flight was accommodated. "Some of those choppers spent as much time in the air with kids as they spent with the Chairman aboard," one CHC employee noted.

Dobbin's business acumen rarely overrode his humanity. On a flight to his fishing lodge in Long Harbour with a group of friends,

Dobbin asked the helicopter pilot to set the craft down for a wash-room break. The pilot chose an open area adjacent to a shack and tower where a provincial wildlife officer was spending the summer on fire-watch duty. The officer, a grizzled veteran of wilderness work, kept the group laughing for some time with his stories and anec-dotes, and the short rest break extended into an hour's impromptu entertainment.

"How long have you been here?" Dobbin asked the old-timer as the group was about to board the helicopter and resume their jour-ney. Ten weeks, the officer answered, with about another ten weeks to go before returning home. "Anything you need?" Dobbin inquired, and the man said he was out of sugar; it would be nice to have some-thing to sweeten his tea, but he would get by.

An hour later, when everyone had disembarked at Long Harbour, Dobbin instructed the helicopter pilot not to shut down the aircraft yet. He entered the cookhouse and emerged with a two-kilo bag of sugar, ordering the pilot to fly it back to the wildlife officer they had met.

"Are you kidding?" the young pilot said. "I'll spend about two thousand bucks in fuel alone to fly it there."

Dobbin gripped the pilot's arm. "Son," he said, "that sugar will mean more to that old fellow than two thousand bucks will ever mean to me. Now get going."

AT SIXTY YEARS of age, Craig Dobbin could have decided to relax a little. Instead, he geared up to extend CHC's size and clout in the same manner as he had been doing for almost twenty years: by playing harder and longer than his competitors. When the opportunity pre-sented itself, he would liquidate them through the simple technique of swallowing them whole. As impressive as his success might have been under ordinary circumstances, the way in which he achieved it—against a challenge as unexpected as it was deadly—remains one of the most remarkable tales in Canadian business history.

8

*There was no question of any scandal when he received his
Irish passport, because he was clearly Irish. But the two things did
happen at the same time, the endowment and the citizenship.*

JOHN KELLY, executive director, The Ireland Canada University Foundation

IN 1992, CHC COULD rightly claim the title of third-largest helicopter services company in the world. Helicopter Services Group
(HSG), a Norwegian firm, was the clear leader measured by gross
income, followed by the U.K.'s Bristow Group. Third place may have
impressed others, but it was never acceptable for Craig Dobbin. CHC,
he was determined, would become the dominant firm in its industry, and he was too impatient to wait around while it grew from
within. He would expand the company through acquisition, and the
beginnings of an opportunity presented itself on November 5, 1991,
through an event in the waters of the Atlantic off the Canary Islands.

On that evening British billionaire businessman Robert Maxwell
fell, was pushed, or was dumped over the side of his luxury yacht,
Lady Ghislaine. Maxwell had been the centre of controversy for
some time; he had been charged with extortion, fraud, embezzle-
ment and even spying on behalf of Mossad, the Israeli intelligence
service. At the time of his death many companies Maxwell controlled were teetering towards bankruptcy, their dilemma the result
of Maxwell's profligate lifestyle and his constant raiding of corporate assets to finance it. Eventually, facts emerged to confirm that
Maxwell had withdrawn hundreds of millions of pounds from the

pension funds of companies he controlled, using the cash to prop up his enormous debts. The process was like bailing water from a sinking ship, and thousands òf employees in Maxwell-controlled firms lost their retirement savings.

Among Maxwell's stable of companies was British International Helicopters, which retained several contracts to service petroleum platforms in the North Sea region. In 1991 the market for helicopter services in the North Sea and immediate waters totalled £168 million. BIH held only 20 per cent of the business, with Bristow owning about half and Bond Helicopters, a subsidiary of the Norwegian firm HSG, claiming the balance. In addition to servicing north and south sectors of North Sea petroleum sites from bases in Aberdeen, the Shetland Islands and Suffolk, BIH provided scheduled helicopter passenger services between Penzance and the Scilly Islands, performed contracted services for the Ministry of Defence, operated two helicopter simulators for pilot training, and was modernizing a fleet of helicopters for the Royal Dutch Navy.

With the collapse of Robert Maxwell's financial empire, BIH became a perfect takeover target for either Bristow or Bond, and both firms announced their intention to bid for it. Bristow made the first bid but abandoned the idea when the U.K. Competition Commission declared its opposition. Bond disclosed its intention to acquire BIH, which would essentially split the industry into two equal-sized competitors. This failed to satisfy the Competition Commission, who feared Bond and Bristow would enter a tacit *entente cordiale*, maintaining barely acceptable service levels and leaving prices to drift higher "unless constrained by customer buying power or the prospect of a new entry," an unlikely prospect. Any new entry, the commission concluded, would need strong financing, a proven safety record, and aircraft and staff that met stringent safety requirements.

But who would want the company? BIH's financial picture was less than enthralling, as shown by the table below:

(£'000)					
	1987	1988	1989	1990	1991
SALES	29,890	30,568	35,512	43,271	45,402
PROFIT/(LOSS)	(1,214)	(822)	(1,962)	588	(971)
PROFIT ON SALE OF FIXED ASSETS	49	1,377	1,763	1,898	18
OPERATING PROFIT/(LOSS)	(1,165)	555	(199)	2,486	(953)
CAPITAL EMPLOYED	24,974	29,614	15,928	25,176	22,964
RETURN ON CAPITAL EMPLOYED	(4.7%)	1.9%	(1.2%)	9.9%	(4.1%)

SOURCE: British International Helicopter/U.K. Competition Commission, 1992

BIH also carried a £22.5-million debt owed to Maxwell Aviation, an obligation Maxwell assumed when he purchased the helicopter firm from British Airways in 1986.

The British government invested substantial effort to maintain an effective competitive climate for helicopter services in its important North Sea oil reserves, encouraged by the giant multinational petroleum companies, who understandably wanted the stiffest competition possible among the firms servicing its offshore rigs. The government also demanded, of course, that any firm bidding for the business boast an impeccable safety record, operate suitable modern aircraft, employ experienced crews, and adhere to unimpeachable maintenance and administrative support programs. The commission searched for a solution to address the concerns of both the oil companies and the government, but its first attempts to locate a saviour for BIH were not promising.

In a report dated August 19, 1992, the U.K. Competition Commission noted that it had contacted almost twenty U.K. and European helicopter service companies to measure their interest in acquiring BIH. About half had responded, including newly formed KLM/Era, owned 51 per cent by KLM Royal Dutch Airlines and 49 per cent by Rowan Companies, an oil drilling operation out of Texas. KLM/Era almost fit the bill, but no company completely satisfied the complex expectations for a successor to BIH. The commission did not look beyond the EU for good reason: an ironclad policy dictated that majority ownership of any EU–operated airline must remain in the hands of EU citizens.

In St. John's, Craig Dobbin watched the situation with interest. North Sea helicopter services revenues approaching $500 million annually, for companies with whom CHC was already dealing? Now there was a prize, and it came with potential entry into the entire European market. The shaky financial condition of BIH failed to dissuade Dobbin. The company's need for an injection of capital was nothing he hadn't encountered over his years of building CHC. And the BIH fleet of Super Pumas and Sikorsky S-61s and S-76s was a perfect fit with CHC. Merging the two companies would be fairly easy, if he could sidestep that pesky requirement for EU citizenship.

In Dobbin's view, the U.K. Competition Commission was practically calling for him and CHC, or someone like them, to step onstage and deliver a happy ending to a dramatic situation. A couple of problems had to be overcome, of course. The first was money; the recent loss of the UN contracts had left CHC with little cash in the bank, but that small detail had never stopped Craig Dobbin before. Robert Foster's Capital Canada firm could tap the necessary source of ready cash, Dobbin believed. And as for the small obstacle requiring Dobbin to carry an EU passport, well, he would deal with that in time.

Borrowing enough money to purchase about 40 per cent of the outstanding BIH shares at a bargain price and pledging the shares as collateral, Dobbin took his first step into the European market. The balance of the company's shares were owned by merchant bankers and BIH employees who, it was soon clear, enthusiastically welcomed the opportunity to sell their shares to CHC with the prospect of continued employment. In a strategic move at odds with his long-held animosity towards unions, Dobbin began wooing the BIH union leaders with promises. If he were to successfully acquire BIH, he assured them, he would restore their pension benefits. With that single move, any hostility the unions may have felt towards a foreign takeover of their firm vanished. Now all Dobbin needed was EU citizenship and several million dollars. *Pas de sweat.*

BIH was categorized as an airline, and the EU reflected a commonly held position throughout the world that foreigners could own no more than 49 per cent of a nation's air carrier. At the outset this did not appear a barrier. Craig Dobbin believed he had a legitimate right to claim British citizenship by birth, qualifying for the passport he needed. When he was born in 1935, Newfoundland was a British colony and confederation with Canada was a distant fourteen years in the future. By definition, Craig Laurence Dobbin was a British subject, right?

Wrong, he quickly discovered. Britain had rescinded that right with Newfoundland's decision to join Confederation, effectively making Newfoundlanders born prior to 1949 citizens of a country the colony was not a part of at the time of their birth. They became Canadians, and that was that. Before Dobbin could acquire BIH, he was informed, he would need to become a citizen of the EU.

The news created a good deal of bitterness in Dobbin, who considered it bureaucratic nonsense. How can you take citizenship away from an individual without his agreement and without any motive for doing so? There would be no avenue around it, however. Not through London, anyway. But perhaps through Dublin.

Under Irish law, anyone whose grandparent was born in Ireland can claim Irish citizenship. Those wishing to claim citizenship through an Irish great-grandparent may be frustrated if their parents were not registered in the Foreign Births Register; parents can only transmit Irish citizenship to children born after they themselves were registered. More damnable bureaucracy. Craig Dobbin sidestepped it with another dose of Irish luck, plus assistance from the extensive networking he had built through his many deep friendships. One of these involved a remarkable Canadian named Mike Wadsworth.

Dobbin had been introduced to Mike Wadsworth a few years earlier through Prime Minister Brian Mulroney. Born in Toronto, Wadsworth attended the U.S. university and football forge Notre Dame on an athletic scholarship. After graduation, he played for the Toronto Argonauts, in the Canadian Football League, from 1966 to 1970 while earning a law degree at Osgoode Hall Law School.

Practising law from 1971 to 1981, Wadsworth was active in print and broadcast media, later completing the advanced management program of the Harvard Graduate School of Business and joining the Crown Life Insurance Company as senior VP of U.S. operations. In August 1989, Mulroney appointed him Canada's ambassador to Ireland. Both Wadsworth and Dobbin were dominant figures in their physical presence and their personalities. "Craig was heroic, like a character out of Steinbeck," Wadsworth's wife Bernadette says, "a sweet song of a man. From the moment he and Mike met, they bonded like brothers." Dobbin turned to his soul brother for the link he needed to hitch CHC to the North Sea market.

MIKE WADSWORTH AND Craig Dobbin met for dinner at the ambassador's residence in Dublin one Saturday evening in early 1993. Other guests included former Irish president Paddy Hillery and John Kelly, registrar and senior vice-president of University College, Dublin, both responding to Wadsworth's invitation. The evening passed cordially, and the following morning John Kelly returned from his weekly morning tennis match to learn that he and his wife had been invited to attend a football match and dine that evening with Craig and Elaine Dobbin at Dromoland Castle.

"Dromoland, a lovely inn, is near Shannon, more than 200 kilometres from Dublin," John Kelly recalls. "I said to my wife, 'And how are we to be there for dinner?' She told me that Craig Dobbin had a jet waiting for us at the airport, and so away we went."

Within a few hours, Kelly and his wife were seated with Craig Dobbin and Elaine Parsons in the stands at Shannon stadium, watching Paddy Hillery toss the ball to start an important football match. After the game, as the group were "sharing a pint or two," in John Kelly's words, Craig Dobbin began discussing his relationship with Ireland.

"He was very emotionally Irish," John Kelly says of Dobbin, "and he told me he wanted to do something for Ireland, and asked if I had any ideas. So I suggested he could inaugurate a chair at the school, for my university, perhaps for Canadian studies. We had chairs for American studies and other cultures, and fish studies and other subjects, but nothing to do with Canada, our nearest neighbour to the west."

Craig Dobbin asked how much it would cost.

"I wasn't thinking about it because I didn't know if he were serious," John Kelly laughs, "so I said, 'Oh, a million pounds should do it,' and he said, 'Okay, it's done.' That easy, it was."

The endowment was made with the understanding that proceedings would begin for Craig Dobbin to become an Irish citizen, a move made easier with John Kelly, Dr. Noel Walsh of University College and Paddy Hillery supporting his application, and Mike Wadsworth proffering advice and opening doors. John Kelly, however, is quick to point out that the agreement had nothing to do with the recent scandals about people buying Irish passports. A few months earlier, reports had surfaced that eleven Irish passports were issued to Sheikh Khalid bin Mahfouz and members of his family and associates in return for several million dollars in payments. (Since then, Mahfouz has been linked, in some quarters, to Osama bin Laden.) "With Craig, there was no question of scandal," John Kelly emphasizes, "because he was unquestionably of Irish extraction."

With surprising speed, it was done. Irish passport in hand—he later obtained Irish citizenship for each of his five children—Craig

Dobbin unrolled his plans to purchase BIH and extend CHC's operations into the busy North Sea petroleum services.

Dobbin's motive for assuming Irish citizenship was not entirely mercenary. His family's association with Ireland, and indeed the affinity between Newfoundland and Ireland, was strong and enduring. The sight of fog rolling in along isolated shores of the Avalon Peninsula on a spring day can be duplicated with remarkable accuracy anywhere on Ireland's west coast, though Ireland's climate is decidedly more temperate than Newfoundland's. Both cultures have much to complain about historically where Britain is concerned, and the jigs and reels in Dublin or Belfast are closely replicated on Saturday nights in St. John's and Marystown. On a broader scale, the historical relationship between Canada and Ireland is deeper than many Canadians realize. At Confederation in 1867, the Irish in Canada were second only to French Canadians in numerical strength, and various political events and personalities have strengthened bonds between the two nations. The Ontario school system, for example, was based on the model of the Irish National School system, and it was in Ottawa in 1948 where then-Irish Taoi-seach John A. Costello announced the intention to declare the Irish state a republic.

The idea of a Newfoundlander providing assistance for Irish students to study Canadian values and culture pleased Dobbin. The Craig Dobbin Chair for Canadian Studies is awarded to the applicant from a Canadian university who, in the opinion of a panel headed by Professor John Kelly, is best qualified "to interpret and promote the study of the historical and contemporary distinctiveness of the peoples, cultures and environment of Canada, as well as Canada's contributions to the world." With its stipend of $75,000 annually, the position is awarded for one year, with the option of a second year of studies based on agreements between the candidate and the university. Craig Dobbin, by every indication, took as much pride in the creation of the chair at UCD as in any of his business achievements.

In addition to the Chair for Canadian Studies, UCD also awards scholarships to Canadian and Irish university scholars engaged in studies relating to both nations. This program too was a product of the meeting between Dobbin and Kelly in the Shannon pub. Study topics for the scholarships have ranged from "Hydro Geochemistry of Irish and Canadian Forests" and "Censorship in de Valera's Ireland and Duplessis' Quebec" to "Acculturation of Irish Traditional Song in Newfoundland" and "Viruses in Irish and Canadian Wastewater Treatment Sludge and Seawater."

According to John Kelly, Craig Dobbin supported this scholarship program inadvertently, a tale Kelly relates with some amusement. "I had told him a million pounds would do the job," Kelly recalls with a smile and a wink, "but at the time the Irish currency was punts, not pound sterling, and Irish punts were valued around eighty per cent of a British pound."

Later that year Craig Dobbin invited key participants in the UCD arrangements to Beachy Cove for the official signing of the agreement establishing the endowment. Dispatching his private jet to Ireland, he brought Noel Walsh, UCD professor of psychiatry; Paddy Hillery, former president of Ireland; Michael Wadsworth; and John Kelly to Newfoundland, adding Antoin Mac Unfraidh, Irish ambassador to Canada, and professor Ken Ozmon, president of St. Mary's University in Halifax.

Meeting the flight at St. John's airport, Dobbin escorted Kelly into one of the offices at CHC Helicopters. "Before we get started on anything else," he suggested, "let's get this money thing out of the way. Then we can relax and play golf for the rest of the week." Sitting at his desk, Dobbin pulled out a chequebook and began writing. "Do I make this out for a million pounds to John Kelly?" he asked.

Startled, Kelly said the cheque should be payable not to him personally but to the National University of Ireland.

"In pound sterling or in punts?" Dobbin asked. John Kelly, with a twinkle in his eye, suggested that pound sterling would be

149

recognition of, and perhaps a tribute to, their brethren in Northern Ireland, and pound sterling it was. Exchanged for the cheaper Irish currency, the total easily exceeded a million punts, and the excess was assigned to fund the Ireland Canada University Foundation, which operates the scholarship exchange program. When the initial funding for that program began to run out, the committee sought sponsors. In 2006–07 these included GF International Advisors Company Ltd., Air Canada, Canada Life (Ireland), Glen Dimplex, Irish Life & Permanent PLC, and the Irish step-dancing troupe Riverdance, for Irish scholars visiting Canada; for the awards to Canadians visiting Ireland the sponsors included CHC Helicopter Corporation, the law firm Ogilvy Renault, Scotiabank and Sprott Asset Management (the latter award exclusive to Carleton University graduates).

Dobbin's efforts to link Canada and Newfoundland with his ancestral home served as something of a catalyst. The Centre for Newfoundland and Labrador Studies and the Ireland Newfoundland Partnership both owe their existence to his initiative in joining the two cultures. John Maher, a professor at the Waterford Institute of Technology, is active in both organizations. "There are sentimental reasons [for Newfoundlanders] to look to Ireland," Maher suggests, "but sentiment will not butter bread." Ireland, Maher suggests, looks to Newfoundland "to learn about strategies for rural development..., for health service models, and for educational paradigms and maritime technology. We do so because there is an ease of communication between our peoples, independent of the national background. We share common-law roots and the British democratic tradition and a language adapted to our respective situations."

Of all the journeys Craig Dobbin took throughout his life, none appear to have given him more pleasure than his periodic visits to Ireland. The country revitalized him, perhaps because he visualized it through the same rose-coloured glasses that Hollywood movies once employed to depict the Emerald Isle. This made his affection for the place no less sincere. He simply responded strongly to the idea of Ireland as his ancestral home. On one visit, he escorted Newfoundland and Labrador Premier Brian Tobin as his guest. Later, on a trek to Waterford, from which several Dobbins had sailed westward more than a hundred years earlier, he presented a painting of St. John's to the city. It remains on display there in the office of the mayor.

HAVING MET THE EU requirement for citizenship, Dobbin directed Robert Foster, via Capital Canada, to recruit backers and negotiate financial terms for his purchase of BIH. Foster brought in two U.K. firms: Brown Shipley Venture Managers and Legal and General Insurance, who agreed to provide US$65 million for the purchase of the BIH outstanding shares. Another US$7.5 million was added by Barclay's Bank of Canada. CHC pledged a substantial number of its own shares to the two U.K. companies as part of the complex deal, buying them back through BIH, now named Brintel Helicopters, within a year. The little helicopter company out of Newfoundland, launched as a means of carrying Craig Dobbin to remote fishing camps, was now tapping into the largest single market for offshore petroleum services.

The year ended on an even higher note. On October 21, 1992, Craig Dobbin was invested into the Order of Canada by Governor General Ramon Hnatyshyn in a ceremony at Rideau Hall. During the investiture, Dobbin was lauded for his business acumen and his philanthropy:

> Widely known as a risk taker, this Newfoundland businessman is the head of CHC Helicopter Corporation, the country's largest such operation. An entrepreneur with a generous nature, he has used his resources and abilities to support health, community and sports organizations. He has made significant contributions to educational institutions, as well as to individuals struggling to better themselves.

Other recognition and honours were to follow, but none gave Craig Dobbin more pride than this one.

John Kelly nominated Dobbin for an Honorary Doctor of Laws degree from University College, Dublin, in 1995, the second time the Newfoundland entrepreneur was recognized in this manner. Somewhat later Dobbin accepted the role of Honorary Consul General of Ireland for Newfoundland and Labrador. He enjoyed the title, as might be expected, and the position required little of his active attention. Inquiries, documents and guidance relating to matters between Newfoundland and Ireland were handled for the most part by Dobbin's personal secretary, Candace Moakler.

According to John Crosbie, Dobbin enjoyed more than the dignity of the position. Crosbie had managed to have himself appointed Mexican Consul General in St. John's. Dobbin had a more credible connection to his own title, and it appears he exploited his role more fully too.

"The provincial government helped out the consulates by giving us a big discount on our liquor purchases," John Crosbie says today, speaking in his downtown St. John's law office, "and we all appreciated it. Then Craig Dobbin got himself appointed the Irish Consul and promptly fucked it up for the rest of us. He bought so much damn liquor that the province took away our discount!"

Craig and Elaine Dobbin with Craig's sons Craig Jr. (*back, far left*),
Mark (*back, centre*) and David (*back, second from right*) and daughters
Joanne (*front, far left*) and Carolyn (*front, far right*), plus their spouses
and children. Craig's mother Rita sits to his left.

Sons David, Craig Jr. and Mark with their father at Long Harbour.

Dobbin, shown here with granddaughter Maria, enjoyed his role as grandfather.

Craig Dobbin with lung transplant team leaders Nancy Blumenthal and Dr. Robert Kotloff. It was "like having a toolbox shoved in your chest," Dobbin said.

The newly married Craig and Elaine, July 1997. The next day Craig was rushed back to the ICU for treatment due to transplant complications.

To strengthen his pitch for giant HSG, Dobbin travelled to Stavanger, Norway, and won over the firm's unionized blue-collar workers.

When Craig Dobbin learned his sealskin coat outraged animal rights
activists, he insisted on wearing it everywhere—except into the U.S.,
where the garment was banned.

In 2000, Craig Dobbin received his third honorary degree, a
Doctorate of Laws from Memorial University. Here the new doctor
poses with M.U. president Axel Meisen (*left*) and Chancellor
and CHC board member John Crosbie.

9

While the accountants may have been looking at the figures
and saying, hey, we're broke, Craig was saying, "We're going to get
this contract, we're going to win this deal, we're going to make
money on it." He believed that he could never, ever fail.

CANDACE MOAKLER, executive assistant to Craig Dobbin

RAIG DOBBIN'S EUPHORIA OF acquiring BIH soon was dampened by hard fiscal reality. The purchase added massive debt
to CHC's books, and the new division would not begin generating income for some time. Coming down to earth from his honours
and his business coup, Dobbin found himself deep in the familiar
bog of overriding debt and underwhelming cash flow.

The impact of the cancelled United Nations contracts continued
to reverberate. The contracts had bridged a difficult period, and Dobbin had no regrets about entering into them, but the company had
not been prepared for their loss. After forecasting estimated earnings of $1 per share for 1993, Dobbin faced the prospect of a net loss
per share for the period, and the losses were substantial enough to
persuade him and the board of directors that a change at the top was
necessary. The change, it was agreed, would involve replacing Pat
Callahan as COO. Late in 1993, CHC announced that Callahan had
resigned as president and COO to pursue other challenges.

"Callahan," someone familiar with the former CHC president suggests, "was done. He was burnt out. It happened to some people at
CHC. If you couldn't keep up with Craig Dobbin, you simply fell by

the wayside." Or perhaps Callahan had found it difficult, as others did, to match Dobbin's high-risk style. "You would be caught within the force of [Craig's] personality," Cabot Martin explains, "and you would have so much respect for his energy and for his basic intelligence that you measured how well you were doing according to his expectations."

For Callahan's replacement, Dobbin located one individual within CHC whom he believed was suited for the job. Rudy Palladina had begun his business career in the marketing department of Bell Helicopter, located north of Montreal. With movie-star good looks and impeccable grooming, he appeared destined for a senior executive position in whatever industry he chose. Palladina rose through the ranks at Bell to become marketing director before being introduced to Craig Dobbin, who offered him a position with CHC in the mid-1980s.

From their first encounter, Palladina was sold on working for the CHC chairman. "Craig Dobbin was one of these guys," he explains, "who, the first time you meet him, you know you're dealing with somebody special." Dobbin explained his plan for building CHC, one that Palladina believed was too ambitious to succeed. Sensing the new recruit's uncertainty, Dobbin promised Palladina he would never be bored working at CHC, and if he had the talent he would really go places. "He could be so persuasive, so charming," Palladina recalls, "that I decided to leave the security of Bell, join a company with a reputation for not paying its bills, and take a substantial pay cut. That's how convincing he was."

Settled in Vancouver as director of CHC's western division when the president and COO position came open, Palladina had little interest in the job. He and his family liked British Columbia, and running CHC was simply not a role he wanted to fill. Besides, by his own admission, Palladina was primarily a salesman, not an executive—as he puts it, "I didn't know a balance sheet from a bedsheet."

It took a telephone call from Craig Dobbin to change his mind. "You haven't applied for the president's job," Dobbin said to Palladina,

154

who explained that he was enjoying west-coast life. "Rude," Craig Dobbin said in a no-nonsense tone, using his favourite adaptation of Palladina's first name, "I want your application on my desk tomorrow." In response, Rudy Palladina sent perhaps history's shortest job application letter: "Craig: I am applying for the job. Rudy."

Palladina believed he was the sole candidate for the position, but Dobbin had two other men in mind. One possessed more senior management experience than Palladina had acquired, and he became Dobbin's favoured choice. As he did on almost every major business decision, Dobbin conferred with Harry Steele, who favoured the same candidate. Steele, however, suggested that the man's strict approach to business dealings would place him in perpetual conflict with Dobbin's from-the-hip style. Palladina, familiar with the Dobbin approach, would more easily adapt.

Dobbin asked Palladina to meet him in Toronto at the Royal York Hotel, where they discussed various topics in a non-committal way. Finally, Dobbin instructed Palladina to meet him the following morning for breakfast, and to bring a pen and a sheet of paper with him. "Here are the ten things I want," Dobbin said without any comment when Palladina arrived. The first goal on the list was to elevate corporate earnings by at least $1 per share for the coming year. Further down the list was an order for Palladina to be in St. John's the following Monday, December 1, prepared to assume the duties of president and COO. "I didn't even learn what my salary would be until sometime in January," Palladina claims.

Dobbin's promise that Palladina would never be bored at CHC proved correct. "He could goad you, flatter you, criticize you and all of that," Palladina says, "but what he did best was challenge you." At times dictatorial in his orders, Dobbin was unforgiving if he sensed resistance. Staff members who balked at relocating their families or taking extended business trips that conflicted with their personal schedules soon found the air around the Chairman growing chilly. There was always room for debate, but once the decision was made there was no room for defiance.

CRAIG DOBBIN PLAYED hard and fair, at least as fair as was necessary to win the game. Hiding aircraft from Steve Hudson, failing to make lease payments on his helicopters for several months and dodging lien-happy bankers were necessary tactics for an entrepreneur building a global business from scratch. In his heart, however, Dobbin believed he never engaged in disreputable activities such as backroom deals that undercut your partners or put greed ahead of ethics and principle. That's why few events in his business career disturbed him more than his civil suit against the giant Boeing aircraft company, which charged that Boeing had engaged in exactly those unethical acts.

Taking a leaf out of Tony Ryan's book, Craig Dobbin had created Aviaco International Leasing to take advantage of his contacts in the aviation industry and, almost incidentally, to dispose of underutilized aircraft owned by his regional airline Air Atlantic. With options on purchasing twenty-five regional aircraft, Aviaco intended to become a global leasing operation, targeting Europe and the Caribbean. Keith Miller, the former president of Eastern Provincial Airways, was installed as Aviaco president, and Craig Dobbin Jr. was dispatched to Barbados to manage the head office in Bridgetown. Aviaco was wholly owned by Craig Dobbin Ltd., and it operated as a separate entity from both CHC Helicopters and Air Atlantic.

It was a bold and basically brilliant move. A recent federal budget redefining certain tax implications for Canadian aircraft leasing firms had reduced their profit potential, inspiring the move to Barbados. While Dobbin never acknowledged it, some consideration may have been given to the greater appeal to clients of visiting Barbados rather than St. John's, especially in winter months. But leasing large-capital equipment in an industry as volatile as air transportation brought its own perils. Aircraft purchases and leasing both involve massive amounts of money committed to companies that frequently teeter on the brink of insolvency, and the risk factor is substantial. Add the apparent habit of certain countries and aircraft suppliers to employ "grease money" as a means of influencing buying decisions, and the business begins to resemble a backroom poker session in Las Vegas.

Perhaps the gambling aspect appealed to Craig Dobbin's "roll the dice" instinct. In any case, Aviaco had paid $24 million to purchase two de Havilland Dash 8-300 aircraft that Dobbin had intended for Air Atlantic. Soon after taking delivery, he arranged to lease the two fifty-seat aircraft through Aviaco to Bahamasair for $250,000 per month over ten years. The Bahamian airline desperately needed new aircraft, and they had approached Dobbin in part because the firm's cash reserves were low and its credit record rather smudgy. Negotiations stretched over a year, trying Dobbin's patience, but eventually a deal was hammered out that required Bahamasair to pay $6 million towards the purchase of the aircraft in return for 55 per cent ownership at the end of the ten-year lease.

On the surface, the contract appeared to favour Aviaco. Subtracting the airline's $6-million deposit, Dobbin's firm would recover $30 million over ten years, and still retain 45 per cent of the planes when the lease expired. Similar terms would be applied to the purchase of more Dash 8s should Bahamasair require them.

Aviaco, Craig Dobbin believed, would open exciting new opportunities. He saw the company as a way to exploit his widening circle of contacts in and around the aviation business, and as the source of a potentially massive cash flow from long-term leases. Unfortunately, Aviaco never succeeded in cashing in on its inaugural deal, the one sending the Dash 8s to the Bahamas.

At the time the deal was settled, de Havilland was owned by Boeing, the Seattle-based aircraft giant. In Dobbin's view, Boeing reviewed the Aviaco/Bahamasair deal and decided to cut out the middleman—in this case Aviaco and Dobbin—arranging a direct sale between Boeing and Bahamasair for brand-new aircraft. That alone might have launched a civil suit against Bahamasair, but Dobbin charged that Boeing and de Havilland officials had retained Duncan Rapier, through Miami-based Sovereign Aircraft Ltd., as a "consultant" to close the deal.

Rapier was by all indications something of a shadowy character. A Canadian citizen, he had been nabbed by the FBI for attempting to sell $25 million in bonds stolen in London by the Irish Republican Army. The adventure apparently did not inhibit his being hired as manager of a luxury Nassau hotel, where he made contact with several highly positioned people within the Bahamian government and exploited the relationships to his own substantial benefit. Rapier, Dobbin charged and the Canadian later admitted, received US$1.14 million from de Havilland to arrange the sale of new Dash 8s to Bahamasair, effectively cutting Aviaco out of the deal. From this "grease money," Rapier passed US$786,000 to two businessmen close to Bahamian government ministers responsible for the operation of Bahamasair.

The Boeing/Bahamasair deal put Aviaco out of business, cost Dobbin millions of dollars, and obliterated his dream of owning a global aircraft leasing operation. In his lawsuit against Boeing and Bahamasair, he initially sought US$900 million in losses and punitive damages, naming among others Boeing chairman and CEO Frank Shrontz and de Havilland president R.B. Woodward as defendants. The action sparked investigations into the matter by the FBI and the RCMP, who initially found nothing. The Bahamian government, however, assisted by Scotland Yard, concluded that Rapier, the government officials and Boeing/de Havilland had indeed engaged in actions that at least appeared to be bribery.

Looking for assistance in his battle against the aviation giant, Dobbin turned to John Crosbie who, as minister of international trade, oversaw the actions of Canada's Export Development Corporation at the time. The fact that a fellow Newfoundlander was claiming maltreatment by a foreign firm added to Crosbie's commitment to help his friend.

Thus began the slow, often excruciating journey of the case through the legal systems of the U.S. and Canada. A Florida district court jury initially awarded Dobbin US$12.2 million, later reduced to US$2.8 million upon appeal. Pursuing the matter in Canada, Dobbin enlisted Crosbie's assistance again, this time calling Crosbie and former prime minister Brian Mulroney as witnesses to support his claim.

Despite the heavyweight presence of a cabinet minister and the confirmed illegal activity of the Bahamian ministers, the trial did not go well. "The judge was a curmudgeon who was looking at retirement in a few months," John Crosbie recalls with more than a little residual bitterness. "For some reason he didn't like Craig or his counsel, and he acted outrageously in my opinion, making the presentation of Craig's case very difficult." Angry, frustrated and demoralized, Dobbin and Aviaco agreed to a confidential out-of-court settlement. In 1996 he sold Air Atlantic to Halifax-based businessman Ken Rowe, and two years later the airline vanished, rolling its operations into Canadian Airlines' Inter-Canadian regional airline system.

PLACING RUDY PALLADINA at the helm freed Dobbin to pursue the two activities that preoccupied him through much of the 1990s: building CHC into a truly global operation and fuming at government incompetence, especially the kind he believed emanated from the office of Clyde Wells, premier of Newfoundland and Labrador. Dobbin expressed his enmity in a 1995 newspaper interview.

"We've learned nothing from Churchill Falls," Dobbin said, referring to the disastrous agreement compelling Newfoundland to sell electricity to Quebec at a tiny fraction of market prices. "The spineless gutless agency, the Canadian Newfoundland Offshore Board, has never had the guts to face up to Hibernia [and] Premier Clyde Wells never had the guts."

The event that so incensed Dobbin was his failed attempt to secure a contract providing helicopter services for Hibernia oil platforms over the first five years of their operations. The contract, worth an estimated $50 million to CHC, went instead to locally operated Cougar Helicopters, partnered with Norway's Helicopter

Services Group ASA. To everyone familiar with the details, it was clear that Cougar was little more than a means to circumvent Canadian restrictions against foreign ownership of air services; the Norwegian firm would perform most of the work and be the major benefactor of the deal. CHC's tender was reportedly $13 million more than the Cougar/Helicopter Services deal, a difference that Dobbin ascribed to predatory pricing and dumping, underwritten by the Norwegian government's open financial support. His demand that Clyde Wells and the Canada-Newfoundland Offshore Petroleum Board cancel the contract was ignored by the Wells government.

Losing $50 million worth of business was upsetting enough, but losing it to the Norwegian firm was doubly galling, because CHC was not permitted to bid on helicopter services in Norway. Legal counsel advised Dobbin that CHC could appeal the contract under the provisions of the Atlantic Accord, designed to favour firms in Newfoundland and Labrador in the sharing of Hibernia and other offshore petroleum earnings. Craig Dobbin always enjoyed a battle, and he was hardly a stranger to civil litigation. He rejected the idea, however. Dragging the case through the courts was not likely to endear him to the large petroleum companies he wanted to do business with. Besides, legal arguments bored him. But wheeling and dealing—that was the source of one of the many twinkles in Craig Dobbin's Irish eyes.

In the spring of 1996 Dobbin dispatched son Mark, now a CHC senior vice-president, to Brintel's head office in Aberdeen, Scotland. There, the younger Dobbin conferred with Paul Conway, a St. John's native whom Craig had parachuted into the commercial director chair of the U.K. operation. Within a few weeks, Mark Dobbin and Conway had negotiated a deal for CHC to purchase 10 per cent of Airlift AS, Norway's second largest helicopter company, with an option to acquire an additional 23.3 per cent at a later date.

Craig Dobbin described the move as "a foot in the door . . . we're now in a position to get a strategic alliance." No one who knew him believed he would be satisfied with one of his feet being used to keep a door open. At some point that door would either open wide or be knocked down. And "strategic alliance," with its suggestion of equal partners working together, was as unlikely as the chance of Dobbin using his polished wingtips for doorstops. Dobbin wanted it all, and he eventually got it.

BACK IN ST. JOHN'S, Craig Dobbin began praising Rudy Palladina's abilities in language that was no doubt meant as much to soothe shareholders as to stroke Palladina. "Rudy is a hands-on grind-it-out watch-the-pennies-and-the-dollars-will-look-after-themselves kind of guy," he said after Palladina's arrival. Others had their doubts. Some familiar with Craig Dobbin and the CHC culture predicted that Palladina would not last long in the position, suggesting he was too Bay Street, too much salesman and not enough manager, too starched collar for Dobbin's inspired seat-of-the-pants style. It was Sylvain Allard and Christine Baird, they pointed out, not Palladina, whom Dobbin had assigned to untangle the defunct UN contracts, enabling CHC to focus on more rewarding opportunities.

Palladina's on-the-job training proved a classic trial-by-fire process. According to Palladina, one year with Dobbin at CHC provided the same amount of experience as twenty years at any other corporation. "Working with Craig Dobbin," Palladina recalls, "was like driving a race car at full speed around an elevated track with no tread on the tires and no guardrail at the edges. You were constantly being challenged to your maximum limits." Those whose limits were too low or who simply failed to respond to the challenge found themselves left behind. This was apparently the thinking behind the assessment that Palladina's predecessor, Patrick Callahan, had been "burnt out" by the pace at CHC.

No record exists of Callahan's reaction to being replaced by Palladina, though it is safe to say that few presidents of large corporations who receive their walking papers ever celebrate the event. While the severance terms provided Callahan by Dobbin are privileged, the CHC chairman's tradition for settling things of this nature tended to be generous. If so, Callahan perhaps disagreed in this instance. Or perhaps he had other beefs. In any case, two years after Rudy Palladina arrived in St. John's to fill Callahan's chair, Callahan announced that he was seeking a substantial new settlement from CHC. The rationale was based on privileged information about CHC's operations that Callahan claimed to possess.

On September 25, 1996, Callahan stated in a letter to CHC's corporate lawyers:

> I was extremely upset to see in CHC Helicopter Corporation's fiscal 1997 annual report and information circular evidence that the company continues to operate as though it is a "private company" by remunerating directly and indirectly its controlling shareholder far, far above any standard. This is done to the detriment of both the company and minority shareholders such as myself. I have spoken to and written management concerning these matters and have received their official response, and this concerns me more than ever about the shareholders' representatives.

At the core of Callahan's grievance was the multi-vote arrangement granting Craig Dobbin 63 per cent of the votes while holding only 27 per cent of outstanding shares and retaining 90 per cent of the options. Given this imbalance of shares and votes, Callahan believed he had a point about the Chairman operating CHC as though it were his own "private company."

Questions of the Chairman's dual-class voting shares were rarely posed, either at shareholders' meetings or in the business press. Depending upon the nature of the agreement, dual-class voting shares can give the owners of multi-vote units a fractional increase in their voting power or an astronomical leap, creating thousands of votes for one share. The subject became central to charges laid against Hollinger International, the corporation directed by Conrad Black, by the U.S. government in 2005. Black and various cronies, the government charged, had employed their multiple voting shares in launching and approving non-compete agreements with purchasers of Hollinger assets. The non-compete deals diverted funds that should have accrued to public shareholders into the pockets of Black and others. (Black and four Hollinger executives were convicted, fined and sentenced to various jail terms.)

Conrad Black undoubtedly used the dual-class advantage to his benefit, but Hollinger, with its multiple voting shares favouring officers and directors, was hardly the most egregious of dual-class corporations. Measuring the power of dual-class voting shares against single-vote, publicly owned shares, two union groups evaluated the voting power dilution—pitting one dual-class share against a single common share—across a number of companies listed on the Toronto Stock Exchange. (An estimated 20 per cent of companies listed on the TSX employ more than one class of shares.) A few examples are shown in the table below.

COMPANY	VOTING POWER DILUTION
GLP NT Corporation	212505.13
AGF Management Ltd	2358.41
Onex Corporation	834.69
Magna International	81.71
Canadian Tire Corporation	23.80
Shaw Communications	19.96
Dundee Corporation	19.58
Atco Ltd.	8.58
Torstar Corporation	7.87
CHC Helicopter	6.62
Four Seasons Hotels	6.34
Newfoundland Capital Corporation	5.06
Bombardier Corporation	3.62

SOURCE: The Disadvantages of Dual-Class Structures to Public Shareholders, National Union of Public and General Employees (NUPGE) and the Service Employees' International Union (SEIU), May 2005

CHC was not among the most leveraged of publicly traded companies, with a 6.62 ratio according to this measurement, although it did outpace Harry Steele's Newfoundland Capital Corporation. Nor does this chart indicate that shareholders of some firms have suffered as a result of the multi-vote shares. Subject to the usual market fluctuations affecting all publicly traded companies, shareholders of AGF Management, Onex Corporation, Magna International, Canadian Tire Corporation and others have profited rather well from the management abilities of top executives. Many of these firms are considered blue chip investments. If dual-class shares provide more power for their owners to make immediate decisions, what does it matter, as long as these decisions eventually benefit shareholders to an acceptable degree?

Craig Dobbin claimed that the purpose of the multi-voting shares was to enable management to act quickly on opportunities that could not wait while various voting groups expressed their concern, or where management perceived a risk/reward situation worth the gamble. Time revealed that this latter advantage could—and did—yield enormous benefits to CHC shareholders who might not have shared Dobbin's shoot-the-works management style.

After departing CHC, Callahan had taken an executive position with another firm, leaving soon after. Salaries and bonuses at CHC had grown more generous in the meantime, a situation that likely grated Callahan, though he claimed the action evolved only from his status as a minority shareholder. Others disagree. "He wanted some of the cash that he believed he had helped create," a former CHC executive suggests.

A fuming Craig Dobbin assured the board he was prepared to answer any questions they might put to him. An agreement was reached in December 1996 when CHC directors decided that a public dispute would not be in the best interests of the corporation. Harry Steele, who retained credibility with and respect from both sides, assumed the duty of negotiating with Callahan and his representatives, eventually reaching a settlement. The former CHC president received only about 20 per cent of his original claim. Moreover, the cash was distributed by one corporate hand; the other corporate hand withdrew various stock options granted Callahan as part of his severance agreement.

By this time, however, Craig Dobbin's attention was directed elsewhere, at a problem that made his ongoing management challenges irrelevant.

10

The doctors said I had four months to live unless I got
myself a new lung. That's when I decided that death was not an option.
CRAIG DOBBIN

IN THE SUMMER OF 1992, Craig and Elaine set out to walk a trail
near the Labrador fishing camp on the way to Craig's favourite
salmon pool. It was a trek both looked forward to on every visit.
In other years Craig had practically galloped along the path, eager
to cast a fly over the water.

This time was different. This time his breathing grew laboured,
his face turned grey, and Craig became strangely weak. Soon he was
using helicopters to carry him to the salmon pools, unable to make
the long walk along the river. Dobbin refused to acknowledge the
seriousness of his condition, even as things steadily worsened. He
was now chronically short of breath, and he had developed a dry
cough. At this point he finally gave in to Elaine's insistence that he
seek medical help.

Physicians consulted in St. John's attributed Craig's shortness of
breath to years of smoking. Elaine refused to believe it, and she persuaded him to consult a specialist at the Lahey clinic near Boston.
There his ailment was diagnosed as idiopathic pulmonary fibrosis
(IPF), a rare genetic disease. Craig Dobbin was puzzled at the diagnosis. Elaine was horrified. Only ten families in Newfoundland and
Labrador were identified as carriers of the gene causing IPF and,
against enormous odds, the families included her own and now

Craig Dobbin's. IPF had struck her sister Peggy, brother Bill and a nephew, resulting in the deaths of all three. Now it was attacking the man around whom she had built her life.

A diagnosis of IPF is essentially a death sentence. In sufferers of the disease, the microscopically thin membrane of their lung sacs, where oxygen and carbon dioxide are exchanged, becomes gradually fibrous in nature. Resembling scar tissue, the leathery texture prevents blood from absorbing oxygen, and over time the membrane hardens into an essentially impermeable material. The specialist at Lahey portrayed the process as grapes drying in the sun, becoming small, wrinkled raisins with time. Inexorably, the lungs become incapable of performing their role, and the patient slowly suffocates. Unlike most diseases of the respiratory system, IPF has no apparent cause. It may be the product of a deficiency in the patient's autoimmune system, but even this is a controversial subject among medical professionals.

There is no cure for IPF; about 50 per cent of sufferers die within two years of the initial diagnosis. The only treatment is the transplant of a healthy lung into the patient's chest, and the respiratory specialist at the Lahey clinic advised Craig to place himself on a transplant list. Returning home, Elaine led Craig on a search for hospitals that would accept him as a prospective transplant patient, a search that proved initially futile. Elaine refused the advice of medical professionals consulted in Toronto and Cleveland. "They essentially told Craig to go home and die," she says with understandable bitterness.

Craig Dobbin's response to the diagnosis of IPF was characteristic: he rejected the idea that he was about to die just when he was achieving the degree of financial success he had always dreamed of. Over the next five years, his breathing growing more difficult and his energy fading, he pressed on with the assistance of oxygen tanks and his own stubborn determination. By 1997, however, even he had to recognize the severity of his condition. Every breath he took sounded like a leaking bellows, and he breathed easily only with the assistance of an oxygen mask. After a CHC board meeting in March 1997, Rudy Palladina prepared himself for the likelihood that he would never see the Chairman alive again.

His health crisis failed to prevent Dobbin from celebrating St. Patrick's Day that year, and he and Elaine hosted the annual party at their Florida condominium. He paid a price. The following morning his breathing was worse than ever. His fingers and his lips were blue. Dobbin was reaching a crisis. With some reluctance he agreed to visit a nearby hospital, where he was diagnosed with pneumonia and blasted with steroids despite Elaine's objections. That evening, she arranged an air ambulance to fly him to Baylor University in Houston to consult Adonnie Frost, the first female medical graduate of Newfoundland's Memorial University and a friend of the couple. Frost confirmed the seriousness of Dobbin's situation. "How long have I got?" Craig asked her. The answer was about six weeks, three months at the most. The time had come for a transplant.

The most critical element in the decision to seek a lung transplant was time—not only the short period Craig Dobbin had before he would die from lack of oxygen, but the maximum time needed to reach the location of an available lung, about two hours. For most patients, this involves registering at a hospital within a two-hour trip of their home in a car or ambulance, and waiting for an organ to become available there. Craig Dobbin had the means to improve his chances of receiving an appropriate lung, and the strength and resolve of Elaine to orchestrate it.

They quickly made a decision to have the procedure completed in the U.S. This provided a larger potential pool of lungs for transplant and a good deal of flexibility in timing and location, but the odds were still not encouraging. An estimated 3,500 patients are awaiting a lung transplant on any given day in the U.S., yet only about 1,000 suitable lungs become available each year.

Drawing on assistance from Craig's niece Margo Johnston, a Florida resident who worked with a firm retrieving organs for transplant, Elaine began plotting the locations of the U.S. hospitals that appeared to have the largest number of transplant organs available and boasted the best record for successful transplant procedures. In many cases, she noted with some chagrin, the donors' families were located in inner-city communities with crime rates that caused a higher incidence of sudden death among their citizens.

Death may not have been an option to him, but Craig Dobbin was enough of a realist to accept it as a possibility, and while undergoing presurgery examinations in Houston he asked Keith Stanford to join him and Elaine there. Over three days they reviewed the estate and drafted a will. With the text in hand they contracted studio time at a local video production facility, where Craig delivered the terms of his will into a camera and onto videotape. With Candace Moakler and Keith Stanford coordinating things, the videotaped will was presented to Craig Dobbin's family at his lawyer's office in St. John's a few days later.

Elaine identified sixteen qualifying hospitals and calculated a location within two hours' flying time of each aboard the Dobbins's chartered Lear jet. The place proved to be Birmingham, Alabama, and Elaine arranged to rent a house for her and Craig near the airport at Bessemer, a Birmingham suburb, with a second house nearby for the two pilots they kept on standby. Of the sixteen hospitals, nine agreed to accept Craig as a potential transplant patient, each asking for and receiving a $1-million refundable deposit to ensure payment. Each hospital was also interested in Elaine, since they wanted to ensure Craig would receive the necessary postoperative care from a concerned and capable partner.

For the next few weeks Elaine, Craig and the pilots occupied the small bungalows, confirming that each of the nine hospitals was monitoring the availability of lungs for transplant and maintaining Craig Dobbin's name on their lists. In addition, Dobbin made periodic visits to each facility to review his condition and undergo various pre-operative procedures.

Among the hospitals on the list was Philadelphia's University of Pennsylvania School of Medicine, where the Dobbins encountered a remarkable nurse practitioner named Nancy Blumenthal. As coordinator of the hospital's acclaimed lung transplant team, Blumenthal directed all phases of the transplantation procedure, from initial consultation and evaluation through the actual surgery, recovery and follow-up. Her credentials were more than impressive. She lectured extensively at the university level on the role of nurse practitioners in transplant procedures and treatment relating to end-stage pulmonary disease, winning recognition for her work with an award for Excellence in Nursing Clinical Leadership. But in her several years of experience Blumenthal had never met a patient quite like Craig Dobbin or a caregiver like Elaine Parsons.

A compact woman with a confident demeanour, Nancy Blumenthal smiles at the memory of her first encounter with Craig and Elaine. "The first person I see is this elegant woman dressed in Chanel who, despite her poise, has fear written all over her face," Blumenthal says, "yet is full of grace, and that was Elaine." Craig Dobbin was a total contrast, wearing a sweat suit, a broad smile and a terrycloth sweatband across his forehead. In the middle of the band, a colourful pin declared, *Don't take your organs to heaven. Heaven knows we can use them here.* "It made him look a little silly, but he didn't care. He was totally without pretence or fear, joking about his predicament." Blumenthal pauses. "He was terribly charming. Sometimes I had to tell him to cut out the charm and just tell me the truth."

Both Craig and Elaine grew to trust Nancy Blumenthal, and a bond developed among the three. "It's very easy to tell someone, in the condition that Craig Dobbin was in, what they want to hear rather than what they *need* to hear," Blumenthal explains. "I had a feeling that other people he had spoken to were not entirely direct with him. Craig Dobbin not only demanded the truth, he was convinced that he could beat this disease. This was not a man who believed he had only another two or three weeks of life ahead of him. His attitude was spectacularly positive, and that was in his favour."

Blumenthal recalls that Dobbin brought the same attitude to this terrifying ordeal as he applied to his business. "He was very analytical about the numbers and procedures, and of course he was not the kind of person who sat around waiting for things to happen. He wanted to *make* them happen, and I had to point out that he really had no control over the situation from this point on." A transplant cannot be undone, Dobbin was told. It was not like a business that could be sold or a marriage that could be ended. Once he was on the list, whether or not a suitable donor was found, the procedure depended on the skills of others and the luck of the draw. "It's easy to sweet-talk a transplant patient and say, 'Don't worry, we'll get the transplant done and you will be as good as new,' but that's a huge disservice to a person who is dying, because you *don't* know, you *can't* know if it will be successful," says Blumenthal.

Craig Dobbin had received little more than hollow assurances from medical professionals up to this point. Their inadequacies became clear when he asked Nancy Blumenthal what it would be like to die from IPF if a successful transplant did not occur. "The man deserved an answer to that question," Blumenthal says with some sorrow, "and it broke my heart that no one had addressed it sooner." She replied with the facts, delivered as gently and directly as she could: he would slowly, inexorably suffocate.

Nancy Blumenthal's blend of open warmth and straight talk made an impression on both Dobbins, but especially on Elaine. At last, someone was providing honest, understandable information for both of them, neither cowed by Craig's personality nor cold to Elaine's concerns.

There is a chance that Dobbin's transplant experience would have been successful in any of the medical facilities located within the two-hour flying radius. But it is impossible to believe that it would have been exceeded elsewhere without the special qualities that Nancy Blumenthal brought to the procedure and the depth of trust she created with Craig and Elaine.

The wait for a suitable lung was made more agonizing when a false alarm on June 23, 1997, sent the Dobbins rushing to the nearby Birmingham hospital. As they were driving back to their rented bungalow, Craig asked Elaine if there was any Irish at home. Elaine knew he meant Irish whiskey and said there might be a drink or two in the bottle. "That won't get it done," he replied and insisted they stop at a liquor store to replenish their supply. Dobbin would not be permitted to drink alcohol after the transplant, so Elaine bent to his wishes. After several nightcaps he drifted to sleep.

The telephone rang at three that morning. It was Nancy Blumenthal. A lung was available. Craig needed to be in Philadelphia in two hours, something of a challenge considering he was still feeling the effects of the whiskey. "I had to get my half-drunk ass out of bed and fly north," he recalled later, laughing at the memory.

The routine the Dobbins had rehearsed in their minds so often worked well. "We were in the air in minutes," Elaine recalls. "At Philadelphia, we didn't look for an ambulance. We grabbed the first taxi we saw, told the driver we would cover any speeding tickets he might get, and took off for the hospital through morning rush-hour traffic. That driver was terrific. When we reached the hospital Craig tipped him a hundred dollars." Within minutes Dobbin was being prepped for surgery, facing a six-hour procedure during which his entire chest would be opened and essentially emptied. "I've had a few drinks," Dobbin informed the nurse who was wheeling him into surgery. "Is that okay?"

"We don't do sobriety tests here," the nurse answered, and he was quickly anaesthetized.

Transplant procedures are by definition invasive, but with the exception of a full heart-lung transplant nothing is more demanding on the skills of the medical team or the physical limitations of the patient than replacing two diseased lungs with one healthy organ.

Among the most critical and arbitrary elements in the procedure is the suitability of the transplanted lung. Of all the most commonly transplanted organs—lung, heart, kidney and liver—the lung is most sensitive to pre-operative damage. The heart, kidneys and liver of a donor who perishes in a severe automobile accident, for example, may be unscathed, but lungs are susceptible to bruising and tearing in such a mishap. Lungs may also be damaged by the aspiration of blood, stomach contents or other materials as a result of the donor's death.

Even before the incident that makes them available, lungs are open to the hostile world, subject to damage from smoking, inhalation of contaminated air in the workplace and other causes. As a result, the availability of suitable lungs is much lower than that of other organs; only about 15 per cent of recovered lungs from donors can be transplanted. To complicate things further, size is a factor in determining the suitability of a donated lung. The chest cavity has a restricted capacity compared with the abdomen, where liver and kidneys are located. Thus, a healthy lung may be simply too large for a patient to receive. In addition, some patients may require a specific—that is, a left or a right—lung, limiting the prospects even more. All of this explains why the average wait for a lung transplant in the mid-1990s was almost two and a half years, and why the incidence of death among waiting patients was higher than that of patients awaiting other organ transplants. Finally, a failed lung transplant cannot easily be corrected. Aside from the challenge of locating yet another suitable lung, the patient's immune system will have been severely weakened, hampering the person's ability to fight infection.

"I define success and failure of a transplant differently than a lot of clinicians," Nancy Blumenthal explains. "I know we are not in charge. We are simply trying to make the most of nature." In a surprisingly candid admission, Blumenthal states that she does not consider death a failure. "I consider a bad death a failure," she says. "If I can at least empower a patient with the understanding of what's going on, I feel as though I have performed an important function no matter what the final outcome." She evaluates her role in the procedure as "a clinical tool," a means of giving information and comfort to patients and their families. She also stresses that she is one member of a large team consisting of nurses, pulmonologists, surgeons, therapists, administrators and others, and says that rating the relative importance of each within the transplant procedure is a mug's game.

No one, however, maintains a closer or more extended relationship between surgical team and patient, from first contact to post-operative follow-up, than the senior nurse practitioner, Nancy Blumenthal's role.

At the time of Craig Dobbin's transplant, the procedure in the U.S. was to allocate suitable organs according to the patient's time on the waiting list—a basic first-come, first-served schedule. That arrangement overly simplified things, however, considering variables such as blood type, lung size and position, and other factors. It took considerable time to move through the list, and a significant number of patients succumbed before a transplant could be performed. In the revised procedure currently in effect in the U.S., a donor-recipient matching system administered by the United Network for Organ Sharing (UNOS) matches available lungs to suitable recipients based on blood type, distance between the organ and the recipient, and a lung allocation score that assesses the type and severity of the lung disease and the likelihood of a transplant proving successful.

Craig Dobbin had been well informed of the transplant procedure, providing him with a realistic assessment of the likely outcome. With characteristic candour he later described the procedure as "like having a toolbox shoved in your chest."

The donor of Dobbin's lung, he later learned, was an inner-city youth who had succumbed to a gunshot wound. Dobbin received the donor's left lung. The right lung was supposed to be transplanted to a patient who could hardly have contrasted more with Craig Dobbin. Dobbin was a wealthy white male from outside the U.S. The other recipient was a poor Afro-American woman. The dissimilarity was more than incidental; access to medical services, including available organs, is a topic of some tension in the U.S., and it is crucial for a transplant team to perform their work with equal consideration for all patients. As it happened in this case, the donor's right lung was discovered to be unsuitable for transplant, and the woman's procedure was cancelled. Sadly, a second transplant attempt sometime later was unsuccessful, and the woman died.

Dobbin's own transplant proceeded without complications. Eight hours after entering the OR, Craig awoke in the hospital's ICU to see Elaine's relieved face smiling back at him.

The following day, Rudy Palladina was meeting with seven CHC divisional presidents in Prince Edward Island. Palladina had been told that the transplant was complete but had received no further word about Dobbin's condition. When he was called from the meeting to take a telephone call he wasn't sure what to expect. With some trepidation he placed the receiver to his ear.

"Rude," Craig Dobbin growled from his bed in the Philadelphia ICU, "where's the share price today?"

11

I could despise the man, love him, hate him, admire him
and love him again, all in the course of one minute.
RUDY PALLADINA, former president and COO, CHC Helicopters Ltd.

C RAIG DOBBIN WAS REQUIRED to ingest about forty different
medications each day for the balance of his life. These included
drugs to suppress his immune system so that it would not reject
the transplanted lung, plus antibacterial, antiviral and antifungal
medications.

No medication is totally devoid of side effects, and the drugs in
Dobbin's new regime brought their own cargo of potential problems,
including high blood pressure, elevated cholesterol levels and the
risk of cancer. For these and other reasons, post-transplant survival
periods for lung recipients are not entirely reassuring. About 85 per
cent survive the first year, but only about half remain alive after
five years, with that figure dropping to one in four ten years after
the procedure. To achieve the optimum results, patients are advised
to follow their medication regimen religiously, monitor their condition regularly, and abstain from alcohol totally.

Dobbin spent three months recuperating in Philadelphia, living with Elaine in a rented condo near the hospital. His new lung
appeared to be performing well, and CHC was back in the control,
via long-distance telephone, of its founder.

No one can expect to remain unchanged after surviving a
sentence of death, and that applied to even the super-confident,

perpetually optimistic Wild Colonial Boy. During the period in Alabama, waiting to hear if a lung would become available, Craig had suggested marriage to Elaine. She rebuffed him. It wasn't the idea of formalizing their relationship that concerned her. It was the risk that others might assume she was taking advantage of his perilous medical condition. She insisted they discuss marriage only after the transplant procedure, and he agreed.

In July 1997, barely two weeks after his transplant, Craig proposed again, suggesting Elaine visit a nearby jeweller to choose an engagement ring of appropriate size. She returned with her selection, accompanied by the jewellery store manager and two burly security guards. Dobbin approved the design but declared the diamond too small. Instead, he ordered a near-duplicate to be made by an eminent Philadelphia jeweller. A few days after the approved ring arrived, while he and Elaine strolled through a park adjacent to the hospital, Craig insisted that the marriage take place immediately. On July 23, 1997, Elaine Parsons, née Davis, became Elaine Dobbin. Brother Derm Dobbin served as best man. Elaine's daughter, Kellee Parsons, was her mother's maid of honour, her son Scott gave the bride away, and Craig's sons Mark and Craig Jr. also attended.

The black Baptist minister who presided over the ceremonies was a man steeped more in the strict fundamentalist guidelines of the U.S. Bible belt than in raucous Irish Newfoundland culture. "He gave a sermon after the ceremony," says Derm Dobbin, smiling at the memory, "saying that Craig would be the boss in the relationship, and Craig and Elaine must not listen to stories from outside the family, they had to do this and not do that. We're listening, not saying anything, Craig and me. But when the minister thundered, 'And there will be absolutely no alcohol in this marriage!', well, the two of us near fell off our chairs."

Smiles and laughter faded the next day, when Craig was readmitted to hospital in serious condition; his body appeared to be rejecting the new lung, and it took two weeks of constant treatment to stabilize his condition.

In September, while preparing to finally leave Philadelphia and return to Beachy Cove, Craig Dobbin wrote to his friend and financial guru Robert Foster, expressing himself in a poignant and rather uncharacteristic manner: "During the past few months Elaine and I have drawn on each other's strengths and I am very lucky to have her. We are extremely happy and if I could have my time back we would have tied the knot years ago."

Many of those familiar with the relationship agree that Elaine brought something to Craig Dobbin's personal and business life that could never have been realized in her absence. "The best work in Craig Dobbin's life was done in his years after the lung transplant," Frank Ryan suggests, "and much of it was achieved thanks to Elaine's contribution."

Each year following his transplant Craig and Elaine made trips to Philadelphia, where assessments were made of his lung's function and of the effectiveness of his medications. During one of Dobbin's early visits, the examining physician reviewed the test results and confirmed that Dobbin's lung, liver, heart and kidneys were functioning well. "Wait a minute," Dobbin interrupted. "Go back to the liver."

"Your liver's fine," the doctor shrugged.

"Does that mean I can have a glass of wine or two?" Dobbin asked.

The physician replied, "Of course." Elaine closed her eyes and said, "Doctor, you don't know what you've started."

Dobbin flashed one of his wide smiles, and from that day forward he enjoyed a glass of wine with meals and kept a bottle of Irish whiskey near his elbow. No alcohol to transplant recipients? Hell, that didn't apply to Craig L. Dobbin.

CRAIG DOBBIN'S COLLEAGUES and employees raved at the restorative powers of the transplant and the renewed energy Dobbin displayed. He also expressed new interest in his assets and liquidity. "He became obsessed with knowing how much he was worth," Keith Stanford says. "For years he had been asset rich and cash poor, and that never seemed to bother him, but after he returned from the transplant he began demanding an e-mail report from me every morning, a more detailed worksheet of every investment he had. Now he wanted to know his net worth that day, every day. He wanted to know how much something had changed from the previous day, and why." Dobbin appeared now to be more concerned about his cash position than any of his other assets, a complete reversal of his approach in the past. It seemed he needed more hard currency and maximum liquidable assets in his personal possession than he had before.

His close call with death did not slow Dobbin when it came to business; many of those who knew him both before and after the lung transplant found him not just more energetic but even more driven to succeed. The transplant also appears to have sharpened Dobbin's focus on matters beyond his business dealings. His marriage to Elaine cemented a relationship that benefited both parties, and he enjoyed the company of his burgeoning flock of grandchildren more than ever. He began earning wider recognition for his achievements in business and finding new ways of assisting others through the power of his expanding wealth.

Craig Dobbin served as patron for the School Children's Foundation of Newfoundland and Labrador, which provided meals for more than 2,000 children in twenty schools across the province. To support its activities, he opened Beachy Cove to the public for various fundraising events. He and Elaine also donated $150,000 to support a research program at a Memorial University genetics lab dedicated to isolating and identifying the gene responsible for IPF, the disease that had almost taken his life.

Many of his charitable acts were smaller and more personal in scope. A year or two after his transplant, Dobbin heard of a brilliant six-year-old St. John's boy, a prodigy who devoured books well above the Grade Twelve level. Learning of the family's limited resources, he arranged for a first-rate computer, complete with CD-based encyclopaedia, to be delivered a few days before Christmas to the boy's home. Other gestures were made to friends and acquaintances, some equally anonymous. Gifts, usually cash, arrived without fanfare, at least one of them reaching seven figures in dollar value to assist an especially favoured friend in dire financial straits.

Dobbin renewed his acquaintance around this time with Brother Brennan, the teacher at St. Bonaventure school whose aversion to corporal punishment had impressed Dobbin and his classmates. Retired from the Newfoundland educational system, Brother Brennan had travelled to the Caribbean island of Antigua, where he spent twenty years donating his services as a teacher and educational consultant. The school facilities in Antigua were very bad, Brother Brennan told Dobbin. Many of the children were bright and ambitious, but their potential would never be achieved, he feared.

Dobbin took two steps to assist his former teacher and some of his students. The first was to donate $300,000 towards constructing a new school on the island. With this in place, Dobbin asked Brother Brennan to choose three high-school graduates from among his students based on their ability, personality and ambition. Dobbin would pay for their travel to and from Newfoundland, their tuition to obtain a degree at Memorial University in St. John's and their expenses, including meals and supplies, as well as providing a comfortable three-bedroom apartment for the duration of their studies. He asked for one condition: upon the completion of their studies, the students must return to Antigua and remain there for two years of work before choosing to venture off the island.

One of the three students proposed by Brother Brennan earned a bachelor of commerce and became an executive with an Antigua hotel-resort chain. Another obtained his teaching certificate, returning to educate children in his own country. The third earned an engineering degree, spending two years in Antigua furthering his studies before entering the Massachusetts Institute of Technology. Today he is a leading engineer with a large U.S. firm. The success of the three candidates is not as surprising as the fact that, during their years in Newfoundland, they never personally met Craig Dobbin. Keith Stanford maintains that Dobbin did not avoid meeting the students; it was simply a matter of schedules that failed to mesh.

WITH HALF AS many lungs as he had been born with, Craig Dobbin appeared to work twice as hard as those around him. CHC's last annual report before Palladina's ascension to the CEO position had recorded significant losses. It took a while to turn things around, but by the time Dobbin returned to the Chairman's office following his transplant CHC had recorded eight consecutive quarters of substantial profit. Much of this turnaround was the result of cost-cutting procedures and efficiency-generating policies engineered by Palladina, Sylvain Allard and Christine Baird. Allard, pulled out of Viking to head the International Division of CHC, and the redoubtable Baird had performed much of the complex work necessary to extricate the company from the UN contracts.

Under the Chairman's direction, this triumvirate shaped CHC into a lean and impressive corporate machine that attracted attention from a new sector of financiers and analysts. Among those impressed with the changes, reflected in the firm's consistent profit performance, were analysts at Newcrest Capital, and Newcrest became a market maker for CHC. In October 1997 the firm led a group to underwrite the issuance of 3 million Special Warrants valued at $13 each. The $39 million reduced the corporate bank debt and financed the expansion of aircraft overhaul and repair operations in PEI and B.C., a move that impressed observers on Bay Street and elsewhere.

Palladina's buttoned-down management style freed Dobbin from many of the day-to-day headaches he had dealt with in the past. That left him to pursue ideas that occurred to him often, according to his wife, in the middle of the night. "He would nudge me awake at four in the morning," Elaine recalls, "and ask me what I thought of this idea or that idea, and I could tell he would be ready, later in the day, to make it happen."

Not all of these things happened as anticipated. Ten years before the explosion in income trust funds that drew Ottawa's wrath, because they drained tax revenue from the federal government's coffers, Dobbin planned to launch the CHC Maintenance Income Trust Fund. Underwritten by First Marathon Securities, proceeds from the offering were to be used to purchase CHC's ACRO Aerospace Division in B.C. and Atlantic Turbines, the CHC-owned engine repair facility in PEI. CHC would continue to provide management and administrative support to the fund and the two subsidiaries. Rudy Palladina opposed the idea. Bay Street appeared to agree with the CHC president, hinting that investment firms would offer little support. The fund, which might have succeeded a few years later when such investments were in fashion, was quietly withdrawn.

Like the income trust fund, many of Craig Dobbin's 4:00 a.m. ideas exemplified the "Ready, fire, aim" philosophy attributed to him by brother Derm. Even when he failed, the failures were magnificent in their scope. An entrepreneur, by definition, is someone who takes advantage of an available situation. If the situation involves government largesse, as a few of Dobbin's ventures did, it's difficult to criticize the recipient.

Sometime before his transplant, Craig Dobbin had a vision of spinning a new company off the business he knew best: operating helicopters. If Newfoundlanders could fly and maintain the complex craft, surely they could damn well manufacture them as well. Not from a standing start; the design and engineering challenges were too daunting. Helicopters, however, represented only one sector of the aerospace industry. With the exception of Brazil-based EMBRAER, aerospace manufacturing centres were located in North America or western Europe. Most were assembly operations with parts and components subcontracted according to quality, price and service. Why couldn't Newfoundlanders participate in manufacturing aerospace components? The more Dobbin pondered the idea the more practical it appeared. Look at a map of the world, he mused. Draw a line from the southwestern U.S. to the centre of western Europe. Bisect the line and head north. Where do you wind up? Newfoundland. An aerospace components manufacturer located there would be closer to the U.S. industry than Europe was and closer to the European industry than was the southwestern U.S. A few hours saved in shipping plus lower labour costs would ensure success, especially if a minimum amount of income was guaranteed from a substantial and favouring customer. Like CHC Helicopters.

With several hundred helicopters in the CHC fleet, Dobbin could justify investing in an operation to repair, rebuild and manufacture parts for his helicopters. To do so, of course, would require proper certification. Once this was obtained, however, the facility could produce components for every aerospace manufacturer in the world.

Things got better. The most celebrated Newfoundland federal politician since John Crosbie, former Fisheries Minister Brian Tobin had recently returned to Newfoundland and won election as premier. Dobbin knew and liked Tobin, who shared Dobbin's opinion that Newfoundland must begin freeing itself from a reliance on fisheries and federal government handouts. Both were shrinking in size and unlikely to return. A high-tech aerospace manufacturing facility would represent a major leap forward for Newfoundland, leapfrogging over the usual ideas being tossed around, those promoting food processing, cucumber agriculture and, yes, fish farms.

The key decision concerned product. Which component should the new company manufacture? Dobbin chose laminates, the fabrication of bonded materials that involves shaping various composite panels. The challenge of blending carbon and glass fibres, metals and thermoplastics into a layered structure meeting tight specifications on size, stability and strength is formidable. Craig Dobbin wanted to prove Newfoundlanders could do it as well as anyone in the world. He had the vision, Brian Tobin had the ambition, and the provincial treasury had the money to get it started.

Negotiations for the project had begun soon after Tobin's government assumed office in 1996 and two years later he and Craig Dobbin announced the launch of Newfoundland Bonding & Composites (NB&C), a subsidiary of CHC Composites, in Gander. The $20.5-million plant covering 5,500 square metres was funded with $9.5 million of provincial money; CHC provided the balance. In return for the province's contribution, CHC agreed to provide 1,000 person-years of employment.

When it opened in July 1999, the CHC Composites plant boasted a number of features that attracted attention in the global aerospace industry. Among its initial forty-seven employees were several engineers and technicians trained at helicopter manufacturers GKN Westland in the U.K. and Augusta in Italy (the two have since merged into AugustaWestland). The facility also possessed one of only two Six-Axis Routers in the world; the other was owned by Boeing. Certified as an Approved Maintenance Organization (AMO), the firm was authorized to perform repairs to off-aircraft structural components, especially those involving composite and metal-bonded techniques. The company promoted itself as "a complete systems solution for the manufacturing and repair of bonded and composite panels."

In the beginning, Dobbin's optimism appeared justified. A memo of understanding from Sikorsky represented a $7.5-million contract for NB&C to produce composite and metal-bonded components for the helicopter manufacturer. CHC joined E.H. Industries, a consortium of Canadian companies with a federal government contract, to construct fifteen AW520 Cormorant search-and-rescue helicopters at a total cost of $593 million. Soon fixed-wing aircraft manufacturer Bombardier came knocking, awarding contracts for CHC Composites to construct panels for its popular Dash 8 turboprop. For a financial cushion, NB&C's parent company CHC Composites drew upon the global line of credit available to *its* parent, CHC Helicopters, to reduce its financing charges. A brand-new company in Newfoundland, it appeared, was about to elbow its way into the wealthy and exclusive club of aerospace manufacturers.

Problems arose, however. Delays in building the plant meant several contract opportunities were missed. Customers grew skeptical. As the new kid on the block, NB&C may have had the qualifications to do the job, but it lacked the experience of more established component suppliers. Timing failed Dobbin when Bombardier, who had promised to be among the largest of NB&C's customers, severely cut back its production schedule during a period of market decline. Other glitches added to the woes. Complications developed with the manufacturing software driving the automated equipment, freight costs rose dramatically, and whispers began to spread about the firm's management capabilities.

The company struggled. In fiscal 2002 it recorded a $4-million loss against sales of only $2.5 million. In July 2004, Dobbin attempted to sell CHC Composites to Skyview, a Beverly Hills investment firm, for US$15.8 million. A forecast of $27 million in sales by 2010 was not sufficient incentive for Skyview, and following several months of negotiations the deal collapsed.

CHC Composites continues to operate in Gander. Although it manages to show an occasional profit, the company marks one of the few times the vision and raw determination of Craig Dobbin could not overcome the hard realities of global business.

Or perhaps Dobbin lost his focus. While launching the composites operation, he was taking an even bigger step towards diversification, aiming to reduce the cyclical impact of the helicopter services industry by spinning off CHC's aerospace overhaul and repair operations into a new publicly traded company. On paper, the move was appealing. Repair and overhaul contracts contributed more than one-third of CHC revenues in 1997 from work performed at Atlantic Turbines Inc. on Prince Edward Island and ACRO Aerospace in British Columbia. Craig Dobbin saw a qualified single-identity operation serving helicopter and various aerospace industries across three markets: Canada, the U.K. and the U.S.

In 1998 Dobbin acquired Hunting Airmotive Ltd., a long-established aviation repair and overhaul facility in the U.K. whose customers included the British ministry of defence. Hunting was licensed by Allison and Rolls-Royce to perform complete engine rebuild services, and by Hamilton Standard to overhaul that firm's aero propellers. These were impressive credentials, and in 1997 the firm's 375 employees had generated $13 million in earnings from more than $60 million in revenue. Dobbin paid $60 million for Hunting, floating the purchase with a $24-million loan from the Bank of Scotland and changing the name to Sigma Aerospace, making it the third piece in the newly assembled company.

All three divisions were rolled into Vector Aerospace Corporation in early 1998, with Mark Dobbin installed as chairman and CEO. Mark was supported by two long-time Dobbin associates: Maxwell Parsons, former CFO of CHC, and Paul Conway, who had been operating U.K.-based Brintel. A first-rate board of directors that included fishing buddy Frank Moores and former Ontario Premier David Peterson was assembled, and an IPO for Vector was issued in June 25, 1998. The original IPO capitalization target had been more than $300 million. When the issue failed to meet its initial target (net proceeds totalled $187 million), CHC absorbed 20 per cent of the available shares and held them for two years before issuing them, netting another $28.9 million.

Dobbin had discussed the concept of Vector as an independent, publicly traded company with Rudy Palladina, who opposed the idea from the beginning. CHC was succeeding at its core business of providing exceptional helicopter service, and its maintenance and repair facilities should be the means of supporting operations, not potential profit centres. Shedding this function from the company through a public offering, Palladina suggested, was totally at odds with the overall corporate strategy.

Palladina's tenure at CHC revealed both strengths and weaknesses, according to those familiar with this period of the company's history. "He was a salesman more than a technician," one source familiar with the company's financial operation suggests.

Top executives benefit from sales and marketing talents, to be sure, but Craig Dobbin perhaps expected other facets to surface in the individual occupying the president's chair, and Palladina's lack of enthusiasm for Vector hardly strengthened the relationship between himself and Dobbin.

The chairman pursued the idea despite Palladina's objections. At a CHC board of directors meeting in Palladina's absence, Vector was born and the IPO scheduled. Upon returning from an extended vacation, Palladina learned of the decision. He packed his briefcase, walked out of CHC's head office, and drove to Beachy Cove, where he submitted his resignation. After a decision with which he had disagreed so long and so vehemently, Palladina explained, he was no longer of any use to either CHC or its controlling shareholder.

To Palladina's surprise, Dobbin accepted his resignation immediately. Sylvain Allard, the CHC chairman knew, was ready to step into the top job, and Palladina's departure provided the opportunity.[*] The pilot who had stumbled awkwardly through his English when first meeting Craig Dobbin, and had originally sought a chance to fly larger aircraft, was now running day-to-day operations for one of the world's largest helicopter companies. As for Craig Dobbin, he enjoyed both seeing his protégé occupying the top executive position in CHC and the prospect of using his Vector IPO earnings to finance the company's ultimate expansion.

---

[*] Palladina disputes this version of events, recalling that Dobbin asked him to "take a couple of days to think it over" and Palladina refused. It has also been suggested that Palladina secured a new position with Aerospatiale before submitting his resignation, assuming it would be accepted. Palladina eventually rose to become CEO of Aerospatiale's North American operations.

12

I thought, Here's a guy who built this company from nothing,
survived that terrible transplant operation, and he still
makes most of the rest of us look as though we're asleep.
And that's just the business side of his life. At his fishing camps
and social events, I hear he was even more dynamic.

PETER GODSOE, former chairman and CEO, Scotiabank

"SYLVAIN ALLARD IS NOT only the best CEO in the international helicopter business," suggests Robert Foster, whose Capital Canada investment firm has had a long association with CHC, "he is also one of the best top executives in Canada, period."

Those familiar with the interior workings of CHC are unanimous in their assessment of the Craig Dobbin/Sylvain Allard partnership. Dobbin's vision and Allard's operational talents meshed perfectly. Unlike Palladina, whose principal talents lay in marketing and crunching numbers, Allard was an operations man who understood every detail of the nuts and bolts—the number of duty hours to be flown, the impact of weather conditions on contract fulfillments, the suitability of equipment and crews for specific functions. In addition to knowing how to manage CHC, someone noted, Allard also knew how to manage Craig Dobbin.

188

Dobbin felt more than confident in elevating Allard into the president and CEO post, especially with Christine Baird's extraordinary abilities at work on the company's global operations. He might also have taken some comfort in CHC's 1998 financial performance, though what could have been a bright picture was somewhat clouded by various developments. From revenue exceeding $350 million for that fiscal year, the company recorded EBITDA (Earnings Before Interest, Taxes, Depreciation and Amortization) of almost $55 million, generating about 75 cents in net earnings per share. The firm's long-term debt-to-equity ratio was a manageable 1.5:1. Not an exceptional performance, perhaps, but reasonable considering the upheavals that occurred in CHC's industry that year.

Dobbin's acquisition of Brintel in 1993 had tipped the first in a line of unstable dominoes. Foreign owners acquired the two remaining helicopter companies serving the valuable North Sea petroleum installations, though in the case of Bristow the acquisition had been limited to 49 per cent, purchased by U.S.-based Offshore Logistics (OLOG). Norway's giant Helicopter Services Group had swallowed Bond Helicopters, making HSG the dominant player on the North Sea stage.

In the midst of this turbulence came a crushing blow. Brintel had long held a $500-million contract with Shell Oil and fully expected to retain it when submitting its proposal for renewal in 1998. Instead, the company lost to newly aggressive Bristow, an event made more painful by a collapse in world oil prices and a corresponding cutback in North Sea production. In the first quarter of 1999 the airport at Aberdeen, Scotland—long established as the world's busiest commercial heliport driven by petroleum services—recorded a year-over-year reduction of 14 per cent in helicopter traffic. Meanwhile, the three giant players continued to vie for contracts in the crowded North Sea, slashing prices in cutthroat action to retain market share. Bristow, with its $500-million Shell deal, was now the largest player, edging out HSG and tumbling Brintel to third position.

None of this stimulated positive thoughts among top executives of the competing helicopter service firms, with the exception of Craig Dobbin. His response to the loss of the massive Shell contract had been tailored several years earlier: when things get tough, it's time to get bigger. As he had with the acquisition of Toronto Helicopters and Okanagan, Dobbin's Jonah prepared to swallow the whale. The whale in this case was Norwegian-owned Helicopter Services Group.

HSG's roots traced back to 1956, ten years before North Sea oil exploration began. The company was operating twenty Sikorsky s-61 craft to and from the offshore rigs when it was acquired by Scandinavian Airline Services (SAS). HSG was among the first European operators to employ Super Pumas, and starting in the mid-1980s the company embarked on a major expansion program. Purchasing Bond Helicopters, it later absorbed Bond's Australian subsidiary, Lloyd Helicopters, and South African–based Court Helicopters in 1996.

Three large helicopter service companies serving North Sea oil rigs, with search-and-rescue contracts on the side, was at least one too many in Dobbin's eyes. He had little interest in Bristow, not wishing to go toe-to-toe with its U.S. string-pullers in Louisiana. Besides, he had heard rumblings of severe discontent at Bristow. The company, once well-managed in a gentlemanly British fashion, was undergoing a swing towards less-than-subtle U.S.-style management. "There has been a lack of attention to customer needs and too much concentration on the almighty dollar," one former Bristow manager observed shortly after Bristow lost a long-held contract with Amoco. "Opinions are not welcomed unless they concur with those of senior management, who would appear to have lost touch with their customers."

Bristow eventually underwent a total restructuring, including a new CEO elevated from his CFO position and a consolidation of support personnel and facilities from elsewhere in the U.K. to Aberdeen. Such turmoil, Craig Dobbin decided, would keep Bristow occupied for a while, reducing its impact on the market. He would leave it to stew in its own juice and focus instead on HSG.

HSG's policies were skewing the industry thanks to funding from the Norwegian government, whose support for the purportedly private company enabled HSG to underprice its services. Those familiar with the industry claim HSG's fees were set as much as 20 per cent lower than those of its competitors; any financial shortfall would be absorbed by public funds. Things had to change.

Sylvain Allard's first inclination was to consolidate operations in the U.K. "We had cash in the bank," he explains, "and excess aircraft. The Norwegians needed more helicopters, so I figured we could do a deal and reduce our debt, or maybe buy their U.K. contracts and leave the rest of the North Sea to them."

Shrinking the company's size was not Craig Dobbin's style, however, and when the Chairman responded with less than enthusiasm for this idea, Allard began exploring a new approach.

"We had a small piece of a Norwegian company called Airlift," Allard continues. "I sat on the board, and it was struggling because it couldn't compete against Bristow or HSG." The linkage paid off when a member of the Airlift board reported a rumour about HSG shareholders being discontented with the company's performance. They had reason to be upset; HSG common shares had dropped from about NOK(Norwegian Krone)100 to barely NOK30 in recent months. This presented Allard and recently appointed CFO Jo Mark Zurel with a new opportunity, and they prepared a flow chart tracing alternative strategies.

Allard's proposal involved choosing among three alternatives. One was to sell the entire European operation and pull back to Canada, debt-free with substantial business in the Americas, Asia and Africa, a standard MBA-dictated move to solidify the firm's financial base. Another would be to pursue Allard's original idea and bid for HSG's U.K. business, paying for a portion of it with surplus aircraft.

"Then I said to the Chairman, 'Here's the other crazy idea,'" Allard recalls. Forget buying the U.K. division, Allard suggested, and make a bid for the entire company. Craig Dobbin's eyes lit up. Now they were talking his kind of business. He immediately had

Candace Moakler locate the name and telephone number of HSG's chairman, Raidar Lund, and placed a transatlantic call to HSG head office in Stavanger, Norway. "Raidar," Dobbin said when he reached Lund, "my name is Craig Dobbin and I want to buy your company."

Lund, doubtless taken aback by the unexpected approach, agreed to meet Dobbin, Allard and Zurel in Norway the following day. Seated in Lund's office, Dobbin repeated his intention as directly as he had in the telephone call. "By the way," he added, "can you recommend a good lawyer and a good investment banker for us?"

"Craig was treating Lund as a friend," Allard explains today. "That was his biggest strength in negotiations. The minute you sat down with him he made you a friend or a part of the circle, and it was a brilliant move." Why ask your opponent to recommend the rest of your team? Because Lund would only propose firms he trusted, Allard points out, making the process comfortable for both sides. Lund recommended two very good firms, including the top mergers and acquisitions law firm in Norway, and without wasting time Dobbin and his team set off to meet with them.

The move was classic Craig Dobbin: skip the formalities, cut the B.S., lay your cards on the table, and do the deal. "You couldn't operate that way today," Sylvain Allard muses. "Too many restrictions. But the Chairman was determined to do it quick and clean, right in HSG's own backyard."

Dobbin was familiar with Norwegian custom and even, to a limited extent, with the Norwegian language. Fifteen years earlier, he and business partner Cabot Martin had set off to negotiate the joint venture with Norwegian engineering firm NorTek and Norwegian Petroleum Consultants (NPC). As usual during these forays, Dobbin set a hectic pace of business meetings, social engagements and the odd extracurricular activity. The climactic event of the journey was to be a formal dinner with their prospective partners and various government dignitaries in Oslo's prestigious Ship Owner's Hall, at which Craig Dobbin planned to make an appropriate toast.

In Bergen on the morning of the banquet, Dobbin and Martin huddled in a sauna, seeking relaxation and some manner of impressing their Norwegian hosts that night. Dobbin decided he would speak to them directly in their own language, a daunting prospect for a man who, in Cabot Martin's words, was "decidedly unilingual." For his language instructor, Dobbin chose an attractive female sauna attendant, persuading her to translate his words into Norwegian and then teach him the pronunciation of each syllable. He dutifully recorded the phonetic guidelines. When she expressed satisfaction with his delivery, he bolted from the sauna to catch the flight to Oslo.

That evening, with everyone in formal dress and the proceedings as tightly scripted as a royal gala, speeches and toasts poured forth. When it was Craig Dobbin's turn, he rose and, in perfect Norwegian, said: "Ladies and gentlemen, I would like to propose a toast to NPC, to NorTek and to the youth of our two nations." He sat down to enormous applause. His hosts were impressed and grateful. More than a decade later, would they be as pleased about his return to purchase one of the country's marquee industries?

SHORTLY AFTER THE New Year in 1999, Dobbin met with Sylvain Allard and a select group of other key personnel at Dobbin's residence in Florida to plot their takeover strategy of HSG. Instead of a full frontal assault on the company, it was decided to create Vinland Helicopters Norway as a separate entity to purchase and hold HSG shares.

"You hear entrepreneurs and investors use the term 'Bet the farm' when talking about a big expansion move or acquisition," Robert Foster observes. "Almost always, there's some hyperbole involved in the suggestion that the company is risking it all and might no longer remain an entity if things didn't work out. Dobbin's deal to acquire HSG was different. This was the only time I have truly seen an entrepreneur bet the farm, the animals, everything."

Under Norwegian securities law, any investor holding 40 per cent of a publicly traded company was required to make an offer to purchase all of the remaining shares. (In Canada and the U.S., the rule applies when an investor has accumulated just 20 per cent of outstanding shares.) To succeed, Dobbin had to commit to acquiring 100 per cent of HSG. Without total control, CHC could not merge with HSG, reduce its costs and, most important, have access to its cash flow in order to service the debt incurred to purchase the company. The idea of gaining less than total control made CHC's financiers uneasy. A scenario in which Dobbin and CHC acquired several million shares, paying inflated prices that slid dramatically when it became apparent that the buyout would not succeed, was easy to visualize. A near miss under those circumstances could mean the end of CHC and massive writeoffs for the company's bankers.

To succeed, the deal would mean access by CHC to a substantial amount of capital, far more than any previous acquisition Dobbin had orchestrated. The first person he called for assistance was Steve Hudson, the investment specialist Dobbin had concealed aircraft from so many years earlier. "He rang me up one morning to announce that he was buying up all the stock of Helicopter Services Group," Hudson smiles. "I said, 'Okay, but with whose money?' and Craig said, 'Your money. You've gotta meet me and help structure this.' He was determined to buy a company even though he had no money to pay for it." Hudson shakes his head in wonder. "Dobbin had balls the size of an elephant." Persuaded either by Dobbin's fiscal testicles or by his shrewd business logic, Hudson pledged $50 million from his Newcourt Capital firm which, along with Dobbin's earnings from the Vector IPO, was enough to purchase 5 million shares, or about 25 per cent of HSG's stock.

Dobbin had not been entirely truthful about his cash position. The Vector IPO had generated a $200-million war chest, merely the ante for the game he wanted to play. Newcourt financing provided CHC with a toehold on HSG, but Dobbin needed substantially more to move the deal forward. To make it work, he would require a single source of capital to cover not only the expected inflated value of HSG shares but CHC's own debts and sufficient capital to fund the merger. Dobbin turned to Robert Foster and his Capital Canada investment firm. Could Foster connect CHC with a source of capital? A very *large* source of capital? As he had in the past, Foster set to work.

Dobbin and Foster established an arrangement with Trilon Financial Corporation, a division of Brascan. Trilon's subsidiaries included Royal Trustco, London Life Insurance, Royal LePage and several other prestigious financial and investment firms.

Under the CHC/Trilon agreement, Trilon purchased 1.1 million HSG shares to fulfill a "Put and Call" options contract with CHC/Vinland. Vinland could call for the shares to be transferred to its ownership at any time before September 30 of that year in exchange upon payment of the original cost of the shares to Trilon plus interest, fees and expenses. If Vinland did not exercise the option, Trilon could require Vinland to purchase them. With this in hand, CHC's ownership reached 30 per cent of HSG in mid-March 1999. Dobbin sought a meeting with the HSG board to discuss CHC's plans in detail.

Despite Dobbin's purchase of Brintel a few years earlier, a transaction that could not have been completed without his possessing an EU passport, the Norwegians balked, claiming they must adhere to their own country's Law on Aviation. This dictated that HSG must be owned and controlled through the votes of at least two-thirds of Norwegian shareholders or shareholders with equal status under European Economic Area (EEA) provisions. Without confirming this requirement had been met, the board was prohibited from transferring the shares, and it referred the entire question to Norway's ministry of transport, who passed the file on to that country's ministry of justice. In the meantime, HSG's corporate advisors set out to locate other potential buyers, including a U.S.-based investment group that expressed interest in the opportunity to buy HSG. How the American company would bypass the requirements of Norwegian law and EEA provisions was never fully explored, but the prospect of watching the deal collapse generated understandable unease for Dobbin.

By now, Dobbin and CHC had committed $48 million to the project, and Dobbin was just beginning. The bill for the outstanding shares of HSG, plus all the associated costs involved in merging debts and obligations from both companies, would be another $500 million or more, an amount only a large chartered bank could handle without wide syndication. Foster got out his Rolodex.

One Canadian bank refused to even discuss the possibility of a deal that large with Dobbin's firm. Another suggested that bankrolling the purchase of HSG through Craig Dobbin would represent a serious mistake by whomever handed over the money. Foster eventually found a bank with pockets deep enough, and its CEO's faith in Craig Dobbin was strong enough to complete the deal.

Peter Godsoe was born in Toronto. He earned both a bachelor of science degree and designation as a chartered accountant from the University of Toronto, followed by an MBA from Harvard. But both of Godsoe's parents had grown up in the Maritimes, and his grandfather's brother, a physician, was present at the birth of John Crosbie. Godsoe enjoys leaning on his Atlantic Canada heritage, prompting one notable figure in the financial world to comment, "Godsoe has a knack for coming on like some shy guy from the east coast, but nobody on Bay Street ever had a more incisive mind when it came to sizing up a business plan." That makes Godsoe's recollection of his first meeting with Craig Dobbin in March 1999 especially pertinent.

"He was larger than life, both in a physical sense and in the tales told about him," Godsoe says in the Scotiabank Tower office made available to him as part of his retirement settlement. It is a bright September day. Several dozen floors below, along Toronto's King Street, pedestrians stroll in the soft autumn air. Godsoe conveys a sense of both relaxation and reserve, weighing each word before releasing it. "If there was a surprise in meeting him, I suppose I was expecting somebody rougher, a kind of outdoors, helicopter-flying guy connected with the oil and gas business. Instead, I found a consummate businessman who knew his numbers inside out."

Dobbin, Scotiabank's CEO quickly recognized, possessed more than charm and confidence. "He could read a balance sheet as thoroughly as anyone," Godsoe says. "His vision of the company and his knowledge of his own firm's numbers in that first meeting were completely and totally impressive. He not only knew his own business intimately, he knew the finances intimately as well. And he wasn't there with his chief financial officer. He came on his own." You could have put Craig Dobbin anyplace in the world, Godsoe suggests, in any financial services organization on any continent, and he would have impressed the person making the decision about whether to support him. "He would look you straight in the eye. He knew what he was going to do, and he knew he would get it done."

"In the end, Peter bet on the man," suggests Robert Foster. To a degree Godsoe did, but he also relied on a team of analysts, led by a Scotiabank senior vice-president who visited St. John's to pore over the financial statements of CHC, evaluate the future of the petroleum services market, assess the abilities of CHC's principal executives, and calculate the risk factor to the bank. Some discoveries were encouraging. The analysts expressed admiration for the managerial talents of Sylvain Allard and Christine Baird, among others. Some of what they turned up was disconcerting. How much would slumping petroleum prices affect CHC? What were the chances of CHC slipping over the edge due to the excessive debt-to-equity, estimated at 4.5:1, resulting from the HSG purchase?

Borden Osmak, the Scotiabank senior vice-president assigned to spearhead the deal with CHC, encountered opposition from the bank's credit department, whose officers were unfamiliar with Craig Dobbin's management style and even less familiar with CHC's industry. Osmak grins as he recalls the credit department's response: "They basically told me to get lost."

From the credit department's point of view, the concept seemed preposterous. Why would a Canadian company even consider taking over a competitor almost twice its size, particularly one operating in its own backyard with the national government providing all the financial backing the target company needed? How could a deal like that possibly succeed? And what about those expensive helicopters CHC owned or leased—what would happen in a market downturn? The helicopters were an asset now, but when they were sitting on the ground they'd be a serious drag on any profits.

"The credit people weren't making a distinction between large commercial helicopters and military helicopters," Osmak suggests. "It takes years to build and sell those big twenty-passenger craft. There's always a market or a job for them somewhere in the world. They were overexaggerating the situation."

The credit department was also missing the point of Dobbin's strategy in acquiring HSG. By keeping its fees artificially low, HSG was preventing everyone in that sector of the industry from earning a reasonable profit. Once CHC acquired the firm and Norwegian government support was lifted, Dobbin's company could elevate its fees about 20 per cent across the board, bringing the cost of servicing North Sea oil platforms in line with costs elsewhere in the world and injecting profit into everyone's bottom line.

Dobbin did not need this kind of opposition and misunderstanding from his primary funding source. He might have gone elsewhere, to one of the larger banks in the U.S. or Europe, but he clearly preferred dealing with a Canadian bank. He also knew and liked both Godsoe and Osmak, so he refused to end negotiations abruptly.

Godsoe was bound to listen to and rely upon the opinion of those delegated to evaluate risks to the bank, but his instincts extended beyond columns of figures and market projections. "It's true, you back the man," Godsoe explains. "If the people you're dealing with have sufficient integrity, knowledge of their business, and get-up-and-go, they're ten times the value of somebody who says, 'Here I am with my Harvard MBA' and who has all the numbers but lacks the passion, the drive and the understanding to make it work."

With Godsoe's tacit approval, plus the enthusiastic support of Randy Hartlen and others at Scotiabank's Halifax office, Osmak pressed forward, wrenching acceptable terms from the credit department and presenting them to the CHC team of Craig Dobbin, Sylvain Allard and CFO Jo Mark Zurel. "They took the proposal," Osmak notes, "went away to discuss it, and came back saying, 'We can do this and this and this.' Once they fulfilled their first promise, everything else fell into place."

The deal was tentatively approved in early April, with Scotiabank agreeing to underwrite the purchase of the HSG shares, CHC's existing debt and other expenses, to a maximum of Can$600 million. Scotiabank's contract with CHC provided financing in two stages. The first stage, enabling CHC to purchase the necessary number of HSG shares, supplied US$400 million at 7.75 per cent. The second step would cover wraparound financing, absorbing CHC's other outstanding debts.

Godsoe may have gone farther out on the limb to assist Dobbin than expected. One option available to Dobbin had been turning to HSG's Norwegian bankers for financing assistance, but he preferred to deal with familiar domestic sources of money. Steve Hudson's Newcourt Finance remained in the picture by providing Can$100 million in mezzanine financing, conditional on the participating banks supporting the transaction. Everything now rested on the shoulders of Godsoe and Scotiabank.

The deal was achieved with some degree of residual misgiving within and beyond the Scotiabank tower. The CEO of a competing Canadian chartered bank declared that Godsoe had made a serious mistake. Reportedly, even Godsoe had some misgivings. "The way I heard it," Mark Dobbin says with a smile today, "for a long time Scotiabank's loan to CHC was the major reason Peter Godsoe had trouble sleeping at night."

The funding was apparently in place, but Dobbin knew money alone was not going to seal the deal that represented the biggest business achievement of his life. It would also require vision, persuasion, negotiation and, what the hell, a little of that good old Dobbin Irish luck. To ensure the latter element at least, he set off for an extended stay in Oslo.

Norway's ministry of justice had yet to hand down a ruling on the EEA provision question when Dobbin, through the Vinland shell, made a public offer on April 26 to purchase all outstanding shares of HSG at NOK45 (about Can$9) per share. This proved a wise proactive move, conditional as it was on Vinland obtaining at least 90 per cent of HSG shares (including those either owned or controlled by Vinland), the successful completion of a due diligence review of HSG by CHC, and the absence of any effective intervention by government and regulatory authorities. The offer to purchase the shares was opposed by the HSG board, who continued to cite the non-EU ownership rule and believed the offered price was too low.

The non-EU rule appeared insurmountable until the Norwegians realized that Craig Dobbin controlled 60 per cent of CHC through the power of his multiple voting shares. In terms of actual share numbers, he owned substantially less than half the company stock. But those multi-voting shares, the same ones that had infuriated former president and COO Pat Callahan, represented a loophole favouring Dobbin, one not available on a one share/one vote basis.

Two weeks after Dobbin's NOK45 per share offer, the Norwegian government declared that CHC met the necessary nationality criteria and could thus be regarded as an EU-controlled company. This should have banished worries expressed by the HSG board about foreign ownership, but to Craig Dobbin's seething frustration it did not. HSG directors demanded a more definitive ruling, scheduling a meeting six weeks later to review the matter.

Dobbin was not going to sit around chewing on herring while the overly cautious Norwegians waited for bureaucrats to decide the future of CHC. He contracted to purchase 1,421,289 outstanding shares of HSG in the interim. Again, to Dobbin's immense frustration, HSG initially refused to permit the share transfer. If one persuasion doesn't work, Dobbin decided, try another. On June 10 he upped the offer for outstanding HSG stock from NOK45 to NOK60, about Can$12 per share.

The one-third increase in share price seems to have had a remarkable effect on the HSG board's assessment of the deal's legal validity. Less than a week after the new price was announced, the Norwegian directors wrote HSG shareholders to confirm that the offer was valid and to comment that it was up to each HSG shareholder to determine if the price was acceptable, still hedging over the question on EEA ownership rules. It all came together—or appeared to—on June 25 when Vinland/CHC recorded ownership or control of 18,799,654 shares of HSG, representing 91.25 per cent of the company. Craig Dobbin was on the brink of heading the largest helicopter company in the world, subject to the due diligence procedure and the release of Scotiabank funds to pay for the shares.

If Dobbin and the CHC board expected the closing of the deal to fall neatly into place, however, they were mistaken—and, in Craig Dobbin's case at least, infuriated. More than a month later, things remained stalled due to a combination of Norwegian red tape and Canadian caution. Among the requirements set by Scotiabank's credit team was an insistence that the debt-to-EBITDA ratio, according to consolidated statements of HSG and CHC, not exceed 5.4:1. The actual ratio was substantially higher than the bank's limit, and Dobbin was forced to sell $61 million in equipment to OLOG, Bristow's 49 per cent owner, to reduce it.

More problems presented themselves. Dobbin and the rest of the CHC team performing due diligence in Oslo discovered that HSG's EBITDA had been dropping in recent months. Current measurements showed it barely 50 per cent higher than CHC's, even though the Norwegian company was twice the size of the Canadian firm.

"It's a great company with phenomenal potential," Dobbin wrote to CHC directors, "but it will have to be cleaned up. The problem is not revenue but unbelievably excessive fat."

Cutting the fat at HSG remained somewhere in the future. Meanwhile, Scotiabank stayed firm on its 5.4:1 debt ratio. The ratio was dependent upon the interpretation of certain figures; the CHC team insisted it had lowered the ratio below the bank's limit, but the bank's credit team persisted in their argument that the magic 5.4 figure remained exceeded.

The impasse created tension not only in Oslo but also on King Street, at the Scotiabank tower. As Dobbin understood it, the Halifax office of Scotiabank, who would be administering the file, was in agreement with CHC and ready to close the deal, as was the bank's policy committee, led by Godsoe and Bruce Birmingham, Scotiabank president. Concerns regarding the debt to EBITDA ratio were being expressed by functionaries in the bank's credit department, who had rejected the terms twice. Overruled on both occasions by Godsoe, Birmingham and the rest of the policy committee, they continued to object. Godsoe and his team could have slapped down the nervous Nellies in the credit department, but they refrained from doing so; the credit bureaucrats were following corporate guidelines, after all. The people at the top preferred that Dobbin and his team find a way to meet the original demands, using Scotiabank's interpretation.

And there was more. OLOG, unhappy with the loss of business to HSG in the previous six months, was looking for a redraft of the agreement before its purchase of the $61 million in "flying assets" could be finalized. Obstacles to the deal flew in through every open window, and Dobbin, impatient at the best of times, expressed his exasperation in a decidedly uncorporate memo to CHC directors on July 28:

The important people at the bank want this deal to happen. [Scotiabank] Credit is against it but the president, the senior vice-president and the Halifax branch are for it. Right now we are mired in numbers, however we are still enthusiastic that we will get the approval. If the thing is turned down you will see a bunch of pissed-off people here at CHC, ten dead fucking Norwegians, and one credit committee shot with balls of their own shit. Regards, Craig.

Five days later, approval for payment of the HSG shares arrived from Scotiabank. Craig Dobbin and CHC had paid Can$206 million for the outstanding shares of HSG, borrowing the agreed-upon Can$600 million from Scotiabank. The CHC executives and board were pleased, the Norwegians remained alive and healthy, and the bank's credit committee was safe from a barrage of any kind fired by the CHC chairman.

"A year after the deal wrapped up," Borden Osmak says, "the Scotiabank credit department told me I could have anything I wanted for CHC. They had turned from lions into lambs as far as Craig Dobbin was concerned, because he delivered on his promises."

Craig Dobbin now stood atop the world's largest helicopter service company, earning more than a half a billion dollars annually through serving the world's most volatile and important energy industry. He ran it all from a desk in St. John's, Newfoundland.

Perhaps, for the first time in his life, he believed he had nothing left to prove.

13

From its beginnings in the murk of a pond bottom,
the dragonfly instinctively ascends, escapes the bounds
of water and luminously traverses the domain of air,
looking and sounding like a miniaturized Sikorsky helicopter.
When Craig Dobbin's commercial diving equipment
malfunctioned at the bottom of St. John's harbour
there was nowhere to go but up, and up he came...
with a momentum that carried him sky-high.

WILLIAM PRYSE-PHILLIPS, professor emeritus, Memorial University

IN JANUARY 2000 THE world, for the most part, followed the human tendency to look with confidence and optimism towards a new millennium. The previous century was arguably the most violent of any in human history, blemished by wars, upheavals and tragedies. Surely the coming decades promised greater peace and prosperity.

Few people could have watched the clock strike midnight on December 31, 1999, with more satisfaction than Craig Laurence Dobbin. He had survived a death sentence, strengthened his personal life and fortune, and built a corporation boasting more than a billion dollars in total assets and half a billion in annual revenue. To someone unfamiliar with Dobbin and the industry he dominated, the view might not have appeared quite so rosy. Along with those assets and income came a long-term debt to equity ratio of 4.6:1, measurably lower than Scotiabank's upper limit but still excessive in the minds of conservative observers. Balancing this, though, as everyone in the industry knew and Peter Godsoe took comfort in, were intangibles that made the debt less onerous. Chief among them were Craig Dobbin's determination and the top management group he had assembled almost entirely in-house. With few exceptions, Dobbin refused to rely on headhunters or anyone else to assess and select the best people to do the job at CHC. Former pilot Sylvain Allard was acknowledged as the best CEO in his industry and considered outstanding top executive material, whatever the business. Christine Baird, director of global operations dealing with everyone from functionaries in volatile African countries to the United Nations secretary-general, maintained CHC's position as an international pacesetter.

The company's board of directors included people who not only marked substantial achievements in their business and personal lives but were also warm friends of the Chairman. Harry Steele was there, as he had been almost from the beginning, along with former Newfoundland Premier Frank Moores; former Newcourt president Steve Hudson (now president and CEO of Hair Club); Senator George Furey; John Fleming, chairman and CEO of Profco Resources Ltd., a B.C.-based oil and gas exploration firm (now Transatlantic Petroleum Corporation); and Craig C. Dobbin Jr. The board's Irish contingent included John Kelly, from University College, Dublin, and Mike Wadsworth, former Argonaut football player and former Canadian ambassador to Ireland, now director of athletics at Notre Dame University.

The quality of middle managers and pilots up and down the line matched that in the executive suite. Without question, CHC represented the class of its industry. The team Dobbin had assembled were seeing that no crisis was unexpected or incapable of being handled smoothly and successfully. His personal finances continued to be monitored and groomed by the irreproachable Keith Stanford, who estimated Dobbin's personal wealth at $100 million.

Even with all of his success, no one familiar with Craig Dobbin would have expected him to settle in front of the granite fireplace at Beachy Cove, sipping Jameson and immersing himself in his scrapbooks. Between his active involvement in the company and his many fishing excursions, he found time to accept a number of proffered honours.

Being named Atlantic Canada Entrepreneur of the Year in 2000 acknowledged Dobbin's success in business, though the competition, sponsored by accounting giant Ernst & Young, gave the national award to WestJet founder Clive Beddoes and his executive group. Earlier that year, Dobbin had been named Newfoundland's Businessman of the Millennium, adding that honour to his Transportation Person of the Year award for Newfoundland and Canada.

Memorial University granted Dobbin his third honorary doctorate, this one a Silver Doctorate of Laws (*honoris causa*). Dobbin had been a frequent benefactor of the university, his pal and former CHC board member John Crosbie was Memorial's chancellor, and the university's recently appointed president, Dr. Axel Meisen, had become a close friend.

The ceremony, carried out with impressive pomp and circumstance, included an introduction by William Pryse-Phillips, a member of the university's medical faculty. Dr. Pryse-Phillips's words struck a poetic note in describing Dobbin's achievements, one that appeared at odds with the rough-and-tumble nature of the recipient yet captured his essence with considerable accuracy. Pryse-Phillips also mentioned a few of the charitable actions Dobbin had undertaken without fanfare. Among his comments:

As Craig Dobbin has always overcome adversity, today I celebrate his return of so much from his business successes to benefit this province and its people. During years of regular and trusted service, he gave back through Air Atlantic a tithe of seats purchased for Memorial, disseminating the skills of members of our faculties of music and of physical education even into the terra incognita of Central Canada. He was a munificent donor to Memorial's opportunity and anniversary funds, and although his charity began at home, the scholarships that he created for Caribbean students and his support of St. Mary's University and of University College, Dublin, witness his global perspective on the needs of others.

Mr. Chancellor, this determined and forceful man has swash-buckled his way up from harbour bottom through the cadre of those content with the middle ground; has audaciously but honestly circumvented the restrictive yokes imposed upon business by those lacking vision; has beguiled Dublin with its own blarney, so that he is now as Irish as his passport; and has infectiously exulted in the life of the land he loves. This loyal, caring, wily risk-taker is himself one of the foxes of Beachy Cove. Vigorous, visual and venturesome, he has added spice to the space of life as a salmon fisherman, as a friend (indeed, a saviour) of an American president, as a confidant of legislators of multiple persuasions, as a percipient patron of the visual arts, and as a visionary who has put aside time for the view. In his support of Irish studies, Craig Dobbin has cherished the past; in business ventures he adorns the present; in philanthropy he has created for the future.

Dobbin's convocation address to the graduates was character-istic of the speeches made at such ceremonies, laden with references to a future that remained in the hands of his audience. He informed them that they needed two degrees to succeed. One they had just earned through their studies. The other was to be acquired from "the University of Life." The rest of his talk was window dressing for a series of short truisms: Dare to dream. Turn adversity into opportunity. Enjoy yourself. Your life is a blank canvas for you to paint upon.

For all of Craig Dobbin's celebrated *joie de vivre,* his words were delivered in a flat, sometimes stumbling manner. Was he overwhelmed by the honour? Intimidated by the sea of faces whose owners had achieved academic standing beyond his own? Probably neither. One on one, or amid a group of confreres at his fishing camp or in a board meeting, Dobbin could be confident and magnetic. He simply wasn't at his best in front of a crowd, reading a prepared statement. Only at the conclusion of his speech did his words lift themselves above his hesitant tone, their impact heightened by his own brush with death. "Most importantly," he advised, "have fun in life. It's a quick trip."

From 2000 on, Craig Dobbin found many ways to have fun in his life, and several of them involved philanthropy. Already recognized as the Outstanding Individual Philanthropist of the Year by the Canadian Society of Fundraising Executives in 1996, he continued to share his hard-won riches with others, motivated in many instances by Elaine. The couple were named Distinguished Patrons of the Renaissance Ball in support of the National Gallery of Canada Foundation, and through CHC Dobbin donated £200,000 to the Benjamin Franklin Endowment Fund, maintaining a restored house on London's Craven Street that the celebrated American revolutionist and kite-flyer kept as his British *pied-à-terre* from 1757 to 1775. His most heartfelt expressions of charity, especially in the years following his lung transplant, were in response to those in need.

In October 2003, Elaine returned home from lunching with a friend whose adult son was severely autistic. Shaken by her friend's near-total dedication of time and resources to care for the boy, Elaine described the challenge facing parents of autistic children
to Craig over dinner that evening. The incidence of autism in Newfoundland and Labrador is substantially above the national average. Like IPF, autism is generally believed to have a genetic basis, perhaps influenced by environmental conditions, and the higher incidence of the malady in Newfoundland and Labrador is beyond curious to those exploring the ailment's cause and treatment.

Looking more deeply into autism in the weeks that followed, Elaine learned many of her assumptions about the ailment were wrong, like those of most Canadians not directly affected by it. Autism, she discovered, is neither a mental disorder nor a form of mental retardation, and it is clearly not a childhood disease; autistic children become autistic adults. The prognosis for treatment was and remains rather bleak, but the idea of writing off those afflicted with it, and ignoring the needs of parents who bear the brunt of caring for their autistic children, was too much for Elaine to accept. She wanted to help those with autism grow as attuned to their world as possible, at all periods of their lives, and she turned to her husband for assistance. With her persistence and Craig's largesse, the Elaine Dobbin Centre for Autism opened in the summer of 2006 on land owned by Memorial University, which leases it to the centre for an annual rent of one dollar. The centre, which had set a goal of $1.5 million for capital costs, exceeded this amount by $400,000, thanks to various contributions, including one of more than a half-million dollars from Craig Dobbin.

Proud as she was of the autism centre, Elaine Dobbin believed her husband should leave more behind to mark both his achievements and his love for Newfoundland and Labrador. In a conversation with Memorial University president Axel Meisen, they discussed the prospect of funding a research centre at the university. Planning for the facility had already begun, and the provincial government was talking about investing $50 million of the estimated $75-million cost. If the Dobbins were to add perhaps $20 million to the province's bounty, payable over four or five years, it would easily justify attaching Craig Dobbin's name to the centre. "Craig loved the idea," Elaine explains, "but he wasn't keen about having his name on the building." Both Elaine and Axel Meisen pressed him on the project. With some reluctance, he agreed that they could settle the question when planning was far enough along.

It is relatively easy to find high-profile examples of Craig Dobbin's charity, but many other such acts went unheralded, if not unappreciated. "Some people described Dad as generous to a fault," Mark Dobbin muses in his Harvey Road office. Through the massive windows behind him, downtown St. John's shines in the sun, with the harbour and the Narrows opening into a splendid vista of the North Atlantic. Generous his father might have been, Mark continues, but foolish he wasn't. "He was no soft touch. Often those who asked did not get. It was those whose need Dad recognized; they're the ones he would move forward on."

CHC WAS NOW a global operation with several thousand employees and extensive facilities in countries on every continent. Craig Dobbin's hard-headed business dealings had powered the firm's successful expansion program, and he continued to watch the earning and expense figures carefully. From time to time, however, he saw the company in the same light he had years earlier, when he realized that the helicopters capable of delivering him and his fishing buddies into and out of some of the most remote regions in Canada had more practical applications.

From 2000 onward, CHC sought and won contracts beyond those associated with petroleum production, though its corporate slogan remained "Moving the industry that moves the world." Some activities involved pilot training for governments and corporations, using the firm's complex flight simulators. The majority of the new contracts dealt with search and rescue services, and the governments of Norway, the U.K., Netherlands, Ireland and Australia still retain CHC in this capacity. If a ship flounders off Galway Bay or the coast of Tasmania, CHC rescue technicians, not the Irish or Australian coast guard or military, are called to hoist passengers and crew to safety and to provide necessary medical care.

Search-and-rescue services have generated multiple tales of heroics among CHC staff around the world, lending a *Mission Impossible* aura to the teams assigned to this duty. In February 2002, a CHC crew member descended a cable suspended from one of the company's Sikorsky s-61 craft ten times in the middle of the night, returning each time with a shivering and near-dead Spanish fisherman. The Spaniards' fishing trawler had been dashed against rocks near Dingle during an Atlantic storm, and the wind and rough seas made rescue by ship out of the question. During the operation, completed in near-total darkness, the forty-nine-year-old CHC crew member was blown into the water twice but managed to remain attached to his rescue line and hoist the fishermen aboard the hovering craft. To local residents it was a rescue unmatched in scope and danger. To CHC staff, it was a mission they had been trained and equipped to perform.

In Australia, CHC averages 300 missions annually over the Great Barrier Reef lining the country's east coast, one-third of them at night and many involving a winch to lift passengers, crew members or vital material from ships a hundred nautical miles or more from the coast. This is far different from the basic transportation services provided to offshore oil rigs, but the company achieves both with almost routine success.

Many CHC services are also performed as charitable acts. When the coast of Southeast Asia was devastated by the horrific tsunami of December 26, 2004, CHC dispatched craft and crews to southern Thailand where they remained for a week, bringing in supplies and medical assistance and bringing out stranded survivors. CHC has conducted humanitarian flights in Bosnia, East Timor, Somalia, Angola, Mozambique, Cambodia, Burundi, Haiti and elsewhere. When a large ore carrier sank near Dassen Island off the coast of South Africa, the resulting oil spill threatened disaster for an estimated 14,000 penguins on the island. In response, CHC sent a Sikorsky s-61 to carry the penguins off the island to safety, each flight ferrying 600 of the somewhat confused birds who, being penguins, had never experienced flight before.

In early 2003, United Nations weapons inspectors flew on CHC helicopters piloted by CHC crews as they scoured Iraq in search of claimed weapons of mass destruction, completing their missions shortly before the U.S.-led invasion of the country and the toppling of Saddam Hussein. Other exploits are the stuff of adventure novels. When a group of explorers found themselves stranded 600 kilometres from the North Pole, it was a CHC helicopter that flew through buffeting winds to locate them and carry them south to shelter. The Australian government even contracted CHC to dispatch helicopters and crews to track a pirate fishing vessel through South Pacific waters for twenty-one days. It's easy to imagine Craig Dobbin wishing he were in the jump seat of one of his craft for several of these adventures, hovering over an exotic location or swooping down on a white-knuckled rescue mission.

Dobbin never forgot the fun aspect of helicopters. His use of them to ferry himself, family, friends and business associates on fishing excursions or "just for the hell of it" flights continued, despite the cost to CHC and the concerns expressed by shareholders and analysts. Many trips were made with audacity and style, such as the time he and Elaine decided to return from the Dobbin home in Florida to Newfoundland by helicopter instead of private jet. The journey was completed in skips and jumps over several days, and, with luggage and golf clubs aboard, Dobbin would often direct the pilot to skim over an interesting-looking golf course. If the course appeared intriguing and the weather was good, he called the club for permission to land in an appropriate open area and play a round. The boldness of the request usually produced assent, and after their nine- or eighteen-hole game, preceded or followed by lunch and drinks in the clubhouse, he and Elaine would board the helicopter, lift off and resume heading north towards home.

CRAIG DOBBIN'S POST-TRANSPLANT years did not leave him entirely dedicated to surveying the brighter side of life. The security of his established and well-managed company, and his constant awareness of life's limits, impelled him to speak out on issues that disturbed him. Hardly cautious when it came to expressing his views in the past, he began delivering them in salvoes of colourful condemnation, especially when the issue was the status of Newfoundland in Confederation.

Despite the discovery of enormous reserves of nickel at Voisey's Bay in Labrador and substantial oil production from Hibernia and other offshore oil fields, Newfoundland and Labrador was still considered a region whose population was driven more by the opportunity to draw unemployment cheques than by the desire to pull their own weight. Efforts to shift employment opportunities to the province, such as Premier Brian Tobin's insistence that Voisey's Bay nickel ore be processed in Newfoundland instead of being shipped to Inco's mill in Ontario, produced animosity rather than understanding among many in Central Canada. In Toronto, financier Seymour Shulich was outraged, suggesting that Prime Minister Jean Chrétien should "pull Tobin's chain" and make him heel. Ontario Premier Mike Harris expressed shock at the very idea of the province claiming the right to process its own resources, and financial columnist Diane Francis preached that "nobody and no corporation owes Newfoundland . . . a living!"

To Craig Dobbin it sounded like the same grumbling in Central Canada about the family's poor relations getting uppity, and it riled him.

"If we're such a drain, such a sinkhole," he bellowed at an October 2000 meeting of the St. John's Board of Trade, "then let us go. Cut us loose, baby. We'll manage our own resources and do what leading economies like Ireland are doing."

Some of his impromptu speech sounded as though it had been crafted by disciples of René Lévesque and Jacques Parizeau rather than by a man who claimed his proudest moment in life was the day the governor general pinned the Order of Canada on his lapel. Dobbin noted that Newfoundland and Labrador sent only seven out of more than 300 MPs to Ottawa, making it easy for the rest of Canada to take Newfoundland's natural resources at any price it pleased. Not one Newfoundlander had ever been appointed to the

Supreme Court of Canada, he pointed out. "The question, my fellow Newfoundlanders," he proposed at the Board of Trade session, "is not 'Who got the most out of Confederation?' It's 'How do we get *into* Confederation?' We're not a have-not province. We are a very rich province. It's just been taken away from us."

Dobbin's words were not empty rhetoric. Newfoundland and Labrador remained beset with a chronic 18 per cent unemployment rate, and the federal government's clawback of 85 per cent of its oil royalties, Dobbin claimed, ensured that the province "will never, ever get out of the hole." The federal government, he suggested, should cancel the royalty clawback ("It gives Canada total power over Newfoundland"); expand the Atlantic Canada Opportunities Agency (ACOA), the equivalent of Ireland's Industrial Development Agency, which had created 100,000 jobs in the republic over nine years; and cancel the federal income tax paid by the province's citizens until Newfoundland and Labrador had created an economy that yielded sufficient long-term permanent jobs.

In March 2003, with two provincial cabinet ministers seated beside him at the head table, Dobbin once again set the cat among the pigeons. His luncheon speech to the Newfoundland Ocean Industries Association blamed the province's "mediocre" politicians for failing to recognize the problems that continued to plague Newfoundland and Labrador. Attacking the government for mishandling everything from the Churchill Falls power project to Voisey's Bay, he roused the crowd to a standing ovation, and the politicians to red-faced apoplexy, with statements such as the following:

This province and the oil companies that work here pump more than 100 million barrels of oil worth more than $3 billion into the economy. Into which economy? Let's check the facts. Ottawa will collect an estimated $550 million in income and other taxes [from Newfoundland and Labrador] this year. Equalization clawbacks will bring another $70 million for the feds. The oil companies, which break even at about $13 a barrel on Hibernia, should make $1.2 billion this year in profit... After clawbacks, this province will earn approximately $30 million in royalties. What a deal we made there! $30 million on the sale of $3 billion worth of oil... Just to put that $30 million in perspective, we make $84 million on video gambling and $50 million on licensing our cars!

We brought a tax base [into Confederation] that yields $1 billion a year in personal income tax for Ottawa. Corporate income tax sends another $500 million to Ottawa. And they give us back $1.1 billion in equalization. We're out $400 million on the deal.

At the university level, only half of the [graduating] class of 2000 were found to still be in Newfoundland. Our youth are gone. It is a tragedy, a shame, a disgrace, that our youth cannot find jobs in their homeland.

I've heard a lot of things about the terms of union over the past few years. I've heard politicians talk at great length about the equalization formula. And sadly, what I've heard more often than not is "the terms of the union can't be rewritten," and "Ottawa will never change equalization." Well, let me tell you, "can't be done" is the rally cry of the meek!

It was classic Craig Dobbin, pulling out all the stops without regard for protocol, etiquette or decorum.

Provincial mines and energy minister Walter Noel, who sat uncomfortably absorbing Dobbin's words at the luncheon, complained later that the comments were offensive to him and to his party. "He comes here and makes a speech like that once a year or so," Noel grumbled to a reporter from the St. John's *Telegram* following Dobbin's presentation, "and we hear nothing from him in between," adding, "You would think he doesn't know what's going on in this province."

For everyone in the audience who heard Dobbin's unchallenged statistics, the people who didn't know what was going on in Newfoundland and Labrador did not include Craig Dobbin. They did include, it appeared, the two elected government members who squirmed through his litany of charges and concerns.

Dobbin's speech continued to resonate. A year after its delivery, a St. John's newspaper reprinted it with the editor's observation that it was "one of the most succinct and passionate statements ever made describing Newfoundland's position in Canadian confederation, and emits a pride that we all should carry . . . One has to ask if anything has changed to make Mr. Dobbin's words any less appropriate."

14

His employees and suppliers respected him so much that they
wanted to see him succeed. And there was always a cost to this. There
was a cost to his employees because they might work longer than they
planned to on some days. And there was a cost to me because maybe
I didn't get the fee I wanted. But people would pay it, they would
go beyond the call of duty for him. It was amazing.

GUY SAVARD, chairman, Merrill Lynch Canada

FROM 2000, CRAIG DOBBIN'S freedom to speak out and to pursue as much happiness as life made available to him was due in part to the smooth functioning of CHC under the aegis of Sylvain Allard, Christine Baird and later CFO Rick Davis, plus the attention paid to Dobbin's personal finances by the shrewd Keith Stanford.

The emergence of CHC into a global entity required attention to subsidiary corporations located in the U.S.A., the U.K., Norway, Denmark, Barbados, Thailand and elsewhere, a conglomerate of almost two dozen firms linked to CHC Helicopter Corporation, with the Chairman's shares held by his Discovery Helicopter Limited.

Much of 2000 was spent consolidating CHC's position. The acquisition of HSG and other purchases over the years had saddled CHC with subsidiaries that were at odds with Dobbin's new focus on core services. Their sale enabled CHC to concentrate on petroleum contracts and search-and-rescue operations, as well as generating cash to reduce the company's debt position. From January to June 2000 CHC sold helicopter companies in Spain (Helicopteros SA—$6.8 million), Norway (Airlift AS and Luftransport AS—$14.7 million), U.K.

217

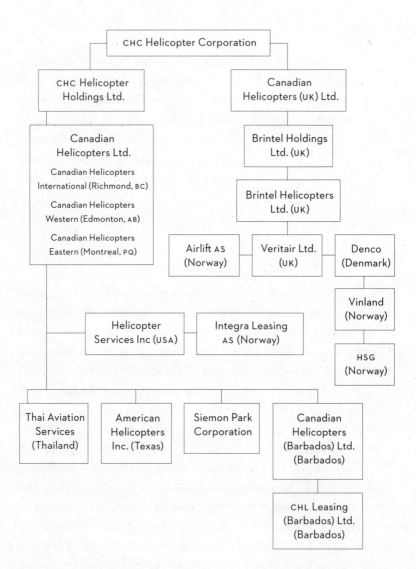

SOURCE: CHC Helicopters Ltd./U.K. Competition Commission

(Brintel scheduled passenger service, Penzance; ministry of defence services in Plymouth and the Falklands; civil police support in Cardiff, Wales—$74.3 million) and Sweden (Heliflyg AB—$6 million).

The opportunities to grow CHC were becoming limited, especially in the petroleum industry. The only offshore production basin in the world without a CHC presence was the Gulf of Mexico within U.S. jurisdiction. Like the EU, U.S. law prohibits foreign control of its aviation operations, presenting a barrier similar to the one CHC had faced in the North Sea. Few doubted that Craig Dobbin would be able to sidestep this provision in a manner similar to the one he employed to acquire Brintel and HSG, but he made no serious efforts to do so.

His reluctance to enter the U.S./Gulf of Mexico market was based, according to Dobbin, on the nature of the business in that region. Most of the locations were compact enough and sufficiently close to shore that single-engine light helicopters could meet all the demands, rather than the medium and heavy Sikorsky and Aerospatiale craft that comprised the CHC fleet. Except for executive transport, Dobbin disliked small helicopters, which carried fewer passengers and less payload and earned less money on each flight. The Gulf, Dobbin noted in an interview with *New Technology Magazine*, was also very volatile, with pricing and earnings rising and falling dramatically and often inexplicably. Still, he admitted, "If a good acquisition came along there, we'd snap it up in a New York second."

The reference to New York came rather naturally. On a cold, rainy day in October 2002 CHC Helicopters celebrated its new listing on the NYSE, moving to the big board from the smaller and less prestigious NASDAQ exchange. The day marked an extraordinary milestone for Dobbin and the company he had launched almost on a whim, a firm that retained its head office operations in St. John's, Newfoundland. From that day forward, CHC shares would be traded alongside the biggest international companies in the world, including CHC customers such as BP, Shell, Norsk Hydro, Statoil, Talisman Energy, Elf and others.

Such an achievement could not go unmarked. Dobbin took his entire CHC executive team to New York for the occasion, along with their spouses and several of his grandchildren, and his ringing of the bell to launch the day's trading—which, coincidentally, marked one of the big board's most impressive rallies in months—was carried on news and business media channels across the world.

To ensure maximum attention to the event, Dobbin had a CHC EC 225 TwinStar helicopter flown to New York City and parked in front of the NYSE, regretting the fact that all of the firm's more impressive Super Pumas were busy elsewhere. Logistics restricted the firm to a static display of the smaller, though still impressive, EC 225. Barely a year had passed since the horrific attacks on the World Trade Center, and no craft was permitted to fly directly over that sector of the city. Still, the sight of the red, white and blue craft in front of the NYSE generated considerable publicity and discussion among the country's leading investment houses.

With celebrations completed and the helicopter, executives and guests returned to their places, Dobbin characteristically warned CHC staff against the danger of complacency. Being listed on the NYSE represented a major step forward and was a source of deserved pride. The challenges, however, were greater than ever, with competitors determined to knock the leader from its perch. The company, Dobbin stressed, must expand into new markets when and where it could, and continue to strengthen its position in existing markets.

Without mentioning it, he was also aware that the company's
position on the NYSE made it more susceptible to the impact of U.S. securities laws, especially those relating to governance. The governance issue had been raised earlier in 2002 by the powerful Ontario Teachers Pension Plan, which maintained a substantial holding of CHC stock in its portfolio.

The pension plan's administrators, among others, were annoyed by CHC's proposal to implement a stock option agreement that investors believed was overly generous. The proposed option plan threatened to dilute the subordinate voting shares by 19 per cent if fully exercised, which was a likely event because the exercise price was below the current stock price, guaranteeing certain profit. Passage of the proposal would have been assured by the CHC chairman's control of 60 per cent of corporate votes, and by the fact that he could lay claim to the largest portion of options. The investor protests won out; CFO Jo Mark Zurel announced an increase in the exercise price, removing the ensured profit. He promised that CHC had "learned a lesson" and that all such actions in the future would be open and transparent.

A more significant development that year drew the attention of Craig Dobbin, everyone on the executive team, and especially the firm's board of directors. The enactment of the Sarbanes-Oxley Act marked the establishment of much higher governance standards than had been previously set for public corporations in the U.S. Officially known as the Public Company Accounting Reform and Investor Protection Act of 2002, Sarbanes-Oxley was a legislative response to a series of securities and accounting scandals that had rocked the U.S. over the previous two years. Enron, Tyco International, Adelphia, Peregrine Systems, WorldCom and other publicly traded firms had suffered enormous shareholder losses, leading to total collapse in some cases, and much of the blame was attributed to unacceptable levels of corporate governance.

Under the rules established by SOX, boards of directors were charged with installing oversight mechanisms for financial reporting in U.S. corporations on the behalf of investors. Making directors both more independent in their decision making and more responsible for their actions (or, in various instances, their inaction) represented a major objective of SOX. The rules were clear: cronyism between top executives and board members would not be tolerated.

Directors must be chosen on the basis of their decision-making ability and their confidence to speak and act in the interests of public shareholders, not in response to the wishes and dictates of top executives.

sox had not been framed with CHC in its sights, but it might have been. From the company's inception, Craig Dobbin had filled many seats on the CHC board with good friends, many of them familiar faces aboard the helicopters scurrying between St. John's and his fishing camps in Labrador and Newfoundland. The qualifications of these individuals to sit as CHC directors were, for the most part, more than acceptable. Few would question the business management abilities of Harry Steele, Robert Foster, David Sobey, Steve Hudson or a dozen others who gathered four times a year to hear assessments of the company's performance delivered by Craig L. Dobbin before voting on measures proposed by the same Craig L. Dobbin.

From 1995 to 2003, either Mark Dobbin or Craig Dobbin Jr. joined their father at CHC board meetings, voting on his proposals; in 2002 and 2003 both were in attendance. In 1995, the year he relinquished his post as Canadian ambassador to Ireland, Mike Wadsworth joined the board, remaining until illness forced his withdrawal in 2003. Frank Moores, former provincial premier and hellraising accomplice to Craig Dobbin for many years, was also a director.

Sarbanes-Oxley changed all of that. Harry Steele, a board member since 1990, was the first to press Dobbin to clean house, or at least the CHC boardroom. Dobbin agreed, and when the 2004 CHC board of directors was announced only Craig Dobbin Jr. and John Kelly remained from the previous group. The rest of the board members were new and exemplary: George Gillett Jr., chairman of Booth Creek Management Corporation; Jack Mintz, president and CEO of the C. D. Howe Institute; Sir Bob Reid, former chair and CEO of Shell UK and of the British Railways Board; and William Stinson, former chair and CEO of Canadian Pacific Ltd. and a brother-in-law to Craig Dobbin via his recent marriage to Dobbin's sister Margo.

Later Dobbin added Don Carty, former chair and CEO of American Airlines, and Guylaine Saucier, chair of the Joint Corporate Governance Committee sponsored by the Toronto Stock Exchange, the Canadian Institute of Chartered Accountants (CICA) and the Canadian Venture Exchange.

This was and remains an all-star board, especially with the addition of CHC president and CEO Sylvain Allard in 2005. Everyone within and outside of the company was pleased with the board's reconstruction, with the exception of Frank Moores. Suffering from the liver cancer that would take his life, Moores was crushed by Dobbin's decision to drop him as a CHC director, a role he had played since 1995. Moores had introduced Craig Dobbin to helicopters, had assisted him in the building of CHC through more means than would ever likely be acknowledged, and counted himself among Dobbin's closest friends and associates. He knew of Sarbanes-Oxley and the need to keep the NYSE-listed CHC board lily-white. Still, his sudden removal from the board rankled him. His feelings failed to destroy their friendship, however, and Dobbin deeply mourned Moore's death in July 2005.

RUDY PALLADINA HAD argued that spinning Vector Aerospace from CHC and launching it as an independent public company would be a mistake. The maintenance and repair division represented a valid profit centre for the corporation, Palladina maintained, and CHC would gain little if anything from the move.

Dobbin's decision was initially proven correct. Cash generated by the Vector IPO enabled him to bid for Norway's HSG and achieve industry leadership, and it provided an opportunity to hand control of an independent company to his son Mark, who had been floating in his father's shadow since obtaining his MBA. Mark, acknowledged as the most ambitious and business-oriented of the five Dobbin offspring, would steer his own ship at Vector. Craig Dobbin expected the addition of seasoned veterans Maxwell Parsons and

Paul Conway to the management team would bring experience and stability. The key decision maker, however, remained Mark.

Among other qualities Mark Dobbin appeared to have inherited from his father was a propensity to expand the company he was managing. Determined to position Vector as a dominant player in the MRO (Maintenance, Repair and Overhaul) industry, he believed Vector needed aggressive expansion to counter a growing trend among original equipment manufacturers to provide aftermarket services.

Soon after the IPO was completed in 1998, Vector had purchased Helipro, a Vancouver-based MRO, for $39 million and folded it into ACRO as a rotorcraft structures specialist. Vector also launched Pathix to distribute software programs used to manage the operation, repair and overhaul of commercial aircraft. In June 1999, Vector purchased Advanced Turbine Technologies and Tower Aviation Services, two Oakland, California-based firms. Advanced Turbine specialized in repairing and overhauling aircraft auxiliary power units. Tower added instrumentation overhaul and repair, effectively expanding Vector's range of services. The two related U.S. firms had recently filed for Chapter 11 bankruptcy protection. Vector financed the $10-million purchase price.

For its 2001 fiscal year, Vector recorded a loss of $13.5 million on total revenue of $347 million. The loss, Vector explained to shareholders, was a direct result of the aftershocks of September 11, 2001. The following year revenue slipped to $317.5 million, creating a net loss of $11.4 million. According to Vector, the company had suffered a major blow when the Royal Saudi Air Force failed to renew its contract with Sigma Aerospace in the U.K. The RSAF represented 40 per cent of revenue for Vector's fixed-wing divisions (Sigma and Atlantic Turbines), and in May 2003 Mark Dobbin announced plans to sell those divisions and concentrate on the global helicopter market, where Vector maintained a leading market position. Other events, however, took over.

Instead of negotiating the sale of Sigma and Atlantic, Mark Dobbin found himself battling a hostile takeover of Vector led by a pair of determined foes. One, Donald V. Jackson, was chairman of Ontario-based Northstar Aerospace, a direct competitor of Vector in the MRO market. Jackson was soon joined by Ken Rowe, who had purchased Air Atlantic from Mark's father five years earlier through Rowe's IMP firm.

Mark Dobbin's public comment on Rowe is politely limited to "He is not well liked in the aerospace business." Rowe plays no favourites when it comes to either industries or geography. He is a major shareholder in Royal Bank of Canada and has sat on its prestigious board since 1985. After the failure of Air Atlantic (an event that quietly delighted Craig Dobbin, who did not care for Rowe or admire him as a businessman), Rowe launched CanJet as a discount airline, a venture he killed in 2006. Rowe's investments have ranged from rubber boot makers to surgical supply manufacturers, among other endeavours, and he is considered a frugal hands-on manager.

In May 2003, Jackson and Rowe failed to win a proxy fight to replace the management team of Dobbin, Parsons and Conway at the Vector annual meeting. At the time, Vector share prices were hovering in the $2.00 to $2.50 range. At some point in the process, the three top Vector executives instituted a corporate clause that would award them, in the event of a hostile takeover, a total of $35 million in severance payments (labelled "forbearance agreements"), a move that outraged Jackson and Rowe. Through 2003 the two men maintained their attack on Mark Dobbin, eventually succeeding in forcing him and the two former CHC executives out of Vector and vowing to dispute their claim to the $35-million settlement. (In April 2007, Vector announced that its new management and Mark Dobbin had agreed on a payment of $5.2 million to its former chairman; Conway and Parsons continued to seek payment for themselves.) Vector, born of two successful divisions of CHC, was now not only out of the CHC orbit but in the hands of a tough competitor.

Would the Vector experience have unfolded as it did with Craig Dobbin rather than son Mark in the Chairman's office? The senior Dobbin provided Mark with advice on strategy and tactics during the process, and no one has questioned the abilities of Mark Dobbin when it comes to making business decisions. Perhaps the point is not the difference between Craig Dobbin and his son but the similarity between the senior Dobbin and Ken Rowe. Both were entrepreneurs at heart, men prepared to engage in hardscrabble tactics whenever necessary to win the day, not to mention the prize. Mark Dobbin boasted substantial intelligence, low-key charm, an MBA and years of experience gained from working alongside his father. But he had never hidden aircraft from a lessor bent on their seizure, never played hardball with a creditor demanding millions in overdue payments, and never sold one half-completed house to obtain the money that would finance two new houses, building his assets like a racetrack tout parlaying his winnings.

IN 2004, CRAIG DOBBIN liquidated all of his real estate holdings, selling them to Northern Property, an Alberta-based firm, for $35 million. In the past, he would have spent the money on a new venture, repeating his tradition of pushing all of his chips into the centre of the table and awaiting the deal. Not this time. This time he had Keith Stanford hand the money to a Montreal investment company to manage for him. Dobbin appeared for the first time to acknowledge the transience of life. There would be no more fish farms or Norwegian technical services; ideas born at four in the morning were destined to fade in the hard light of reality.

The exception was his partnership with brother Derm in the St. John's Fog Devils, a semi-pro hockey team saddled with the challenge of playing all of its away games on the Canadian mainland. Travel and accommodation costs almost ensured the Fog Devils would struggle financially. The brothers didn't care. They revelled in the joint venture, two Newfoundland boys whose business successes allowed them to enjoy their wealth any damn way they pleased. The $2-million investment was peanuts to Craig Dobbin and it was fun, something to share with his brother and a means of adding to the pleasure of being a Newfoundlander.

Dobbin had another interest as well. Sometime earlier, he and Elaine had chosen an oceanfront building lot in Reddington Beach on Florida's gulf coast. They wanted a larger, more elaborate winter retreat than their condominium near St. Petersburg, and Elaine took charge, working with architects and designers to create a southern showplace. Beachy Cove is spectacular in a brute force manner, an expansive expression of money and power. Reddington Beach is more elegant and refined. Its Spanish colonial–inspired exterior provides only a hint of its interior luxury and comfort. The master bedroom opens to an extended balcony overlooking the Gulf of Mexico. The garden and swimming pool are flanked by sculptures and landscape features, and the estate is appealing enough to draw curious beach walkers up to the home, where they peer through doors and windows in curiosity and envy. For Craig Dobbin, perhaps the most pleasing feature was his Florida office, equipped with video conferencing equipment to keep him in touch with CHC locations around the world.

Less than 3 per cent of CHC's revenue was now being earned from Canadian sources. The balance came from more than thirty foreign countries and the efforts of 3,400 employees in CHC facilities around the world, a development that made Craig Dobbin more grateful than ever for the talents of Christine Baird, director of global operations. As proficient as Baird might be, however, Craig Dobbin knew the importance of visiting CHC facilities, making connections with deal-makers in each locale. After his lung transplant he and Elaine made several globe-circling tours in the firm's corporate jet.

Most of these visits went smoothly, often marked by formal receptions hosted by high-level government officials. Those who greeted them were not entirely cordial, however. Landing in Ghana late one night, the couple and their aircrew were brusquely hustled into a darkened room while military authorities inspected their baggage. The attitude of the soldiers distressed Elaine, but not nearly as much as their scrutiny of the couple's personal belongings. Needing a mass of medications daily, Craig Dobbin travelled with a miniature pharmacy of tablets, capsules and other drugs. Elaine grew convinced that they would be charged with drug trafficking, a fear compounded by the couple spending more than an hour in what the Ghanaians claimed was security but felt to the Dobbins like detention. Eventually they were released without charges being laid, and they avoided Ghana on future trips.

One reason for Dobbin's visit to Africa had been an assessment of the need for CHC services in petroleum-producing countries on that continent, particularly Nigeria, Chad and Cameroon. CHC had little presence in those countries, and in late 2003 the company purchased Schreiner Aviation Group, a Netherlands firm with several contracts in the region. The $140-million acquisition added fifty helicopters to CHC's fleet and ensured its dominance in Africa.

DOBBIN'S FORMATION OF CHC from various companies created remarkable growth, but it produced something of a mishmash in terms of organization. HSG in Norway continued to retain its identity under the Vinland umbrella, which in turn reported through Denco in Denmark to Brintel out of Aberdeen, Scotland. Another Norwegian arm, Airlift AS, and Veritair Ltd. in the U.K. were also linked to Brintel. Operations in Australia, Thailand, Texas, Barbados and Africa maintained their individual identities as well. In addition, CHC offices in Richmond, B.C., where Christine Baird had located in 1998 to run the global division, expanded enormously when Sylvain Allard and his staff joined her in a massive new building there. The decentralized setup created confusion within CHC and among its clients. "We were reaching the point where we were stepping on each other's toes," Candace Moakler explains. "At times, one or two divisions would be making pitches against another division for the same job. Clients began asking just who CHC was. Something had to be done."

In search of a solution, CHC retained a group of Norwegian management consultants, who recommended that the company consolidate all divisions as CHC and bring the head office and operations people together in one location. Instituting these moves, the report concluded, could save the firm as much as $200 million. Presented to the board of directors of a publicly traded company, the proposition could not be ignored.

The most contentious issue was the location of the new head office. Three alternatives presented themselves: Aberdeen, Scotland; St. John's, Newfoundland; and Richmond, B.C. Aberdeen, while it harboured a substantial number of people and aircraft in a newly constructed facility, was soon discounted. CHC was a Canadian company owned primarily by Canadians, Craig Dobbin insisted. It must remain in Canada.

When CHC first attracted national and international attention, much had been made of the St. John's location of its head office. Why there, of all places? Why not? was Dobbin's usual reply. No one loved Newfoundland and Labrador more than he did, and no one more fervently wanted people to see what Newfoundlanders could do when they took on the world. "I'll never move this company," Craig Dobbin stated repeatedly, and few who heard him speak those words doubted his promise.

The benefits of moving to British Columbia, however, were now too compelling. In 2004, CHC's Richmond facility employed 350 people, about ten times as many as the office in St. John's. As painful as it might have been to admit, Dobbin knew it was easy to attract employees to B.C. Vancouver was being touted as one of the world's great cities. St. John's had more than its share of charm, but it lacked the international cachet of the west-coast location. Besides, the Richmond office, repair and storage facilities were new and efficient. Could the cost of abandoning them and building a similar structure in St. John's be justified if the company consolidated in Newfoundland? It could not.

On June 30, 2004, a reluctant and somewhat embarrassed Craig Dobbin announced that the headquarters of CHC would be transferred to Richmond, B.C. Aberdeen, Scotland, would become the site of a second division, CHC European Operations, and a new division, Heli-One, would be established, also in Richmond. Serving as CHC's leasing, repair and overhaul support group, Heli-One would occupy separate quarters near the head office.

Craig Dobbin would maintain a small office in St. John's with minimal staff. Most employees in St. John's, he proposed, would be offered similar positions in British Columbia. Few accepted. In St. John's CHC had been a wonderful employer, a vibrant company that did interesting work, paid excellent salaries and benefits, and maintained a warm, family-style atmosphere. No one wanted it to change. "On some Friday afternoons," Candace Moakler recalls, "Mr. Dobbin would send an e-mail out to everybody saying, 'Shut 'er down and let's go fishing!' It drove people like Sylvain mad, but most would laugh and remind themselves how much they liked working there."

Other companies based in Atlantic Canada have encountered pressure to relocate their head offices, usually to central Canada. Among them is the grocery chain Sobey's, whose head office location in Stellarton, Nova Scotia, has made it difficult in some instances to attract senior management. The Sobey family adamantly refuses to move the office, even to Halifax, not because of disagreement with the practicalities of the idea but because such a move would contradict their corporate culture. Sobey's, whose shares are publicly traded, remains a family-dominated corporation with deep roots in Stellarton. Any benefits of operating in Montreal, Toronto or Vancouver, David Sobey has said, would be countered by the myriad distractions of the cities, a perception supported by a story widely circulated among Toronto's Bay Street financiers.

According to the tale, a man was recruited from a small city to fill a top-level executive position at the Toronto head office of one of the Big Five chartered banks. The candidate announced he would accept the offer only if it were written into his contract that he did not have to attend any afterhours social occasions hosted by the bank for its major clients or senior executives. Spending time with his family in their home was more important to him than schmoozing with stuffy, predatory business executives at some boring banquet. If he were expected to be present at these social events, he insisted, he would prefer to stay where he was, midway up the corporate ladder instead of perched near the top. The man got his wish.

Jo Mark Zurel, CHC's CFO, initially travelled to British Columbia, but after some time in Richmond chose to return to Newfoundland. His highly regarded replacement, Rick Davis, proved another example of Craig Dobbin's knack for spotting exceptional talent and encouraging the individual to grow and develop within the organization. Davis, brought into the CHC fold through Vector, was moved to CHC and assigned to establish and implement moves that would bring the company into compliance with Sarbanes-Oxley.

Many in CHC believe the company's corporate culture vanished with the move west. In St. John's, CHC reflected the character of Craig Dobbin, creating a unique corporate history and persona. It was "that amazing helicopter business run out of Newfoundland by that wild, shoot-the-dice Irishman." In British Columbia Dobbin was a name, not a legend, another dark-suited chairman of the board. Few in and around Vancouver knew his background, nor cared. Fewer still felt the deep-rooted loyalty to the firm that St. John's workers did. Jobs like those offered by CHC are scarce in Newfoundland; in Vancouver they are plentiful. As a result, west-coast workers are transient, more committed to their individual fortunes than to those of the company employing them.

Business leaders understood and approved Dobbin's decision to relocate CHC. So did newly elected Newfoundland and Labrador Premier Danny Williams. Sorry to see the company and the jobs leave the island, Williams was enough of a businessman to appreciate the wisdom of the decision. Other premiers before him, notably Clyde Wells and Brian Peckford, might have railed and gnashed their teeth at the decision. Williams shrugged and wished Dobbin good luck.

Like Williams, Dobbin could not argue against the astuteness of the move. His primary concern was embarrassment at contradicting his promise. He would adjust, of course. But it was difficult, supremely difficult. The four-and-a-half-hour time difference between Vancouver and St. John's had been a small problem in the past. After the move of the head office to B.C., it became a nagging irritation. Always an early riser, Dobbin would try to be patient while waiting for early afternoon to arrive on the Avalon Peninsula before he could speak to anyone at head office in Richmond. He felt the same distancing at the couple's winter home in Florida, the same fear that he had lost control of the company.

When Sylvain Allard and his wife, Robyn, moved to B.C., Craig Dobbin secretly purchased their ranch home in Portugal Cove. Situated on an inland pond and nestled among trees at the foot of a hill, the home had always appealed to Elaine. It may have lacked the drama of Beachy Cove, but it exuded a warmth and coziness that their oceanside mansion could not match. Craig Dobbin presented Elaine with the key to the new house concealed in a small silver jewel box, a surprise gift, and she was delighted. It would be her home, they agreed, after Craig was gone.

In Florida, Dobbin purchased something of a toy to assuage his concern about the corporate move to B.C.: a new Rolls-Royce saloon, in an unusual dark-brown metallic colour, perfect for cruising up and down the Gulf Coast. "I would never take this to Newfoundland," he chuckled, knowing such extravagance would be seen in a less flattering light.

Elaine Dobbin recalls that her husband later regretted not spending more time at the head office in Richmond. In the opinion of others, moving the firm to British Columbia saved the company money, but it may have cost Craig Dobbin dearly. "The move to B.C. took the wind out of his sails," one former CHC employee suggests, adding darkly, "Some think it helped kill him."

When Dobbin repeated financier Steve Hudson's pants-down gesture at Dobbin's seventieth birthday party, he offered Hudson a kiss as a bonus.

Former pilot Sylvain Allard abandoned his flying career to assume CEO duties at CHC Helicopter Corporation.

Christine Baird ventured into remote regions on behalf of CHC, earning her position as President, Global Operations.

The world's offshore oil rigs could not function without helicopter service—most of it provided by CHC.

CHC helicopters and crews provide search-and-rescue services for several countries, including Australia, Ireland and Great Britain.

After her husband's death, Elaine Dobbin assumed various roles, including hosting the awards ceremony for the Ireland Canada University Foundation in Dublin.

15

I loved Craig. He was a bigger-than-life friend who loved his family,
loved going out to fish the hallowed rivers of his beloved Canada,
and loved his many friends. I have had an exciting life, and one of the
best days in that life was the day I met Craig Dobbin. Life is a little
different without that great big outgoing Irishman around.

GEORGE H.W. BUSH, former U.S. president

THROUGH MUCH OF THE summer of 2005, Elaine Dobbin focussed on one event above all: Craig Dobbin's seventieth birthday on September 13. They had marked eight years since Craig received his new lung. Her husband had bettered the average survival period, and he remained in generally good health. But each day forward, Elaine knew, represented a small miracle. Reaching the biblical three-score-and-ten was a reason for anyone to be grateful. For her husband, it was reason to celebrate in an unprecedented manner. She wanted to show how much she loved him and how much he was loved by others.

The location for the party was obvious. It had to be Beachy Cove. The guest list would be extensive, at least three hundred. Demonstrating the ability that convinced John Crosbie and others she could have assumed management of CHC in her husband's absence, Elaine orchestrated the event over several weeks, and on September 9, 2005, guests arrived from across Canada, the U.S. and Europe. Many were accommodated in rooms filling two floors of the Fairmont St. John's hotel. The guests included Quebec Premier Jean Charest, Newfoundland and Labrador Premier Danny Williams, former federal cabinet minister John Crosbie, nurse practitioner Nancy Blumenthal from Philadelphia, and others. Not every guest could boast such status or notoriety. Long-time loyalists such as Clayton Parsons, the "Old Soldier" upon whom Dobbin depended to ship parts around the world and be at his desk in any weather, were seated among more prominent guests and welcomed with just as much warmth. Following a pre-banquet reception, guests were ushered into a massive tent for an elaborate meal, followed by dancing to a live orchestra and entertainment featuring Nancy Walsh and other Newfoundland headliners.

Speeches were minimized. Video presentations carried birthday wishes from George H.W. Bush, Harry Steele, Guy Savard and others, all wishing their friend a happy birthday. The most memorable message was delivered by Steve Hudson, former Newcourt Capital CEO. In his presentation, Hudson reminded Dobbin of the greeting sent to Hudson's wedding roast fifteen years earlier in which Dobbin made a $5,000 donation to Hudson's favourite charity, offering to double the amount if Hudson dropped his trousers and mooned the Canadian financial community in attendance. Now it was Hudson's turn. In his video Hudson doubled the bet, agreeing to donate $10,000 to Elaine Dobbin's favourite charity, raising it to $20,000 if Dobbin would repeat the gesture.

When the lights came up, everybody in the tent knew what to expect. Suggesting that women at nearby tables move back and avert their eyes, the seventy-year-old birthday boy ceremoniously removed his jacket, loosened his tie, unhitched his belt, lowered his trousers and provided everyone who chose to look a view of his seventy-year-old bottom. Nothing else about the spectacular celebration—the entertainment, the meal, the setting or the extensive fireworks display—would be as memorable to those who attended as that moment.

"Craig had so much fun at that party," Elaine Dobbin smiles, "that he never asked me how much it cost. And it's a good thing he didn't."

CRAIG DOBBIN'S DECISION to liquidate his real estate holdings had been perceived by many as a means of helping him concentrate on CHC activities. It may also have signalled his recognition of the need to arrange his holdings in anticipation of preparing his estate. This appears to be the motive behind his attempt to privatize CHC in 2006, a move he had discussed with Keith Stanford nine years earlier when he tape-recorded his will for video presentation to his children. "When I die," he had confided in Stanford, "I don't want to leave any companies. I want all cash."

Dobbin's concern was that the company he had assembled over so many years would not survive the turmoil he expected to be created by his passing. Although son Mark exhibited good managerial skills, none of his children appeared interested in assuming total direction of CHC, hardly a surprise. History confirms that the progeny of most driven, visionary entrepreneurs do not share the degree of obsession that drove their parent to such high levels of achievement. Nor could they be expected to. The circumstances of their lives and the environment in which they develop are dramatically different from those of the company's founder, and their goals and aspirations often contrast just as sharply. Exceptions exist, especially in Atlantic Canada, where the Irvings, Sobeys, McCains and others have succeeded in transferring management responsibility within the family. But none of these empires was built with the reckless audacity of Craig Dobbin. Their development was steady and structured, following traditional business management guidelines.

Neither of Craig Dobbin's daughters chose to participate in the business. His sons were another matter, though the degree of both their involvement and their success ranged widely. Craig Jr., while filling various corporate roles in response to his father's wishes, seems not to have found his footing as a manager. His work record within CHC is extensive, but his achievements are limited. In 1991, he was appointed marketing director for GPA Helicopters, a small CHC division. He moved from there to become manager of corporate planning for Air Atlantic, and later a director for the airline. In the midst of this activity he was dispatched to Barbados to run the disastrous Aviaco leasing in that country. That ended when he was appointed president of the ill-fated Sea Forest Plantation cod aquaculture operation in 1995, and for the ten-year period between 1996 and 2006 he served as general manager of Canadian Northern Outfitters Ltd., the corporate entity managing his father's fishing lodge at Long Harbour. In 1998 Craig Sr. tapped his namesake to become a director of CHC, followed a year later by appointment as director of marketing for CHC Composites Ltd. It was another short stay. In 2002, Craig Jr. left the composite operation to serve as a CHC vice-president.

Craig Jr.'s affable older brother, David, has directed his attention towards the hospitality industry rather than CHC Helicopters or any of its offshoots. In mid-2007 David's Repechage Restaurant Group managed a chain of pubs and restaurants under the Elephant & Castle brand, with more than twenty locations throughout North America.

This left Mark Dobbin to step into his father's shoes, perhaps blazing new trails with the same dash and élan. It would never happen. Elegant, intelligent and capable, Mark Dobbin is not the visionary his father was, though that qualification excludes an enormous number of people. Mark's personality could never dominate CHC in the manner his father's had for a number of reasons, including the fact that CHC now boasted a competent managerial staff prepared to function with or without the presence of Craig Dobbin Sr., especially after the head office relocation to B.C. With that move, Craig Dobbin began evolving from a hands-on manager into an inspirational spirit whose physical presence, although warmly welcomed and acknowledged, was no longer necessary.

Craig's nephew Brian Dobbin has demonstrated entrepreneurial vision and determination similar to his uncle's. The younger Dobbin developed Humber Valley Resort near Deer Lake, an upscale four-season destination incorporating more than 150 chalets abutting an eighteen-hole championship golf course. Its isolated location has proved no deterrent to attracting wealthy guests from Europe. In fact, the locale has an appeal crafted by Brian Dobbin's brilliant marketing strategy, which included positioning unknown Newfoundland as an exotic destination and having European airlines add Deer Lake to their periodic (seasonal) flight schedules. It's clear to most people that Brian Dobbin's success is based upon a blend of genes and emulation.

Brian is the son of Dr. Patrick Dobbin, the oldest of Craig Dobbin's siblings, and he spent the first four years of his working career alongside his successful uncle. Brian's employment included filling the role of "half nephew, half son and half friend," in which he performed chores ranging from picking up Craig Dobbin's luggage at the airport to writing his speeches, and participating in extended sessions of a card game called Growl. "Basically it's forty-fives with a different twist," Brian Dobbin explains, "and enough ways to mess the other players up that they growl at each other. Thus the name."

Other lessons were more subtle but much more valued, such as the importance of perspective. Hold your hand two inches from your face, Craig Dobbin lectured his nephew, and you don't know what you're looking at. Hold it at arm's length, and you get the whole view. Never forget the importance of standing back to survey things.

Another piece of advice dealt with the significance of respecting the individual in negotiations. Whether the situation involves two nations trying to end a war or two men arguing over a barrel of fish on a pier, the older Dobbin lectured his nephew, it all comes down to two individuals. Their skill at bargaining and the relationship maintained between them will determine the outcome. "That was his gift to me," Brian Dobbin says, "his most important lesson.

Always understand and respect what the other guy needed from the deal." And what of his uncle's own personality, negotiating style and business relationships? "He could be a bull," Brian Dobbin admits, "but he was never a bully."

AS CONCERNED AS he was for the future of CHC, Craig Dobbin also feared that his passing would create stress and upheaval among his extended family. Almost twenty-five years had gone by since Dobbin had left Penney, and almost ten years since he and Elaine married in Philadelphia. Few second wives assume the role of stepmother totally free of acrimony from within the family, and Elaine was no exception. She would always be viewed by some as an interloper, an outsider. It was left to Mark Dobbin, who perhaps best understood and appreciated the contribution Elaine made to his father's life, to act as a bridge between Elaine and Craig's sons and daughters.

Family events at which Craig's daughters, Carolyn and Joanne, were present could be strained if Elaine were also involved, and it often took the force of Craig's personality to impose a veneer of tranquillity. Nothing could obstruct Dobbin's delight in his grandchildren, however. He loved being "Poppie" to them, loved rollicking with them, teasing them, surprising them and at times spoiling them. He also dispensed wisdom when the opportunity presented itself. "Poppie," his grandson Zack asked him on one occasion, "you're rich, aren't you?" Dobbin agreed that he was. "Then why do you still work so hard?" Zack queried.

Craig Dobbin gave it some thought before replying. "Life, Zack," he said in classic grandfatherly manner, "is like water-skiing. When you stop, you sink."

CRAIG DOBBIN WANTED the two proudest achievements in his life—his talented and gifted family and his global corporation—to prosper after his death, and in April 2006 he took steps that he hoped would ensure it.

Outlining his strategy to Keith Stanford, he announced he would privatize CHC, purchasing all the outstanding shares before selling the entity to a private owner, retaining perhaps 10 per cent for his estate. The legacy he would leave his children and grandchildren would not involve the vibrant corporation he had created. It would consist almost entirely of cash.

None of this was explained when CHC broke the news in mid-March 2006 that the company was in sales talks with two U.S. private equity firms, the Blackstone Group and the Carlyle Group. The CHC chairman, media were informed, planned to retain between 10 and 14 per cent of a privatized CHC, as well as minority board representation rights and protective provisions. Analysts assumed the motive was greater financial return for the controlling shareholder, speculating that CHC's share price did not reflect future profit opportunities from the burgeoning global petroleum industry. News of the plan, along with industry suggestions that CHC stock was undervalued, immediately drove share CHC prices on the TSX up by almost 14 per cent to $30. Dobbin, the analysts suggested, would have to pay at least $32.50 or even $35 per share for a total purchase price in the neighbourhood of $1.5 billion.

Speculation boiled for six weeks. How much would Dobbin have to pay? Who would eventually own the company? How much profit could current shareholders expect to earn from their shares? Would CHC remain a Canadian firm?

The outcome was anticlimactic. On April 27, CHC announced that talks had ended and no further effort would be made to privatize the company. Share prices immediately dropped 5 per cent. No reason for ending the talks was provided.

"We came down to the one-yard line," Keith Stanford explains, "and Craig just believed he wasn't getting enough for the company he had spent so much of his life building." The difference was relatively small, a few million dollars on a deal involving substantially more than a billion dollars. When neither side budged, negotiations ended. Other sources suggest alternative reasons. Some shareholders believed the rumoured price of $30.00 to $32.50 per share was too low. Adding to their dissatisfaction was the behind-closed-doors negotiation, which caused many to suspect that the deal would favour the Dobbin family, perhaps leaving them with a stake in the privatized firm.

Craig Dobbin's reluctance to settle may have had less to do with money and more to do with being distracted by his failing health. Events were occurring that he could not ignore and that he would not acknowledge to anyone but Elaine. Throughout 2005, his sleep had grown restless and his breathing laboured, and that summer he had suffered a seizure so debilitating that Elaine feared he had died. Revived by paramedics, he agreed to travel to Philadelphia for examination at the hands of a medical team led by Nancy Blumenthal.

The Philadelphia nurse practitioner had remained close to the Dobbins. Her professional association with Craig included regularly scheduled visits by him and Elaine to monitor the condition of his transplant, but it was Elaine who instigated many of these sessions at the U.S. hospital. Knowing her husband would refuse to visit a local physician if a health matter arose, Elaine would alert Nancy Blumenthal in Philadelphia, and the nurse practitioner Craig Dobbin admired so much would place a call seemingly out of the blue to Beachy Cove, asking how Craig was and suggesting he schedule a visit over the next few days for an examination.

"We called it our 'Come to Jesus talk,'" Blumenthal laughs. "I would say, 'Look at you—your eyes are bloodshot, you're obviously not feeling your best, you have to clean up your act.' And he would smile and agree with me." He must watch his diet, Nancy Blumenthal lectured him after each examination. He should also get more exercise and ease up on the drinking. Moderation, however, was not a philosophy that Dobbin understood. Early in 2006 he and Elaine, accompanied by Christine Baird and other CHC executives, took off for one of their extended, gruelling, round-the-world excursion, visiting CHC facilities and customers in a dozen different countries.

Visiting Florida that summer, Craig invited Harry Steele to the Clearwater airport to show off his new private helicopter. Steele noted that the craft had skids, not wheels, meaning it couldn't land at Long Harbour or Adlatuk, and Dobbin explained that he would build landing pads at all of his locations so he could land anywhere in the new machine. Steele wondered about that—not about building the pads, but about Dobbin's claim that he would continue to fly back and forth to the fishing camps. Dobbin wore Gucci slippers, not shoes, that day because his feet were so swollen. Steele believed his friend's end was near, and so it appears did Craig Dobbin. It was Steele to whom Craig turned a few weeks later when reviewing his will, mentioning friends, associates and CHC employees he wanted to recognize after his death. "Did I leave anyone out?" he would ask, and whenever Harry Steele mentioned someone Craig would add his or her name. Finally Harry begged off, fearing his friend's generosity could dilute the estate severely.

Terry Young, the caretaker at Beachy Cove, believed Craig's end was near as well. Working in the garden that summer he could hear his boss gasping for breath clear across the massive lawn in front of the house. Sometimes Dobbin's coughing fits appeared endless, shaking his large body and leaving him so weak that he had to lean against a wall to recover enough strength to continue walking. The bulk, the life, the sheer physical presence of Craig Dobbin was diminishing, it appeared, with each day.

During one of the routine examinations she conducted, Nancy Blumenthal pulled Craig out of Elaine's earshot and lectured him more like a concerned friend than a health professional, troubled by his excessive use of alcohol and general disregard for his health. "You've got to be more responsible for yourself," she advised him, "and for Elaine. What is Elaine going to do without you?" The guilt tactic appeared to work. He grew sombre, more attentive to her words. "Most of the people surrounding him wanted to give Craig whatever he wanted," Blumenthal suggests, "not necessarily what was good for him. I was always honest, always upfront, and I think that's why he listened to me."

Nancy Blumenthal, however, was unable to change Craig Dobbin's pace and lifestyle entirely. Even the cancer he developed could not do that.

Since his seventieth birthday, Dobbin had felt his energy dwindling, and he began suffering abdominal pain. X-rays revealed tumorous tissue in various locations of his body, but none of the biopsies performed over several months identified them as cancerous. Given the multiple drugs Dobbin had been taking to suppress his immune system, the appearance of cancer would not be surprising. No primary source of the cancer could be located, however. The tissue was acting like cancer and appeared on X-rays as cancer, but the hospital was unable to find cells to prove the existence of the disease.

In August 2006 Dobbin paid his final visit to the Philadelphia hospital. While he was there, an oncologist suggested the hospital staff cease the painful tests on Dobbin in their search for the primary cancer. "Essentially, he said that making the diagnosis was not going to change the outcome," Blumenthal explains. "That's what the doctor said to us. What Craig overheard was that it was not cancer, which was not the same thing at all, and he and Elaine left, Craig smiling and Elaine looking concerned."

Craig and Elaine called Blumenthal from the bar in their hotel. They were sharing a bottle of champagne, Craig told her, celebrating the news that the oncologist was ending the tests, interpreting the decision as evidence that he was cancer free. "I suspect that he knew better, and in her heart Elaine believed differently," Blumenthal says, her voice dropping, "but that's what he wanted to sit on. They needed to believe it, and they needed to get home."

Just as Craig and Elaine were about to return to Beachy Cove, though, they received a telephone call from friends and neighbours in Florida who were planning a party that very evening. "Have a good time," Craig wished them. Then, hanging up, he turned to Elaine and said, "We're going to Florida."

They arrived in time to crash the party, surprising everyone with their presence. It was like old times, sharing drinks and jokes, Craig's presence convincing most of those in attendance that nothing, not even cancer, was going to defeat Craig Dobbin. In truth, the impromptu visit was more than a means of enjoying the company of their friends. It was a way of saying goodbye.

Within a few days, Craig called Sylvain Allard to discuss the upcoming CHC annual general meeting, scheduled for late September in Vancouver. He had not been feeling well all summer, he confessed to Allard. When Allard asked about the problem Dobbin, perhaps for the first time as blunt as the situation required, replied, "Sylvain, I'm toast."

Sylvain Allard could not believe it. "What're you talking about?" he asked, almost laughing.

"They're looking everywhere for the cancer," Dobbin replied. "They can't find fuck all, and they keep bullshitting me, but I'm ready, Sylvain. I'm ready."

Dobbin maintained a positive facade. In mid-September he and Elaine flew to Guy Savard's country home in the Eastern Townships of Quebec to attend a black-tie dinner. Savard and a number of partners, including Paul Desmarais, were developing a private golf club, and Dobbin was invited to participate. "He arrived looking like a million dollars," Savard recalls, "enjoying himself and never complaining at all. I couldn't believe it when he died two weeks later. Just couldn't believe it."

On the flight to Vancouver on September 27 to attend the CHC AGM, Craig and Elaine were accompanied on the CHC corporate jet by Craig's sisters Rita and Margo, Margo's husband Bill Stinson, Craig Dobbin Jr. and, surprisingly, Keith Stanford. Over almost twenty-five years of service with Craig Dobbin, Stanford had never flown on the company aircraft, turning down all invitations from the CHC chairman as part of his determination to separate his professional obligations from his personal relationships. This year Stanford had planned to attend the AGM in Vancouver, knowing the precarious state of Dobbin's health. Adhering to his policy, he booked a commercial flight, arriving at the St. John's airport only to learn the flight had been cancelled. For the first time, he asked if he could join the others on the CHC flight to B.C.

The previous day, Stanford recalls, Dobbin had learned he had only a short time to live. That soon became evident. During the flight, oxygen was administered to the Chairman when he lost consciousness. In Vancouver, Craig and Elaine were whisked to their two-storey condominium on Howe Street, where he appeared to recover his strength.

The following morning, Dobbin insisted on travelling to the CHC head office in Richmond, calling Christine Baird to let her know he was on his way. "He always loved having people around him, loved visiting and chatting with the employees," Baird says. "So when I heard he was coming I did my usual routine. I went around the office and told everyone the Chairman was on his way, and we should gather in a group and greet him when he arrived, like we always did."

Christine Baird had no idea of the seriousness of Dobbin's condition until he entered the building. The sight of him shocked her and the twenty or so CHC staff gathered nearby, and she quickly escorted him to her office, closing the door for privacy. He collapsed in a chair and in a hoarse whisper told her he was dying. They both cried openly and unashamedly, and he told Christine Baird how intensely proud he was of her and all that she had accomplished. Neither of them was willing to leave the other's company until Sylvain Allard arrived, noting it was almost time for the board meeting.

Dobbin handled himself well at the board meeting. The directors, concerned about his appearance, suggested he skip the AGM.

But Dobbin insisted he could chair the event, and he and Sylvain retired to rehearse their speeches. In past years, their meetings of this kind had been relaxed, almost recreational, the mentor and his protégé exchanging ideas in a genial atmosphere. This was different. Clearly in pain, Dobbin told Allard he was being medicated with OxyContin, a particularly powerful analgesic. They completed the rehearsal, then set out for the meeting, where the CHC chairman managed not only to conceal his condition from the shareholders but to toss humorous asides into his speech.

Returning to his condominium in downtown Vancouver, Dobbin took to bed, unable to accept Allard's invitation to accompany him on a visit to CHC's new facility, being constructed at nearby Boundary Bay. Elaine grew concerned. She could see the severity of her husband's condition, and she feared he would not survive a journey back to Beachy Cove, where he wanted to spend his last few days.

Craig's sons Mark, David and Craig Jr. had returned to St. John's following the AGM. Barely twenty-four hours after their arrival in Newfoundland they received an urgent telephone call from their aunt Rita, Craig's sister, advising them to come back to B.C. because their father could die momentarily. None of the sons believed this to be a possibility. Of course their father was ill, but he had been ill for some time. Surely they could remain in Newfoundland and await their father's arrival there? Rita was adamant. If they could not get a scheduled flight to Vancouver they had better charter one and bring their sisters with them. Later that day the five Dobbin children boarded a flight west.

In Vancouver, Craig Dobbin agreed to an injection of antibiotics and a blood transfusion, both conducted at a nearby hospital where he remained overnight. Elaine and Rita sat with him until dawn. At eight the next morning the chartered jet bearing the entire family took off for St. John's. It was Tuesday, October 3.

Settled in his Beachy Cove second-floor bedroom, near the soaring windows with their dramatic view of Bell Island, Craig Dobbin appeared to relax and gain strength. Elaine alerted friends to the situation, inviting them to Beachy Cove for their final goodbyes and a mass to be celebrated by Father Kevin Molloy, who had contributed much to the family's spiritual comfort over the years.

Among those who arrived the next day were Sylvain Allard, flying in from New York City with news that the company continued to be viewed favourably there, and that business dealings he and Dobbin had long discussed were going forward. Pleased with the news, Dobbin smiled and said, "We had one hell of a ride, didn't we?" His hand-picked successor agreed that they sure as hell had.

Keith Stanford arrived as well, and the camaraderie the two men had built up over almost a quarter of a century infused their meeting. They discussed the daily financial reviews Stanford had provided over so many years, and Dobbin's total trust in Stanford's integrity and honesty. "Too bad we couldn't close that last deal," Dobbin said, meaning his effort the previous year to privatize CHC and amass the cash for his estate. "We were so close."

Stanford expressed mock anger. "Hang on a second," he said. "What do you mean *we* were so close? I sold everything I was supposed to sell, all those properties and such. You only had to sell one company, and you fucked it up." The two men laughed while others, out in the corridor, dried their eyes and awaited their turn to visit.

Craig had asked to see Steve Hudson, the man from whom he once concealed $40 million in aircraft and who was now enclosed within Dobbin's inner circle of friends. Elaine had contacted Hudson in Wichita, Kansas, and without hesitation he flew directly to St. John's. Sharing several minutes of Craig Dobbin's diminishing time, the two men reminisced, Dobbin advising his younger friend to "do everything you want to do" before asking Hudson to wait nearby because he needed sleep. Six hours later, Dobbin awoke to ask for Hudson, and this time the two men, major players in the country's highest corporate and financial strata, embraced each other. Dobbin kissed Hudson and told him he loved him.

All of the Dobbin children were present, and Elaine had asked them to invite their mother, if she wished to attend. Penney Dobbin arrived, absorbing the grandeur of Beachy Cove for the first time, a residence so at odds with her own lifestyle. She and Craig shared private time together.

Dobbin was ready to go. He wanted the mass said, the good-byes exchanged, the ceremonies completed. Elaine gathered family and friends at his bedside, then told him they couldn't begin until Father Molloy arrived on a flight from Florida. Craig Dobbin's eyes narrowed and, in a voice that recalled the strength he once had, he barked, "Who's paying for his damn ticket?" Everyone laughed, wishing to remember the Wild Colonial Boy this way.

Father Molloy celebrated mass Thursday evening. At its completion, some family and friends returned to their homes. Others remained at Beachy Cove. A hospital bed had been installed, and a twenty-four-hour nurse was in attendance. The next evening, a full moon rose after sunset, its rays illuminating Conception Bay, the dark shadow of Bell Island brooding across the open stretch of water. His bed positioned to give him a view of the scene, Craig Dobbin absorbed it during brief periods of consciousness. He told Elaine that she would miss the view beyond the window when she moved after his death, and he offered to leave her both Beachy Cove and the legendary Rolls-Royce. She refused both. She loved the house he had purchased for her on Hogan's Pond. She did not need Beachy Cove or that tank of a car. She needed nothing in her life except him. No man, she assured him, could have made any woman any happier than he had made her.

Craig Dobbin died just after dawn on Saturday, October 7, at 6:51 a.m. The nurse passed the word to family and friends gathered on the ground floor of the house at Beachy Cove. Most burst into tears and hugged each other, sharing their grief.

Instead of remaining with the others, Terry Young stumbled outside to blink away his tears. The muscular groundskeeper, whose devotion to Craig Dobbin was exceeded by nobody, circled the house to stand and mourn alone on the brink of the cliff high above the bay. From the west, out of the mist that frequently gathers along Conception Bay in autumn, he watched Craig Dobbin's personal helicopter approach, skimming over the water towards Beachy Cove. Reaching the house, the craft rose in the air until it was level with the window of the bedroom where Craig's body lay. It hovered there for a moment, as though waiting for someone to board. Then it gently floated higher and turned north, its rotor blades flashing in the rays of the rising sun. Terry Young watched as the red, white and blue craft grew smaller and then vanished in the clouds above Bell Island.

16

Think where a man's glory most begins and ends,
And say my glory was: I had such friends. —W.B. YEATS
Quoted by GEORGE H.W. BUSH to mark the passing of Craig L. Dobbin

N THANKSGIVING DAY, MONDAY, October 9, the massive Basilica of St. John the Baptist in St. John's grew crowded with mourners. Each received an ornate, full-colour program whose front cover displayed a smiling Craig Laurence Dobbin in tuxedo and black tie. The program's back cover showed the same man, younger and smiling more broadly, next to a salmon river with a CHC helicopter parked on the shore.

For the most part, it was a traditional Roman Catholic funeral. "Be Not Afraid" was the gathering hymn; "How Great Thou Art" served as the recessional. Father Kevin Molloy celebrated the mass and read the homily. Major roles in the service were assigned to the next generation. Craig Dobbin's granddaughter Christine Rose delivered the first reading, followed by grandson Zachary Dobbin, reading from Second Corinthians. Prayers of intercession were offered by granddaughters Gillian Dobbin, Megan Dobbin and Isobel Dobbin-Sears. Grandchildren Kelly Rose, Tim Rose, Jane Holloway, Sally Holloway, Elli-Jo Holloway, Jake Dobbin, Heather Dobbin, Maria Dobbin and Michael Dobbin participated in the offertory procession.

Two CHC helicopters circled in the sky above the church while an honour guard of CHC directors assembled below. Many of them, including Don Carty, Sir Bob Reid and John Kelly, had travelled a considerable distance to pay their respects. Mourners in the pews included Newfoundland and Labrador Premier Danny Williams, Lieutenant-Governor Edward Roberts, actor and TV personality Mary Walsh, and former Newfoundland Premier Brian Tobin. Quebec Premier Jean Charest, in Boston when he learned of his friend's death, arrived after quickly chartering a small Beechcraft King Air propeller-driven plane to carry him to St. John's.

Emotions flowed back and forth between pride at Dobbin's life and accomplishments among those who had been close to the CHC chairman and sorrow at his passing, especially when celebrated Newfoundland vocalist Shelley Neville sang "On Eagle's Wings." Through it all Elaine remained disconsolate, supported by her sons Rob and Scott.

In his eulogy, Guy Savard recalled Craig Dobbin as "a tall and beautiful man with the smile of a child opening his gift on Christmas morning. Those of us who were coming in [to his fishing camps] were in fact his gifts. He loved to have company and was looking forward to taking our money at the card table." Savard ended the memory of his friend by describing a photograph of Craig and Elaine taken at the black-tie dinner in the Eastern Townships two weeks earlier: "Craig is standing tall, with Elaine sitting beside him. He is looking up at the sky as though he is talking to the angels and saying, 'I am coming. Now—here's the deal.'"

Harry Steele's eulogy was more poignant, noting that not everyone from Beachy Cove, Newfoundland, gets to ring the bell at the New York Stock Exchange. "Time spent in his company went faster," Steele explained, "and the laughter was louder. Craig had this great Newfoundland gift of taking on life as if it were made for him." Then, his emotions threatening to choke off his words, he said: "I'm a happy and better person to have known Craig Dobbin."

At the close of the service the coffin, bearing Celtic crosses, was carried from the church, with sons Mark, David and Craig Jr., brothers Dermot and Barney, and Craig's nephew Brian as pallbearers. Local reporters spoke to many gathered on the steps of the church. Brian Tobin noted how Craig Dobbin did many good works out of the public eye. "He was a great giver to people privately, anonymously," Tobin noted. "He had a big heart—a competitive heart, to be sure, but a big heart as well."

Danny Williams expressed thanks for Dobbin's willingness to become involved in political issues, supporting the province's goals. "When we had to take on Ottawa," Williams recalled, "he was one of the few businesspeople who was very outspoken. Craig was there, and I'll never forget him for that."

Jean Charest was more reflective. "He was life itself," Charest said sadly. "He was one of the most exceptional Canadian citizens I have ever known."

As the hearse and limousines pulled away, the helicopters made a final circle above the mourners remaining on the basilica steps.

Following cremation, Elaine divided Craig's ashes into three portions. She would spread one at each of the fishing camps and reserve the other to be interred beneath a massive black granite monument near St. Philips, to be set on a low rise within view of Conception Bay.

CRAIG DOBBIN'S ESTATE was divided among sixty-two people. Both the number of people recognized and the degree to which they shared in the estate is testimony to the care he took to reward those who mattered to him. Son Mark was named sole executor and trustee. Mark and his four siblings received all the shares of Discovery Helicopters Incorporated, the holding company whose assets included a substantial portion of outstanding shares of CHC Helicopters, plus the Beachy Cove property. Craig Dobbin received his father's shares of Canadian Northern Outfitters, operators of the Long Harbour fishing camp. Harry Steele was given his friend's shares in Adlatuk, the Labrador fishing camp.

Elaine Dobbin inherited a numbered company with substantial assets, as well as the cabin Craig had built for her at Devil's Lake, a considerable amount of cash, and one week each year at the two fishing camps. Each of Elaine's children was remembered with an inheritance, as were Nancy Blumenthal and Craig's former wife, Penney. Dr. Bruce Rosengard, the Philadelphia surgeon who had successfully transplanted a lung into Craig Dobbin almost a decade earlier, received a substantial sum. Derm Dobbin inherited his brother's share of the St. John's Fog Devils hockey team. (Unfortunately, the Fog Devils could not overcome the burden of their heavy travel expenses, and Derm sold the team in early 2008.)

CHC employees for whom Craig Dobbin felt a special fondness, due to their dedication and character, were recognized with cash or other assets, including pieces from the exceptional collection of art on the walls of Beachy Cove. Groundskeeper Terry Young, butler Dean Churchill, Dean's mother Winnifred Churchill, secretary Candace Moakler, "Old Soldier" Clayton Parsons and others inherited portions of the estate. Keith Stanford's loyalty and energy earned him the highest cash inheritance next to Elaine's, plus a fund for the education of Stanford's two teenage daughters. Guy Savard's daughters received lifetime annuities. George H.W. Bush was granted one week each year at either fishing camp, with the accompaniment of up to thirty friends, for his lifetime.

Fissures in the relationship between Elaine and the Dobbin family appeared during this time. Some were more nagging than upsetting. Elaine had planned to keep her husband's Mercedes-Benz, but family members claimed it. The Dobbin children also declined to commit their portion of the $20 million promised by their father and Elaine to the Craig L. Dobbin research facility at Memorial University, much to Elaine's disappointment.

More painful to her was the withdrawing of access to many Dobbin grandchildren, who had played a major role in her life and her husband's while he was alive. Mark, the most responsive of the Dobbin sons and daughters to Elaine, maintained the relationship between her and his three children.

Elaine occupies the home on Hogan's Pond, wintering in Florida and continuing to support various charities. She serves on the

New Capital Campaign committee striving to raise $280 million for Memorial University. Among the campaign's goals is the creation of the research centre she hoped would be named for her husband. Her son and daughter, Scott and Kellee, remain nearby; son Rob lives with his wife in Hamilton, Ontario. Among the goals Elaine has set is having the St. John's International Airport renamed the Craig L. Dobbin Airport.

MARK DOBBIN WAS appointed non-executive chairman of the board of CHC, representing the Dobbin family as controlling shareholders of the company with 61.7 per cent of voting power. On various occasions he noted that any decision made by the board of directors and implemented by management to increase the value of the family shares would have to also increase the value of publicly held shares.

The new chairman had a good relationship with the board and with top management at CHC, but he remained realistic. "There's this huge void that is never going to be filled," he said in December 2006. "My father wasn't a shadow. He was a presence that you wanted to be around . . . If anybody tells you that stepping into the chair of an international corporation, the most successful helicopter company in the world, is not challenging, [they are] either delusional or not being honest. It's very challenging."

Speculation drove CHC stock upwards after Craig Dobbin's death on the assumption that the Dobbin family would sell their holdings, probably as a block to a private investor. Such a move, observers noted, would run afoul of the requirement for majority ownership by Europeans if the takeover firm planned to continue operating in the North Sea and elsewhere. Most market analysts continued to favour the worldwide company.

Things changed on a Friday in February 2008 when Sylvain Allard publicly announced an agreement had been reached with Connecticut-based First Reserve Corporation to purchase all outstanding shares of CHC at a price of $32.68 per share. The share price, a fat 49 per cent above the closing price the previous day, represented a substantial windfall for shareholders. For Mark Dobbin and his four siblings, it was a payday of enormous proportions. Based on figures from the company's September 2007 annual report, the estate owned 33,150,000 shares, including 22,000,000 ordinary shares that carried no market value. This left 5,426,462 Class A shares and 5,555,432 Class B shares. At the proffered price, the 10,981,894 shares yielded $358,888,296 to be divided among Craig Dobbin's five children.

In total, First Reserve was committing $3.7 billion. About $1.5 billion would be paid to the Dobbin family and other shareholders, while $800 million would be earmarked for CHC corporate debt. First Reserve also assumed responsibility for $1.4 billion in other liabilities, primary aircraft leases.

In a statement following the announcement, Mark Dobbin declared, "There is a time for everything, and the time for our family to be the controlling shareholder of CHC, particularly in light of the value the First Reserve deal represents, in my mind [it] had come and gone." Adding that the decision had been based on the best interests of the company's shareholders, Mark Dobbin noted that if the Dobbin family were not going to be the long-term stewards of the company, "then we really had the responsibility to examine offers like the First Reserve offer."

The words from First Reserve and CHC were reassuring when it came to maintaining the company's Canadian identity. Certainly there was no reason to question the capabilities of Sylvain Allard, Christine Baird, Rick Davis and the balance of the B.C.-based team. Still, niggling concerns remained. Among the most problematic was the question of the EU's rule against non-European control of operations in its waters, particularly the North Sea. No one believed First Reserve could qualify, as the Dobbin siblings had, for EU citizenship status. No one believed, however, that First Reserve would venture so far into a deal with such a premium price offer without taking this factor into account and finding ways to stickhandle around it.

Meanwhile, more than a billion dollars flowed into bank accounts in the name of Dobbin and former shareholders of lesser size.

THE FULL IMPACT of Craig Dobbin's life will be measured by means other than monetary.

Some weeks after the funeral, Elaine made one of her first unaccompanied forays out of her home on Hogan's Pond. Admitting to a heavy right foot when behind the wheel, she was pulled over by a police officer who informed her she had been speeding.

"I told him I didn't realize how fast I had been driving," Elaine says. "I told him I was late for an appointment and agreed that I probably had been driving too fast."

The officer requested her driver's licence and vehicle registration slip, and stood near her car studying the documents for some moments. Finally he asked if she were Craig Dobbin's wife. Elaine said yes, she was.

He handed the licence and registration back to her. She should be getting a ticket, he told her, but she wouldn't. Not this time. Her husband, he explained, had been very good to his family during a family emergency, picking up the costs of their airfare. The officer had never forgotten the generosity.

"Mrs. Dobbin," the officer said before returning to his cruiser, "please slow down."

Elaine Dobbin indeed drove the rest of the way more slowly, her vision obstructed by tears.

Sources & Acknowledgements

LAINE DOBBIN INSPIRED THE story of her late husband's remarkable life; my wife, Judy, and I are thankful for her warm and gracious support.

Harry Steele, whose affection for his friend rivals Elaine's, was exceptionally generous with his time and advice. Harry's remarkable life deserves a book as well, though his modesty and sense of privacy will doubtless preclude any such project.

Mark Dobbin's gracious assistance granted me special insight into his father's life and access to essential elements of the story. Robert Foster's familiarity with so many aspects of Craig Dobbin's life and his generosity with time and facilities were equally important. Sylvain Allard proved invaluable in explaining much of Craig Dobbin's character and business strategy. And no one was able to portray Craig Dobbin's extraordinary personality and business acumen with more perception and colour than the delightful Keith Stanford.

Everyone I consulted about their experiences with Craig Dobbin was supportive. Their continuing admiration and affection for him became something of a need to share their stories, and I am deeply appreciative of the time and effort they invested on behalf of this book. Among those who offered their assistance in many different ways were Jim Appleby, Christine Baird, Nancy Blumenthal, Carol Brydges, George H.W. Bush, Kellee Carter, Premier Jean Charest, Barry Clouter, Bob Cole, John and Jane Crosbie, Nancy Crowley, Brian Dobbin, Derm Dobbin, Margo Dobbin, Rita Dodge, Bob Dunne, Colleen Field, Tana Fulton, Christina Gagno, Ronan Gaynor, Bob Glass, Peter Godsoe, Bob Gosse, Natalie Haywood, Steve Hudson, J.C. Jones, Kim Kornic, Tom Mabry, Cabot Martin, Maureen McCarthy, Axel Meisen, Candace Moakler, Michel Montaruli, Sheila Nugent, Patrick O'Callaghan, Borden Osmak, Dr. Ken Ozmon, Rudy Palladina, Clayton Parsons, Rob Parsons, Scott Parsons, Sir Bob Reid, Jim Roache, Frank Ryan, Guy Savard, Seymour Schulich, William Stinson, Brian Tobin, Marion Tucker, Sean Tucker, Bernadette (Bernie) Wadsworth, Trish Williams and Terry Young.

In Dublin, I was fortunate enough to enjoy the company and absorb the wisdom of the remarkable John Kelly, Paddy Hillery and Walter Kirwan. In Waterford, John Maher was a genial host and an essential link to local sources, including Eamonn McEneaney and Mayor Cha O'Neill.

Craig Dobbin's vibrant life generated an appropriate volume of press coverage on his speeches and other activities, and many descriptions in this book have been drawn from those sources. Thanks to the exceptional generosity of Dr. Axel Meisen, former president and vice-chancellor of Memorial University of Newfoundland, I was granted access to the university's extensive media files on Craig Dobbin and CHC. With the kind cooperation of university librarian Colleen Field, quotations and descriptions were drawn from the following publications: *Canadian Business, The Globe and Mail—Report on Business Magazine*, the *Halifax Chronicle-Herald,* *The Irish Times, Maclean's, The New York Times* and the St. John's *Telegram.*

Much of the correspondence relating to CHC corporate activities, including exchanges between Craig Dobbin and John Lecky and those between various CHC directors, was drawn from Robert

Foster's Capital Canada files. The files were also the source of a good deal of financial data related to acquisitions by Sealand and CHC.

Other sources included *Codfathers: Lessons from the Atlantic Business Elite* by Gordon Pitts (Key Porter, 2005), *Everything I Needed to Know about Business . . . I Learned from a Canadian* by Leonard Brody and David Raffa (Wiley, 2005) and *No Holds Barred: My Life in Politics* by John Crosbie (McClelland & Stewart, 1997).

Everyone at Douglas & McIntyre provided first-rate professional support for the book. I especially appreciated Scott McIntyre's good-natured interest, plus the superb editing assistance of Barbara Pulling, Susan Rana and Ann-Marie Metten. They did what all good editors do: they made this a better book.

Index

263